LINEAR B
AN INTRODUCTION

J.T. HOOKER

PUBLISHED BY BRISTOL CLASSICAL PRESS
GENERAL EDITOR: JOHN H. BETTS

Cover illustration: drawing of KN Sc 230

First published in 1980 by
Bristol Classical Press
an imprint of
Gerald Duckworth & Co. Ltd
61 Frith Street
London W1D 3JL
e-mail: inquiries@duckworth-publishers.co.uk
Website: www.ducknet.co.uk

Reprinted 1990, 1994, 2001

A catalogue record for this book is available
from the British Library

ISBN 0-906515-62-9

Printed in Great Britain by
Antony Rowe Ltd, Eastbourne

CONTENTS

page

Acknowledgments   v
Preliminary note   vii
List of abbreviations   ix

Part One   1
    1: The Aegean Bronze Age   3
    2: Writing in the Aegean Bronze Age   7
    3: The decipherment of the Linear B script   19
    4: The Linear B inscriptions   35
    5: The language of the Linear B texts   49

Part Two   81
    1: Knossos sword tablets: the Ra set   83
    2: Sheep and wool tablets from Pylos and Knossos:
       PY Cn and KN D   85
    3: Knossos cloth and wool tablets: the L series   95
    4: Groups of women: the Pylos A series   101
    5: The assessment and distribution of bronze: PY Jn   107
    6: The o-ka set: Pylos An tablets   123
    7: Inventories: Pylos Ta tablets   127
    8: Land tablets: E texts from Pylos and Tiryns   133
    9: Religious texts from Knossos, Pylos, and Thebes   151
   10: Wheel and chariot tablets: the Knossos S series   163
   11: Spice tablets: the Mycenae Ge set   169
   12: Assessments of various commodities:
       M and N tablets from Pylos and Knossos   171
   13: Inscribed jars, sealings, and labels   179

Part Three   183
    Index 1: Linear B words   185
    Index 2: Greek words   193
    Index 3: Linear B inscriptions discussed   199

Plates   201

ACKNOWLEDGMENTS

I wish to thank Mr. John Betts for undertaking the publication of this book and for giving me much active encouragement. Professor Anna Morpurgo Davies, Dr. John Killen, and Dr. Jean-Pierre Olivier read the typescript and sent me lists of comments and criticisms which have enabled me to make many improvements to the text. I am most grateful to these colleagues for their interest and their help: they must not, of course, be held responsible for any of my statements or omissions. I thank Mrs. Jean Bees and Mrs. Brenda Timmins for executing the figures, and University College for defraying certain expenses. I am indebted to the following for help in obtaining photographs and for permission to publish: Dr. Olivier, Dr. Ingo Pini, Professor Anna Sacconi, the American School of Classical Studies at Athens.

University College, London   J.T. Hooker
August 1980

A new printing has given me the opportunity of making some corrections and revising the bibliographies.

April 1983   J.T.H

PRELIMINARY NOTE

Despite the existence of a large number of books and articles dealing with the Linear B texts and their interpretation, we have in English no introduction to the subject as a whole. *Documents in Mycenaean Greek* by Ventris and Chadwick and Palmer's *Interpretation of Mycenaean Greek texts* are works of considerable authority and prestige, but neither of them is entirely suitable for the student who has some knowledge of Greek and wishes to have access to the Linear B material: *Interpretation* is too polemical and partisan for his purpose, while the second edition of *Documents* is arranged in a manner which is more likely to confuse than to help him. It is hoped that the present *Introduction* will be found to set out the relevant facts as simply as possible. Part One places the development of the Linear B script against its historical background; the earlier varieties of Aegean writing are discussed, and Ventris' decipherment of Linear B is described; attention is then paid to the extant types of Linear B inscriptions and their classification; finally the Mycenaean dialect of Greek is examined in some detail. In Part Two, the reader is taken through a number of important Linear B texts. These are presented first in a 'normalized' transcription of the Linear B characters, so as to induce familiarity with the lay-out of the original texts, secondly in transliteration, and thirdly in translation where this is possible. Part Three contains the indexes.

Many matters concerning the Linear B script are still disputed, and it is often necessary to take up a position on these. But an attempt has been made to indicate alternative interpretations; moreover, each section is equipped with a full bibliography. After perusing this *Introduction,* the reader will be ready for more advanced works like *Documents, Interpretation,* and other books and papers cited in the bibliographies.

Further help is afforded by the following publications:
Nestor·(Madison 1957-1977, Bloomington 1977—): monthly list of all publications in Mycenaean and related fields, indexed annually.
Studies in Mycenaean inscriptions and dialect (London 1953-1975, Cambridge 1976—): annual index of publications on Linear B and the other Aegean scripts. (Consolidated edition of *Studies* for the years 1953-1964 by L. Baumbach, Rome 1968).
E. Grumach *Bibliographie der kretisch-mykenischen Epigraphik* (Munich 1963) and *Supplement* I (Munich 1967): classified and indexed list of all publications up to the end of 1965.
S. Hiller and O. Panagl *Die frühgriechischen Texte aus mykenischer Zeit* (Darmstadt 1976): detailed discussion of the various classes of Linear B texts, with bibliography.

LIST OF ABBREVIATIONS

AA	*Archäologischer Anzeiger* (Berlin)
AAA	Ἀρχαιολογικὰ ἀνάλεκτα ἐξ Ἀθηνῶν (Athens)
ABSA	*The annual of the British School at Athens* (London)
AC	*L'antiquité classique* (Brussels)
AC(CT)	*Acta classica* (Cape Town)
AC(D)	*Acta classica* (Debrecen)
AE	Ἀρχαιολογικὴ ἐφημερίς (Athens)
Aevum	*Aevum: Rassegna di scienze storiche, linguistiche, filologiche* (Milan)
AGI	*Archivio glottologico italiano* (Florence)
AIV	*Atti dell'Istituto Veneto di Scienze, Lettere ed Arti* (Venice)
AJA	*American journal of archaeology* (Princeton)
AJP	*American journal of philology* (Baltimore)
Altertum	*Das Altertum* (Berlin)
AM	*Acta mycenaea* (ed. M.S. Ruipérez)(Salamanca 1972)
AntCret	*Antichità cretesi: Studi in onore di D. Levi* I-II (Catania 1973-1974)
Anthropos	*Anthropos: Internationale Zeitschrift für Völker- und Sprachenkunde* (Freiburg, Switzerland)
AO	*Archiv orientální* (Prague)
AR	*Atti e memorie del 1° Congresso Internazionale di Micenologia* (Rome 1968)
Archaeology	*Archaeology: A magazine dealing with the antiquity of the world* (New York)
Archaeometry	*Archaeometry: Bulletin of the Research Laboratory for Archaeology and the History of Art* (Oxford)
Arion	*Arion: A quarterly journal of classical culture* (Austin)
ASAA	*Annuario della Scuola Archeologica di Atene e delle Missioni Italiani in Oriente* (Rome)
Athenaeum	*Athenaeum: Studi periodici di letterature e storia dell'antichità* (Pavia)
AVEM	Y. Duhoux *Aspects du vocabulaire économique mycénien* (Amsterdam 1976)
BASOR	*Bulletin of the American Schools of Oriental Research in Jerusalem and Baghdad* (Baltimore)
BCH	*Bulletin de correspondance hellénique* (Paris)
BICS	*Bulletin of the Institute of Classical Studies* (London)
BIFG	*Bollettino dell'Istituto di Filologia Greca dell' Università di Padova* (Rome)
BJRL	*Bulletin of the John Rylands Library* (Manchester)
BN	*Beiträge zur Namenforschung* (Heidelberg)
BSL	*Bulletin de la Société de Linguistique* (Paris)

CAH	*The Cambridge ancient history* (Cambridge)
CM	*Colloquium mycenaeum* (ed. E. Risch and H. Mühlestein)(Neuchâtel/Geneva 1979)
CRAI	*Comptes rendus de l'Académie des Inscriptions et Belles Lettres* (Paris)
DI	*Donum indogermanicum: Festgabe für A. Scherer* (ed. R. Schmitt-Brandt)(Heidelberg 1971)
Documents	M.G.F. Ventris and J. Chadwick *Documents in Mycenaean Greek* (Cambridge 1973²)
EC	*Estudios clásicos* (Madrid)
Eirene	*Eirene: Studia graeca et latina* (Prague)
EM	*Etudes mycéniennes* (ed. M. Lejeune)(Paris 1956)
Emerita	*Emerita: Revista de linguistica y filología clásica* (Madrid)
Eranos	*Eranos: Acta philologica suecana* (Gothenburg)
Eunomia	*Eunomia:* Supplements to *Listy filologické* (Prague)
Europa	*Europa: Festschrift E. Grumach* (ed. W.C. Brice) (Berlin 1967)
FF	*Forschungen und Fortschritte* (Berlin)
Glotta	*Glotta: Zeitschrift für griechische und lateinische Sprache* (Göttingen)
Gymnasium	*Gymnasium: Zeitschrift für Kultur der Antike und humanistische Bildung* (Heidelberg)
Hermathena	*Hermathena: A Dublin University review* (Dublin)
Hesperia	*Hesperia: Journal of the American School of Classical Studies at Athens* (Baltimore)
Historia	*Historia: Zeitschrift für alte Geschichte* (Wiesbaden)
IBK	*Innsbrucker Beiträge zur Kulturwissenschaft* (Innsbruck)
IF	*Indogermanische Forschungen* (Berlin)
Interpretation	L.R. Palmer *The interpretation of Mycenaean Greek texts* (Oxford 1963)
JCS	*Journal of classical studies* (Kyoto)
JHS	*The journal of Hellenic studies* (London)
JNES	*Journal of near eastern studies* (Chicago)
JRAS	*Journal of the Royal Asiatic Society* (London)
Kadmos	*Kadmos: Zeitschrift für vor- und frühgriechische Epigraphik* (Berlin)
Klio	*Klio: Beiträge zur alten Geschichte* (Berlin)
Kokalos	Κώκαλος: *Studi pubblicati dall'Istituto di Storia Antica dell'Università di Palermo* (Palermo)
Kratylos	*Kratylos: Kritisches Berichts- und Rezensions-organ für indogermanische und allgemeine Sprachwissenschaft* (Wiesbaden)
KS	Κυπριακαὶ σπουδαί (Nicosia)
KX	Κρητικὰ χρονικά (Iraklion)

Language	Language: Journal of the Linguistic Society of America (Baltimore)
LB	Linguistique balkanique (Sofia)
Lingua	Lingua: International review of general linguistics (Amsterdam)
LP	Lingua posnaniensis (Poznan)
MDOG	Mitteilungen der Deutschen Orient-Gesellschaft (Berlin)
Mémoires I	M. Lejeune Mémoires de philologie mycénienne I (Paris 1958)
Mémoires II	Ib. II (Rome 1971)
Mémoires III	Ib. III (Rome 1972)
MH	Museum helveticum (Basel)
Minoica	Minoica: Festschrift J. Sundwall (ed. E. Grumach) (Berlin 1958)
Minos	Minos: Revista de filología egea (Salamanca)
MIO	Mitteilungen des Instituts für Orientforschung (Berlin)
Mnemosyne	Mnemosyne: Bibliotheca classica batava (Leiden)
MS	Mycenaean studies (ed. E.L. Bennett)(Madison 1964)
MSS	Münchener Studien zur Sprachwissenschaft (Munich)
MX	Μνήμης χάριν: Gedenkschrift P. Kretschmer II (ed. H. Kronasser)(Vienna 1957)
Names	Names: Journal of the American Name Society (Berkeley)
Numen	Numen: International review for the history of religions (Leiden)
OA	Opuscula archaeologica (Lund)
OLZ	Orientalistische Literaturzeitung (Berlin)
OpAth	Opuscula atheniensia (Stockholm)
OR	Opuscula romana (Stockholm)
Orbis	Orbis: Bulletin international de documentation linguistique (Louvain)
PCCMS	Proceedings of the Cambridge Colloquium on Mycenaean Studies (ed. L.R. Palmer and J. Chadwick)(Cambridge 1966)
Platon	Πλάτων: Δελτίον τῆς 'Εταιρείας 'Ελλήνων Φιλολόγων (Athens)
PP	La parola del passato (Naples)
QU	Quaderni Urbinati di cultura classica (Urbino)
RA	Revue d'archéologie (Paris)
RAL	Rendiconti della (Reale) Accademia dei Lincei (Rome)
RBPH	Revue belge de philologie et d'histoire (Brussels)
REA	Revue des études anciennes (Paris)
REArm	Revue des études arméniennes (Paris)
REG	Revue des études grecques (Paris)

RF	*Rivista di filologia e di istruzione classica* (Turin)
RhM	*Rheinisches Museum für Philologie* (Frankfurt)
RIL	*Rendiconti dell'Istituto Lombardo* (Milan)
RP	*Revue de philologie* (Paris)
RPL	*Recherches de philologie et de linguistique* (Louvain)
Saeculum	*Saeculum: Jahrbuch für Universalgeschichte* (Freiburg/Munich)
SC	*Studii clasice* (Bucharest)
SCO	*Studi classici e orientali* (Pisa)
SG	*Siculorum gymnasium* (Catania)
SGIIL	*Studies in Greek, Italic, and Indo-European linguistics offered to L.R. Palmer* (ed. A. Morpurgo Davies and W. Meid)(Innsbruck 1976)
SL	*Studi linguistici in onore di V. Pisani* II (Brescia 1969)
SM	*Studia mycenaea* (ed. A. Bartoněk)(Brno 1968)
SMEA	*Studi micenei ed egeo-anatolici* (Rome)
SMSR	*Studi e materiali di storia delle religioni* (Rome)
SPFFBU	*Sborník Pracĺ Filosofické Faculty Brněnské University* (Brno)
Sprache	*Die Sprache: Zeitschrift für Sprachwissenschaft* (Wiesbaden/Vienna)
SSL	*Studi e saggi linguistici* (Pisa)
TAPA	*Transactions of the American Philological Association* (New York)
TPS	*Transactions of the Philological Society* (Oxford)
VDI	*Вестник древней истории* (Moscow)
VY	*Вопросы языкознания* (Moscow)
WJ	*Würzburger Jahrbücher für die Altertumswissenschaft* (Neue Folge)(Würzburg)
Word	*Word: Journal of the Linguistic Circle of New York* (New York)
ZA	*Živa antika* (Skopje)
ZVS	*Zeitschrift für vergleichende Sprachforschung* (Göttingen)
2ICretStud	Πεπραγμένα τοῦ Β' Διεθνοῦς Κρητολογικοῦ Συνεδρίου (Athens 1968)
3ICretStud	Πεπραγμένα τοῦ Γ' Διεθνοῦς Κρητολογικοῦ Συνεδρίου (Athens 1973)

PART ONE

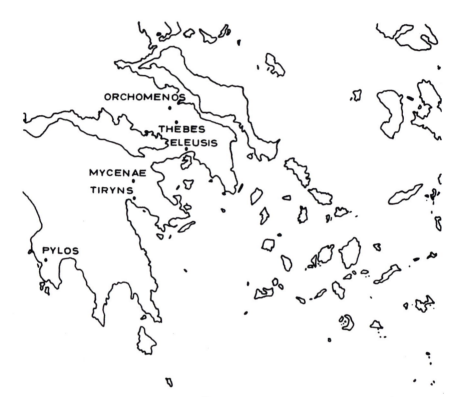

ORCHOMENOS

THEBES
ELEUSIS

MYCENAE
TIRYNS

PYLOS

CHANIA

KNOSSOS

SKETCH MAP
OF THE AEGEAN
SHOWING
FIND-PLACES
OF LINEAR B
INSCRIPTIONS

1   THE AEGEAN BRONZE AGE

§ 1   Exploration in Crete near the end of the last century and
at the beginning of the twentieth revealed that a distinctive civilization had flourished there in the Bronze Age. Large complexes
of buildings (conventionally called 'palaces') were excavated at
Knossos in the north of Crete by Sir Arthur Evans and his colleagues, at Phaistos in the south by the Italian School, and at Mallia
to the east by the French. Other important sites which were known
by the early 1900s are Palaikastro, Gournia, Tylissos, and Ayia
Triada.   More recently, two major settlements of palatial character have been uncovered at Zakro in eastern Crete and at Chania in
the west.   To the culture represented at these and at other Bronze
Age sites in Crete Evans gave the comprehensive name 'Minoan', after
the Minos who, according to Greek legend, had ruled at Knossos in
the heroic age.   The 'Minoan' period was divided by Evans into
three chronological phases: Early Minoan (EM), Middle Minoan (MM),
and Late Minoan (LM).   Only Middle and Late Minoan will be of much
concern to us here, since only in these epochs was writing (in the
true sense) practised in the Aegean area.

§ 2   Early in MM (c. 1850 B.C.), palaces were built at Knossos,
Mallia, and Phaistos: hence this epoch is sometimes known as the
Early or First Palatial Period.   Alterations and additions were
constantly made to the palaces throughout MM; at Knossos, for instance, the so-called Domestic Quarter was constructed to the east
of the Central Court.   The great brilliance of this era is reflec-
ted not only in the elaborate plans of the palaces and houses but
also in the artefacts, above all the gems and polychrome pottery,
which have been recovered from Minoan settlements and caves.   The
Minoans of the First Palatial Period were an outward-looking people.
The MM settlement on the Cycladic island of Melos was excavated
many years ago.   But Minoan wares of fine quality were taken to
places far beyond the Aegean: to Egypt and the coasts of Syria and
Palestine.   Conversely, the arts of the Minoans, especially their
frescoes and pottery, display a number of Egyptian motifs.   At the
end of MM (c. 1570), the Cretans made their first close contacts
with the 'Helladic' civilization of mainland Greece.   The inter-
action of Minoan and Helladic, above all in the Shaft Graves at
Mycenae but at other Peloponnesian sites as well, led to the rise
in Greece of a new culture, now called 'Mycenaean'.

§ 3   The brilliance of the MM epoch was dimmed, but not exting-
uished, by a series of natural disasters which affected the Cretan
sites late in the period.   Before the end of MM, the palaces were
reconstructed on a still larger scale: a process which initiates the
so-called Second Palace Period.   In this era of expansion, Minoan
artefacts were even more widely spread in the traditional markets
of the eastern Mediterranean than in the First Palace Period. Minoan settlements were planted in Rhodes, at Miletos in south-west
Anatolia, and perhaps also in Cyprus.   Minoan 'colonies' are found
in the Cyclades, especially at Melos and Thera.   At the same time,
the Greek mainland was deeply penetrated by the styles and habits of
Minoan Crete; on that side of the Aegean, an almost complete fusion
between the Minoan and the Helladic cultures was effected.

§ 4   During the fifteenth century, the Second Palace Period came
to an end at almost all sites except Knossos and Chania. With these
exceptions, the principal Minoan sites were destroyed and abandoned.
Knossos itself, while surviving as a palatial site for two or three
generations longer, underwent profound changes in its way of life.
The burial of 'chieftains' in elaborate built tombs with spears and
other weapons, the depiction of warriors on frescoes, and the mention of great quantities of warlike equipment on the Knossos Linear
B tablets give a militaristic colouring to this period (called by
Evans LM II), which had previously been lacking.   The pottery produced in the Knossian workshops was now of a rather stereotyped and
grandiose character, exemplified by the large three-handled jars of
the 'Palace Style'.   The devastation of Knossos early in the fourteenth century brought to an end the Second Palace Period in central
Crete; but the Minoan civilization continued to flourish, without a
break, at Chania.   Other sites in the island, for example Knossos
and Palaikastro, enjoyed a modest recrudescence of material culture
in LM III (1400-1200), even though the 'palatial' way of life had
vanished.   There is some evidence of trade between Crete and the
Greek mainland in LM III.

§ 5   After the end of Knossos as a palatial site, the Mycenaean
civilization of the mainland pursued an independent career, which
reached its acme in the fourteenth and thirteenth centuries.   In
this period (Late Helladic III) there arose palaces at Mycenae,
Tiryns, Pylos, Thebes, Orchomenos, and Volos, and possibly at Gla
and Athens.   The massive 'Cyclopean' circuits of stone which en-
closed the citadels at many Mycenaean sites (especially at Mycenae,
Tiryns, and Gla) stand in marked contrast to the unwalled and un-
fortified palaces of Minoan Crete.   During this mainland Palace
Period, virtually the whole of Greece as far north as Thessaly was
penetrated by Mycenaean culture which, however, made only sporadic
contact with Epirus and Macedonia.   The Cyclades, but not Crete,

were drawn into the Mycenaean orbit. The Mycenaeans at first equal-
led and later surpassed, in both scale and extent, the trading activities previously engaged in by the Minoans.   Walled Mycenaean
settlements are known at Miletos and Iasos in Anatolia, while the
large number of Mycenaean tombs in Rhodes points to the existence of
Mycenaean colonies there.   The most important deposit of Mycenaean
pottery in Egypt, dating from c. 1375, was found at Tell-el-Amarna.
Cyprus and the Levant have yielded such large quantities of Mycenaean pottery as to suggest a very lively trade between Greece and the
eastern Mediterranean which continued for well over a century.   Mycenaean wares have been found at some coastal sites in Sicily and
southern Italy.   The long-established trading-links with the Balkans
and with central Europe were maintained.

   § 6   The Mycenaean Palace Period was brought to an end at about
1200, with the destruction of all the mainland sites named above,
with the exception of Athens and Volos.   A period of re-occupation
ensued at many sites, but by the eleventh century nearly all the typical marks of the Mycenaean civilization had disappeared, and 'sub-
Mycenaean' was giving way to the culture of the Protogeometric period.

                                  ***

   The Aegean Bronze Age: S. Marinatos and M. Hirmer *Crete and Mycenae* (London 1960); M.I. Finley *Early Greece: the Bronze and Archaic
ages* (London 1970); H.-G. Buchholz and V. Karageorghis *Prehistoric
Greece and Cyprus* (tr. F. Garvie)(London 1973); P. Warren *The Aege-
an civilizations* (London 1975).
   Minoan culture: A.J. Evans *The Palace of Minos at Knossos* I-IV
(London 1921-1935); J.D.S. Pendlebury *The archaeology of Crete*
(London 1939); R.W. Hutchinson *Prehistoric Crete* (Harmondsworth
1964[2]); F. Schachermeyr *Die minoische Kultur des alten Kreta* (Stutt-
gart 1964); S. Alexiou *Minoan civilization* (Iraklion 1969); M.S.F.
Hood *The Minoans* (London 1971); G. Cadogan *Palaces of Minoan Crete*
(London 1976).
   Mycenaean culture: W.D. Taylour *The Mycenaeans* (London 1964);
G.E. Mylonas *Mycenae and the Mycenaean age* (Princeton 1966); E.T.
Vermeule *Greece in the Bronze Age* (Chicago 1972[2]); J. Chadwick *The
Mycenaean world* (Cambridge 1976); F. Schachermeyr *Die ägäische Früh-
zeit* II (Vienna 1976); J.T. Hooker *Mycenaean Greece* (London 1977).
Early Mycenaean: G. Karo *Die Schachtgräber von Mykenai* (Munich 1930-
1933); G.E. Mylonas Ὁ ταφικὸς κύκλος Β τῶν Μυκηνῶν (Athens 1973).
Late Mycenaean: P. Ålin *Das Ende der mykenischen Fundstätten auf
dem griechischen Festland* (Lund 1962); V.R.d'A. Desborough *The last
Mycenaeans and their successors* (Oxford 1964).   Post-Mycenaean:
A.M. Snodgrass *The dark age of Greece* (Edinburgh 1971).

The Minoan and Mycenaean expansion: A.J.B. Wace and C.W. Blegen *Klio* 32 (1939) 131-147; H.J. Kantor *AJA* 51 (1947) 3-103; A. Furumark *OA* 6 (1950) 150-271; F.H. Stubbings *Mycenaean pottery from the Levant* (Cambridge 1951); W.D. Taylour *Mycenean pottery in Italy and adjacent areas* (Cambridge 1958); S.A. Immerwahr *Archaeology* 13 (1960) 4-13; K. Bittel *MDOG* 98 (1967) 17-23, *Gymnasium* 83 (1976) 513-533; V. Hankey *ABSA* 62 (1967) 107-147, *BICS* 19 (1972) 143-145; F. Schachermeyr *Ägäis und Orient* (Vienna 1967); *Bronze Age migrations in the Aegean* (ed. R.A. Crossland and A. Birchall)(London 1973); *Acts of the International Archaeological Symposiums 'The Mycenaeans in the eastern Mediterranean'* (Nicosia 1973) and *'The relations between Cyprus and Crete, ca. 2000-500 B.C.'* (Nicosia 1979).

2   WRITING IN THE AEGEAN BRONZE AGE

The purpose of writing among the Minoans

§ 7   The Minoans were the inventors of writing in the Aegean.
Not only did they initiate the art, but throughout the Bronze Age
they were responsible for its principal developments and innovations.   In time, the Minoan scripts were taken over by other peoples, such as the Cypriots and the Mycenaeans, who used them for
their own purposes.   The question, to what extent the Minoans were
indebted to any foreign system in the creation of their scripts,
cannot yet be answered satisfactorily: it seems certain, however,
that some of the earliest signs used in Minoan writing were derived
from Egypt.

§ 8   Two fundamental questions need to be answered.   What did
the Aegean peoples use writing for?   What stages in the history of
writing are represented by their scripts?   The probable answer to
the first question is that the invention of writing in Crete was called forth not by a desire to communicate but by economic necessity.
It seems that the Minoans, and after them the Mycenaeans, had two
main objects in writing: to confirm ownership and to make records.
Only the inscriptions found on some Minoan cult-objects, especially
the so-called libation-tables, fall a little outside these categor-
ies.   There is, as yet, no direct evidence that the Minoans or the
Mycenaeans ever wrote any literary or historical text, or even sent
a letter from one city to another; but the analogy of contemporary
cultures makes it highly probable that they did in fact use writing
for these purposes.   From first to last, and especially in the
Late Bronze Age, Minoan-Mycenaean writing was confined to very few
centres; and it may be suspected that the number of people who were
able to read or write the scripts was at all times very small.

The three stages of Minoan writing

§ 9   The successive stages of Minoan writing were elucidated by
Evans in 1909 on the evidence of his discoveries at Knossos:
       The written documents from the Palace of Knossos and its im-
       mediate dependencies now amount to nearly two thousand.   The
       overwhelming majority of these clay documents, including the
       first discovered, presented an advanced type of linear
       script — referred to in the present work as Class B — which

was in vogue throughout the whole of the concluding period of
the Palace history. But the course of the excavations brought
out the fact that the use of this highly developed form of
writing had been in turn preceded in the 'House of Minos' by
two earlier types — one also presenting linear characters,
described below as Class A, the other, still earlier, of con-
ventionalized pictorial aspect, recalling Egyptian hierogly-
phics.   *Scripta Minoa* I 18
Evans called the earliest stage of Cretan writing indifferently Pictographic or Hieroglyphic.   Here the term Pictographic only will be
used, to avoid confusion with the Egyptian and the Hittite Hieroglyphic scripts.

§ 10   The general picture presented by Evans in this early publication is an admirably clear one, and in its broad outlines it is
still valid to-day.   Three great scripts arose in Crete during the
Middle and Late Bronze Age (c. 1900-1200).   The earliest (Pictographic) system flourished from the beginning of the period.   At
some undetermined point within Middle Minoan must be placed the development of the Linear Script A.   At *Scripta Minoa* I 28-29, Evans
observed that examples of the Linear A script had been found in the
First or Early Palace at Knossos, which was devastated late in the
Middle Minoan period.   Most, and perhaps all, of the Linear B inscriptions from Knossos date from the destruction of the Second or
Late Palace, c. 1375.   No precise date can yet be assigned to the
recently discovered Linear B inscriptions from Chania.   We thus
have a satisfactory *terminus ante quem* for the creation of both Linear A and Linear B; but there is no *terminus post quem* for the creation of either.

The Pictographic script

§ 11   The Cretan Pictographic inscriptions are of two main
kinds: those carved on seal-stones and those incised on objects of
clay, such as tablets, labels, and four-sided bars.   The inscriptions on seals probably do not belong to a different chronological
stage from those on clay: it is likely that the greater stylization
displayed by the former arises from the more intractable nature of
the material used.   An impressive seal makes it probable that this
type of inscription still had the function of marking ownership:

(i)

(ii)

(iii)

The heraldic character of the cat on side (i) is plain to see.   In
such a context it is possible, as Evans suggested, that the sign-
groups on each of the three sides represent the spelling of official
names and titles. The groups themselves recur on other Pictographic
texts, sometimes in different combinations or in a different order.
To judge from the analogous stage in the development of other
scripts, there is little doubt that some at least of the signs in
Cretan Pictographic are phonetic, that is to say they represent the
actual sound or syllables of the spoken language. Two of the signs,
Ħ on side (i) and 𝛶 on side (iii), survive into both the Linear A
and the Linear B scripts.   The seal is interesting in yet another
respect to the student of writing.   Side (iii) presents an amalga-
mation of more than one sign so as to form a ligature or monogram: a
scribal practice which is still frequently in the Linear A inscriptions and, rather less often, in those of Linear B (§ 75).

§ 12   The Pictographic seals are, for the most part, chance discoveries.   The clay documents, on the other hand, come from the so-
called Hieroglyphic Deposit in the West Wing of the Knossian Palace.
The simplest type of document in this deposit does no more than record a number of objects illustrated: it therefore forms part of an
inventory of a kind still commonly attested in Linear A and Linear
B.   For example in P. 101c (according to Evans' numeration in
Scripta Minoa I), which is to be read from right to left:

We can detect two essential elements in this simple type of record:
an 'ideogram' (that is, a sign which represents an actual object)
and a numeral.   So the GRAIN-JAR ideogram followed by the numeral
170 records the presence of 170 measures of grain, while the next
group indicates 160 arrows; unless, of course, the script is already
sufficiently developed for the ideograms to have a significance beyond what they ostensibly signify.   The small cross to the right of
the ARROW ideogram is perhaps an ideogram-marker, as Grumach suggested (*Minoica* 162-191).

§ 13   A rather more complex type of record is represented by a
group of signs consisting of double axe + grain-jar + crooked line
(P. 103d):

Here the numeral 1640 is preceded by the sign-group.   If the × is
rightly diagnosed as an ideogram-marker, we have a record of 1640
objects denoted by the DOUBLE AXE ideogram (perhaps objects of cult
significance, in view of the sacral connotations of the double axe
in Minoan ritual).   In that case, the two following signs, the
grain-jar and the crooked line, may be functioning either as further
ideograms (in some way modifying the DOUBLE AXE) or as phonetic signs
which perhaps spell out the word already represented by the DOUBLE
AXE ideogram.   It would not be surprising to find the grain-jar,
for instance, acting sometimes as an ideogram and sometimes as a
phonetic sign: such a double function is well attested in other
Bronze Age scripts, as well as in Linear A and Linear B.

§ 14   The clay disc from Phaistos, to which Evans devoted a chap-
ter in *Scripta Minoa* I, stands completely outside the main Pictographic and Linear traditions of Minoan Crete. For this and other reasons, it was considered by Evans to be an import from Asia Minor.
This view of its origin is still sometimes maintained, but it was
made less tenable by the publication in 1935 of an axe from Arkalochori, which bears fifteen inscribed characters evidently related
to those of the Phaistos Disc and which there is no reason to think
was not manufactured in Crete.   Since the script of the Phaistos
Disc and that of the Arkalochori Axe are not directly related to the
Pictographic system in use at Knossos, it seems likely that several
different kinds of picture-writing were being developed simultan-
eously during the Middle Minoan period.

The Linear A script

§ 15   During Middle Minoan, the Pictographic script, or a script
related to it, was transformed (perhaps over a considerable period)
into a neater, more orderly, and more cursive kind of writing in
which the pictorial elements were stylized still further.   The new
script was called by Evans Linear A.   Until recently, Linear A was
thought to have replaced the Pictographs all over Crete towards the
end of Middle Minoan. The transition between Pictographic and Linear A is exemplified by inscriptions on a clay bar found at Mallia
and dated to a late stage of Middle Minoan:

side (a)

side (b)

The signs on this bar are already well on the way towards the shape
they acquire in Linear A, and so it can be presumed that the process
of developing the latter script had begun some time before.   There
is no ground for believing that the Linear A script was created in
order to meet the needs of a new language.   The very existence of
such a document as the Mallia bar means that we must not think of a
clear break between Pictographic and Linear A, but rather of a grad-
ual change from the one to the other.   Levi's discoveries at Phaistos show that there the transition from Pictographic to Linear A
took place at an earlier date than in the north and east of Crete.

§ 16   The total amount of known Linear A material is very small.
Apart from a few inscriptions on stone libation-tables and other
sacral objects, most of our Linear A texts come from the archive of
Ayia Triada, a site near Phaistos, which was destroyed by fire during the fifteenth century B.C. (LM Ib).   The archive comprises some
150 small clay tablets (some of them now very fragmentary), containing records of transactions made or stocks held.   A few examples
will illustrate the main types of inscriptions present in the Ayia
Triada archives.   HT 114, a tablet inscribed on both sides, is of
simple structure, as the following analysis will show:

heading.		10 measures of WHEAT
list of com-modities		7 measures of BARLEY
		1 measure of FIGS
		1 measure of WINE
		3 OXEN (?)

heading.		
commodity		8 measures of WINE

§ 17   What the respective 'headings' convey is unknown, but the number of possible meanings is quite small: thus, they could denote the place where the commodities were produced, collected, or recorded, or the persons who were involved in their production, distribution, or delivery.   The meaning of the ideograms in Linear A is not known for certain, and for the present purpose their use has been deduced from the way in which similar ideograms are employed in Linear B.   The system of numerals may be compared with that of the Pictographic script:

	Pictographic	Linear A
1	ϽＯＲＩ	ᛁ
10	•	• or ‒
100	＼	o
1000	◊	✛

The Linear A system of numerals is much the same as in Linear B, except that in the latter script the sign ‒ has become the standard for 10.   Unlike the Linear B script, Linear A possesses an extensive system of fractional numerals.

§ 18   HT 88 appears to contain two lists, each with its own 'heading':

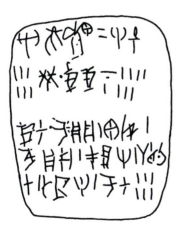

heading :

list :

heading :

list :

total .

The purpose of neither list is very clear.   The presence of a MAN
ideogram as the first member of the first list might be supposed to
indicate that a number of personnel were being recorded, and it is
possible that the two signs which come second do represent personal
names or occupations; but third in the list comes the sign Ψ, which
has been interpreted as the ideogram for FIGS, followed (perhaps) by
a phonetic rendering of the word for 'figs', before the numeral '7'.
The second list may consist of personal names (and in that case the
purpose of making the record would be made plain in the 'heading').
The text ends with the commonest sign-group in the Ayia Triada tablets, indeed the only sign-group whose meaning is beyond all dispute:
✝✝. From the way it is used (as in this text), the group must mean
'all' or 'total', since it is regularly found with a numeral which
represents a total of the numbers in a preceding list.

     § 19   Roughly a hundred Linear A signs are in common use.   Of
these, about a dozen occur singly in lists before numerals. In contrast to these signs, which may confidently be regarded as ideograms,
the remainder appear in groups, and are best interpreted as phonetic
representations of syllables.   As in Linear B (and perhaps in the
Pictographic script) some characters have a double function, acting
either as ideograms or as phonetic signs.   The most important text
for observing the relationship between ideograms and phonetic signs
is the damaged tablet HT 31.   This contains a 'heading' of obscure
import followed by a list of receptacles:

Since all the ideograms obviously represent vessels of different
shapes, it is likely that the sign-groups

Υ日ʊ

ʈϙʊ⚑ī

likewise spell the names of vessels, only in these cases the names
are spelt phonetically.   The most interesting feature of the inscription is the insertion of a sign-group in small characters over
each ideogram. It is probable, but not certain, that each of these
groups forms a phonetic spelling of the name of the vessel with
which it is associated.   (Cf. E. Peruzzi *Minoica* 287-293).

The diffusion of Linear A; the Cypro-Minoan script

§ 20   The expansion of Cretan trade during the Early Palace Period and at the beginning of the Late Palace Period resulted in the
spread of Minoan writing to the Cycladic islands and probably to the
mainland of Greece as well.   Isolated marks and groups of signs have
long been known from Phylakopi in Melos; and these have now been
joined by scattered finds from Keos, Kythera, Naxos, and Thera.   So
far as is known, writing was no longer practised in the Cyclades after the wane of Minoan influence at the end of the fifteenth century.

§ 21   The examples of writing which come from Cyprus are of much
greater significance.   As early as 1909, Evans discussed the Bronze
Age inscriptions on clay balls from Enkomi in eastern Cyprus (*Scripta
Minoa* I 68-73).   After examining the close resemblances between some
Enkomi signs and those of the Linear systems in Crete, he concluded
that all three scripts were interconnected.   It was clear also that
a direct line linked the Bronze Age Cypriot script, which Evans named
Cypro-Minoan, and the syllabary which flourished in Cyprus during the
classical period.   The phonetic values of the classical Cypriot syllabary had been known for a number of years when Evans wrote the
first volume of *Scripta Minoa*.

§ 22   Further examples of inscribed clay balls from Cyprus may
now be added to those known by Evans; while the discovery of long
inscriptions at Enkomi, dating from a late epoch of the Bronze Age,
attests the use of writing there for purposes other than the making
of simple records.   The earliest extant Cypro-Minoan tablet, dated
to the sixteenth century, displays a form of writing clearly derived
from the Minoan Linear A script:

It therefore seems likely that writing was introduced to Cyprus by
Minoan traders before the Mycenaean expansion to the eastern Mediterranean.

***

The Aegean scripts: A.J. Evans *Scripta Minoa* I (Oxford 1909)'; B.
Gaya Nuño *Minoïká* (Madrid 1952); S. Dow *AJA* 58 (1954) 77-129; H.
Jensen *Die Schrift in Vergangenheit und Gegenwart* (Berlin 1958[2])
111-126; A. Bartoněk *Altertum* 5 (1959) 16-34; I.J. Gelb *A study of
writing* (Chicago 1963[2]) 91-97; J. Friedrich *Geschichte der Schrift*
(Heidelberg 1966) 64-70; H.-G. Buchholz *Frühe Schriftzeugnisse der
Menschheit* (Göttingen 1969) 88-112; E. Grumach *Allgemeine Grundla-
gen der Archäologie* (ed. U. Hausmann)(Munich 1969) 234-267; A. Heubeck *Archaeologia Homerica* III (Schrift)(Göttingen 1979) X 1-73.
    The Cretan Pictographic script. *Corpora:* A.J. Evans *Scripta
Minoa* I; F. Chapouthier *Les écritures minoennes au palais de Mallia*
(Paris 1930). Joins: E.L. Bennett *Minoica* 36-40. Additional
material: F. Chapouthier *BCH* 62 (1938) 104-109; H. Van Effenterre
RA (6th ser.) 49 (1957) 205-208; E. Grumach *Kadmos* 1 (1962) 153-162,
2 (1963) 7-13, 84-97, 6 (1967) 6-14; S. Alexiou *Kadmos* 2 (1963) 79-
83; O. Pelon *BCH* 89 (1965) 1-9; E. Grumach and J. Sakellarakis *Kadmos* 5 (1966) 109-114; J.-P. Olivier and J.-C. Poursat *Kadmos* 10
(1971) 16-19.   Structure of the script: H.Th. Bossert *Šantaš und
Kupapa* (Leipzig 1932) 7-21; F. Chapouthier *Minos* 1 (1951) 71-76; L.
Deroy *Minos* 2 (1952) 34-56; E. Grumach *Minoica* 162-191, *FF* 36 (1962)
115-119, *BJRL* 46 (1964) 346-384, *KX* 18 (1964) 7-14; W.C. Brice *BJRL*
48 (1965) 56-68; M.-L. and H. Erlenmeyer *Kadmos* 4 (1965) 1-4; P.
Meriggi *Kadmos* 12 (1973) 114-133, *AntCret* I 172-181; P. Faure *Kadmos*
14 (1975) 1-7; J.-P. Olivier *PP* 31 (1976) 17-23; D. Schürr *Kadmos* 17
(1978) 8-15; A.A. Molchanov *VDI* 157 (1981) 116-133.
    The script of the Phaistos Disc.   First edition: A. Della Seta
RAL (5th ser.) 18 (1909) 297-367.   Revised editions, with detailed

photographs: J.-P. Olivier *BCH* 99 (1975) 5-34; Y. Duhoux *Le disque de Phaestos* (Louvain 1977).   Structure and interpretation: A. Cuny *REA* 26 (1924) 5-29; G. Ipsen *IF* 47 (1929) 1-41; G. Neumann *Kadmos* 7 (1968) 27-44; W. Nahm *Kadmos* 8 (1969) 110-119, 18 (1979) 1-25; V. Georgiev *LB* 19 (1976) 5-47, *VDI* 139 (1977) 52-60.   Origin of the script: C. Davaras *Kadmos* 6 (1967) 101-105; E. Grumach *2ICretSt1* 281-296.   Comparison of the signs with those of Linear A: D. Schürr *Kadmos* 12 (1973) 6-19; W. Nahm *Kadmos* 14 (1975) 97-101.

The script of the Arkalochori Axe: S.Marinatos *AA* (1935) 252-254; N.K. Bouphidis *AE* (1953/2) 61-74.

Proto-linear and Linear A inscriptions from Phaistos: G. Pugliese Carratelli *ASAA* 35-36 (1957-1958) 363-388.

The Linear A script.   *Corpora:* W.C. Brice *Inscriptions in the Minoan Linear script of class A* (Oxford 1961); G. Pugliese Carratelli *Le epigrafi di Haghia Triada in lineare A* (Salamanca 1963); L. Godart and J.-P. Olivier *Recueil des inscriptions en linéaire A* I (Paris 1976), II (Paris 1979), III (Paris 1976).   Index: J. Raison and M.W.M. Pope *Index transnuméré du linéaire A* (Louvain 1977).   Frequency of signs: D.W. Packard *Minoan Linear A* (Berkeley/Los Angeles/London 1974).   New material: E. Grumach *Kadmos* 1 (1962) 164-165; S. Alexiou *Kadmos* 2 (1963) 14-16; M.S.F. Hood and J. Chadwick *ABSA* 57 (1962) 73-74; M.S.F. Hood *Kadmos* 3 (1965) 111-113; A. Morpurgo Davies and G. Cadogan *Kadmos* 10 (1971) 105-109; J.-P. Olivier and O. Pelon *BCH* 95 (1971) 433-436; C. Davaras *Kadmos* 11 (1972) 101-112, 20 (1981) 1-6; S. Alexiou and W.C. Brice *Kadmos* 11 (1972) 113-124, 15 (1976) 18-27; N. Platon and W.C. Brice 'Ενεπίγρα-φοι πινακίδες καὶ πίθοι γραμμικοῦ συστήματος Α ἐκ Ζάκρου (Athens 1975); L. Godart and J.-P. Olivier *BCH* 100 (1976) 309-314; I.A. Papapostolou, L. Godart, J.-P. Olivier Γραμμικὴ Α στὸ μινωικὸ ἀρχεῖο τῶν Χανιῶν (Rome 1976); J.-P. Olivier, O. Pelon, F. Vandenabeele *BCH* 103 (1979) 3-27; E. Hallager *Kadmos* 19 (1980) 9-11; J.-P. Olivier, L. Godart, R. Laffineur *BCH* 105 (1981) 3-25; W.C. Brice *Kadmos* 21 (1982) 9-14; R. Janko *Kadmos* 21 (1982) 97-100; J.-P. Olivier *Rayonnement grec: hommages à C. Delvoye* (Brussels 1982) 15-26; M. Tsipopoulou, L. Godart, J.-P. Olivier *SMEA* 23 (1982) 61-72; M.A. Vlasaki and L. Godart *SMEA* 23 (1982) 51-60.   Relationship with other scripts: M.W.M. Pope *Aegean writing and Linear A* (Lund 1964).   Structure: J.L. Myres *Minos* 1 (1951) 26-30; G. Pugliese Carratelli *ASAA* 30-32 (1952-1954) 7-19; G.P. Goold and M.W.M. Pope *Preliminary investigations into the Linear A script* (London 1955); A. Furumark *Linear A und die altkretische Sprache* (Berlin 1956), *OR* 11 (1976) 1-21; P. Meriggi *Primi elementi di minoico A* (Salamanca 1956); G. Neumann *Glotta* 36 (1958) 156-158, 38 (1960) 181-186, 39 (1961) 172-178; E. Peruzzi *PP* 11 (1956) 434-448, *Minos* 5 (1957) 35-40, 6 (1958) 9-15, *Minoica* 287-293, *Word* 15 (1959) 313-324, *Le iscrizioni minoiche* (Florence 1960), *VY* 9 (1960/3) 17-27, *Minos* 8 (1963) 7-14; W.C. Brice *Kadmos* 1 (1962) 42-48, 2 (1963) 27-38, *Europa* 32-44; S. Luria and I.D. Amusin *VDI* 86

(1963) 198-201; R. Kamm *Orbis* 16 (1967) 242-268; E. Grumach *BJRL* 52 (1970) 326-345; J.T. Hooker *JRAS* (1975) 164-172; J.-P. Olivier *Le monde grec: hommages à C. Préaux* (Brussels 1975) 441-449; L. Godart *PP* 31 (1976) 30-47, *SMEA* 20 (1979) 27-42; Y. Duhoux *Études minoennes* I: *le linéaire A* (Louvain 1978); C. Consani *SSL* 21 (1981) 225-249. Diffusion of the Linear A script outside Crete.   Aeolian Islands: L. Bernabò Brea *Minos* 2 (1952) 5-28; G. Pugliese Carratelli *Kokalos* 1 (1955) 5-9.   Keos: J.L. Caskey *Kadmos* 9 (1970) 107-117.   Kythera: J.N. Coldstream and G.L. Huxley *Kythera* (London 1972) 205-206. Melos: C.C. Edgar and A.J. Evans *Excavations at Phylakopi in Melos* (Hellenic Soc. suppl. paper 4)(London 1904) 177-185; A.C. Renfrew and W.C. Brice *Kadmos* 16 (1977) 111-119.   Mycenae: E. Grumach *Kadmos* 1 (1962) 85-86. Naxos: N. Kontoleon *Kadmos* 4 (1965) 84-85.   Thera: S. Marinatos *Excavations at Thera* IV (Athens 1971) 43-45.

    Writing in Cyprus.   General: J.F. Daniel *AJA* 45 (1941) 249-282; J.V. Karageorghis *RA* (1958/2) 1-19, *KS* 25 (1961) 43-60.   Cypro-Minoan: H.-G. Buchholz *Minos* 3 (1955) 133-151, 6 (1958) 74-85; O. Masson *EM* 199-206, *Ugaritica* III (Paris 1956) 233-250, *Minos* 5 (1957) 9-27, *Ugaritica* VI (Paris 1969) 379-392; E. Masson *Minos* 10 (1969) 64-77, *SMEA* 11 (1970) 73-102, *Étude de 26 boules d'argile inscrites trouvées à Hala Sultan Tekke* (Gothenburg 1971), *CRAI* (Jan.-Mar. 1973) 32-60, *Cyprominoica* (Gothenburg 1974), *CM* 397-409.

3   THE DECIPHERMENT OF THE LINEAR B SCRIPT

The Linear B script

§ 23   The emergence of the third and last kind of Aegean writing, Evans' 'Linear B script', is usually placed in the fifteenth
century B.C.; but there are good reasons for supposing that it took
place at a considerably earlier date.   Since the structure of Linear A is still imperfectly known, it is not easy to surmise why a
new script was needed at all.   So far as can be seen, Linear B differs from Linear A in two important respects: in the *internal structure of the system* and in the *external form of the signs*.

§ 24   With regard to the *structure,* we have observed that the
lists on the Linear A tablets commonly consist of separate signs
(which appear to be ideograms) and sign-groups (which seem to represent the syllables of actual speech): it is only rarely that
ideograms and phonetic signs are combined in the same expression.
On the other hand, Linear B regularly employs a phonetic group
followed by an ideogram, both group and ideogram referring to the
same object.   This kind of 'double writing', as it is sometimes
called, is well exemplified by the first Linear B text to be studied
below (§ 168).

§ 25   So far as the *external form* of the two scripts is concerned, both make use of about the same number of syllabic signs.   Some
of these they share, but each script contains many signs peculiar to
itself.

§ 26   From facts already adduced, and also from other consider-
ations, Evans realized that the three main kinds of Cretan writing,
though closely related to one another, had not evolved by a simple
process of development: Linear A replacing Pictographic and in its
turn being superseded by Linear B.   In Evans' own words:
> The obvious conclusion that the linear class of Script B,
> which at Knossos supersedes the other, is simply a later out-
> growth of Class A, does not sufficiently explain the phenome-
> na with which we have to deal.   It is true that the general
> *facies* of these later Knossian documents is more advanced.
> The records are often much fuller and the tablets larger;
> there is a smaller selection of characters and a less compli-
> cated system of compound signs.   At the same time, the con-
> clusion that Class B was merely evolved out of the other is

precluded by the fact that several of the signs belonging to
it are not found in Class A, and that some of those which are
shared by both 'signaries' appear in a more primitive form
upon tablets belonging to Class B.   The two systems, which
contain a large proportion of common elements, must on the
whole, therefore, be regarded as parallel to one another, and
it is probable, as already suggested, that the usage of Class
B in the Remodelled Palace of Knossos to a certain extent co-
incided in time with the continued use of Class A at Phaestos
and Hagia Triada.   (*Scripta Minoa* I 38).

§ 27   Subsequent excavation in Crete and further reflexion on
the nature of the scripts have confirmed the accuracy of Evans' dia-
gnosis.   The history of Cretan writing should not be seen as a development which was uniform in all parts of the island; on the contrary, there was probably a good deal of overlapping, with different scribal schools moving at different speeds, though in the same
general direction: that of simplifying and standardizing the reper-
tory of pictorial signs.   Again, while it is obvious that the Linear B script shares many of its features with the earlier Linear A
system, other elements have a closer affinity with the Pictographic
script.   In consequence, it is best to think of Linear B as a re-
lation of Linear A, but not a direct descendant of it.

§ 28   Evans placed the Linear B inscriptions from Knossos at the
end of the Late Palace Period at that site, which to-day is usually
dated c. 1375.   That date, or a date close to it, is still the most
probable one, despite the objections brought by Palmer against Evans'
methods and reasoning.   A much later date, however, must be assigned
to the large deposits of Linear B inscriptions found at Pylos in 1939
and again in the post-war years.   These belong to a late phase of
Late Helladic IIIb (c. 1200); and this is the approximate date also
of the few texts discovered at Mycenae in the 1950s and at Tiryns in
the 1970s.   The date of the tablets from Boeotian Thebes cannot be
determined with certainty until the associated pottery is published
in full; from what is known at present, they appear to be roughly
contemporary with the Pylos texts.

§ 29   As well as inscriptions scratched on clay tablets and sealings, which formed the bulk of the extant Linear B material (§§ 63-
65), short texts painted on the side of large clay vessels are known
from a number of mainland sites, including Eleusis, Mycenae, Orchomenos, Thebes, and Tiryns, and from Knossos and Chania in Crete (§ 66).
The dates of their fabrication fall within the fourteenth and fifteenth centuries.

Preliminaries to the decipherment

§ 30   The Linear B tablets gave, at first glance, little hope of
achieving a successful decipherment, in the absence of any bilingual
text.   They bear short inscriptions issuing from the bureaucratic
apparatus of the Bronze Age palaces, and consist of little more than
lists of people, beasts, and commodities;   records of transactions;
descriptions of land-holdings; and the like.   The first difficulty
confronting the would-be decipherer arises from the physical state of
the tablets, since most of them are broken, worn, or burnt to a greater or lesser degree. Again, the inscriptions are extremely brief and
terse, revealing little by way of syntactic structure. A third difficulty is associated with the subject-matter of the texts. As these
deal extensively with people and places, a large number of the words
they contain will be proper names.   Whereas proper names provided a
starting-point for the decipherment of Persian cuneiform in the nine-
teenth century, they could not help with Linear B. Some of the Persian texts were recognizable as 'royal' inscriptions, and of course
the names of many Persian kings were already known.   But no clue
existed as to the language in which the Linear B texts were written,
and the personal names they contained were likelier to be those of
quite humble individuals than of kings. It is true that place-names
did play a part in the decipherment of Linear B, although not at an
early stage (§ 49).

§ 31   On the other hand, a closer and more systematic examination
of the Linear B material revealed some features which seemed at the
very least to reduce the number of possibilities.   Most important
of all, the structure of a Linear B inscription is such as to provide
a context within which the meaning of the whole must be sought, and
outside which it is not permissible to go.   The range of meaning is
delimited by the ideogram which is present in most of the complete
texts (§ 76).   Many years before a convincing decipherment of the
script as a whole was arrived at, Evans found it possible to assign
hundreds of the Knossos tablets to clearly-defined groups, solely on
the evidence of the ideograms: *Palace of Minos* IV (London 1935) 694-
732.

§ 32   Another encouraging fact which emerged from an inspection
of the Linear B tablets was that, if some signs were clearly ideograms (pictorial representations of persons or objects), the analogy
of contemporary writing-systems in the Near East suggested that the
remaining sign-groups were phonetic in character; and, when it was
observed that the number of such signs was about ninety,   it became
reasonably certain that one was dealing with a *syllabary*:   that is,
a system in which each phonetic sign represents a syllable of the
language in question.

§ 33   It therefore seemed likely that the Linear B signs which
occur in groups were 'syllabograms'.   If the system as a whole
was in fact a syllabary, it could be exploited in an important way
to yield some preliminary indications of the principles upon which
the language was constructed.   The sign-groups had to be examined
to see if they gave evidence of grammatical inflexion.   If such an
examination had positive results, some information would have been
acquired about the syntactic structure.   Since the inscriptions
available were very short, it was unlikely that this information
would enable the language to be identified immediately; but at least
it would be possible to exclude from the discussion a whole range of
languages of quite different structure.

§ 34   The first essential step of methodically isolating sign-
groups which showed appearance of grammatical inflexion was taken by
Alice Kober.   At *AJA* 52 (1948) 97, she set out a series of possible
noun-paradigms, in which the centre and bottom rows seem to be grammatical variants of the words in the top row:

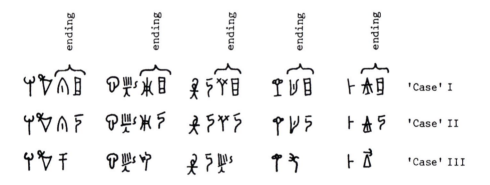

§ 35   The change of form was so regular in certain words that it
could be predicted and, since these words appeared to be nouns and
seemed to be inflected according to the same rule, Miss Kober felt
tempted to assign them to the 'first declension' of the 'Minoan' language.   On the basis of the observed patterns of inflexion, she reached some tentative conclusions about the phonetic relationships of
the signs themselves.   Thus, in the first column of the above table,
if each sign stood for an open syllable of the type *ba* or *ti*, it was
highly likely that the third sign in lines 1, 2, and 3 would begin
with the same consonant: that consonant would represent the last
sound of the stem of the noun, while the vowel would represent the

ending.   By applying this principle in all her columns, Miss Kober
constructed what she called a 'tentative phonetic pattern' of five
pairs of signs, each of which seemed to share the same consonant:

	vowel 1	vowel 2
consonant 1	⋔	干
2	⅍	伊
3	Ŷ	屮ˢ
4	ⱱ	才
5	⋔	Ἀ

The following words of Miss Kober accompany this reconstruction:
> The assumptions on which [this figure] is based are the foll-
> owing:
> (1) *B* is a simple syllabary each of whose phonetic signs re-
> presents a consonant-vowel combination, with the possibility
> that either may be zero, that is, that pure consonant or vowel
> signs are possible.   This assumption has not been proven, nor
> is it provable at present.   It may, indeed, be entirely erro-
> neous.   It is used by the author whenever it is necessary, in
> following out an argument, to see what would be implied in
> terms of a syllabary, because the number of phonetic signs in
> *B* closely approximates those of the Cypriote syllabary, which
> is of the type described...   When some *type* of syllabary must
> be postulated, it seems only sensible to postulate a type
> which is simple and at the same time agrees with the few facts

at our disposal; other types require either too many signs
(for example, the cuneiform) or too few (like Sanskrit).
(2) The second assumption is that the stem of each of the five
words includes the initial consonant of the penultimate signs
of "cases" I and II, and of the final signs of "case" III.
(3) The third assumption is that all the words in the first
five columns ... belong to the same "declension" and that the
vowel following the last consonant of the stem is the same for
all of them in "cases" I and II, and changes to another vowel,
which is the same for all, in "case" III.   Since all three
assumptions are unprovable, [the tentative phonetic pattern]
has no validity.   If, however, an inflection pattern can be
restored for *B* and a reasonably complete phonetic pattern can
be constructed on the basis of this inflection pattern, using
assumptions similar to those above, and we find that the phonetic relationships are mutually confirmatory, the validity of
the original assumption might be proven by this very fact.   At
this stage, no such proof is possible.   *AJA* 52 (1948) 98 n. 46.
It may be noted that, with regard to *every pair* of signs in Miss Kober's tentative phonetic pattern, her deductions have been proved
correct.

Ventris' decipherment of the Linear B script

§ 36   Once the foundations had been laid by Alice Kober, Michael
Ventris was able to make rapid progress towards the decipherment of
the script.   From the beginning of 1951 until June 1952 he circula-
ted to interested persons a series of Work Notes on Minoan Language
Research, in which he recorded his changing opinions and took account
of the transcription of the Pylos tablets (1951).   The Work Notes as
a whole are characterized by immense industry and thoroughness.   If
the methods used in them fall a little short of the austere string-
ency of Miss Kober's, Ventris brought to his study, in more than ad-
equate compensation, an unsurpassed flair for isolating important
problems and tenacity in probing them.   His principal fault is that,
in common with many other would-be decipherers of the Linear B
script, he could not always resist the temptation of translating
whole words, just as they stood, using the frail evidence of the
Cypriot script and the contextual guide offered by the ideograms.
For a number of years before 1951, Ventris had had the fancy (it was
little more) that Etruscan, or a language closely related to Etruscan, underlay the Linear B inscriptions;[1] and the reader of his Work

[1]   Compare his contribution to his own questionnaire *The languages of the Minoan and Mycenaean civilizations* (London 1950) i.

Notes, aware of the conclusions he was soon to reach, is constantly disconcerted by allusions to Etruscan words and the attempt, half-hearted though it may be, to fit the inflexional pattern of the 'Minoan' language into an Etruscan frame-work.

§ 37 Ventris saw at the outset that Miss Kober's identification of examples of grammatical inflexion offered the only valid approach to a systematic decipherment. He therefore began by collecting all the instances then known of sign-groups in which the last sign or the last two signs showed a variation of such a consistent and predictable kind that it could reasonably be attributed to grammatical inflexion. As a result of this investigation, he published on 28th January 1951 the first of his phonetic 'grids'. In this, he arranged the commonest Linear B signs so as to indicate those which appeared to share a common consonant. A simplified version of this 'grid' will illustrate his procedure:

CONSONANTS	VOWEL 1 -nil? (-o?)	VOWEL 2 -i?	OTHER VOWELS? -a -e -u?	DOUBTFUL
t-?	〒	⋂		⊕
r-??	⟨sign⟩	Ϝ	↑ ⟨sign⟩	
ś-??	Ψ	⋔	⟨sign⟩ ⟨sign⟩	
n-?? s-??	⟨sign⟩	⟨sign⟩	Ϋ	
l-?	†	⟨sign⟩		
h-??	⟨sign⟩		⟨sign⟩	
θ-??	⟨sign⟩		⟨sign⟩	⟨sign⟩
m-? k-?	⊖			⟨sign⟩
				⟨sign⟩ ⟨sign⟩

In constructing this 'grid', Ventris went much farther than Miss
Kober had ventured to do and, by pressing into service what little
the Cypriot syllabary had to suggest about the nature of the signs,
he tentatively assigned actual phonetic values to a few of the signs
which constantly recur in word-endings.

§ 38   Two principal trends are apparent in Ventris' Work Notes,
arising from his extremely detailed study of the Pylos inscriptions:

§ 39   In the first place, he introduced greater refinement into
Alice Kober's concept of grammatical 'cases'.   For example, he
found that Miss Kober's 'Case II' could be sub-divided (so far as
its form was concerned) into five secondary types, depending on the
behaviour of the vowel in the last syllable of the stem: this was
sometimes left unchanged, and sometimes altered in various ways.

§ 40   Next Ventris carried out a statistical analysis of the inscriptions from Pylos, not only for the distribution of syllables
within a word (which we have been considering hitherto) but also for
the distribution of words within a text.   It was found that the very
rigidity of word - order in some classes of tablets could be made to
yield valuable information, when subjected to a penetrating analysis.

§ 41   The so-called E tablets from Pylos (§§ 248-274) were particularly productive.   These records of grain-allotments associated
with land-holdings have a rather complex structure, whose precise
nature has not, even now, been completely elucidated.   It is clear,
however, that two groups of inscriptions can be distinguished within
the E series, one group having been written at a later time than the
other.   The important fact which Ventris seized upon is that the
structure of these inscriptions is, to a large extent, stereotyped,
so that the behaviour of different sign-groups in identical contexts
can be studied easily.   It says a great deal for the thorough-going
character of Ventris' enquiry that he carried out, in Work Note 14,
no fewer than 159 analyses of the structure of E tablets. An outline
of one of these analyses is presented on the opposite page.   It was
vital in the working-out of the decipherment, and it furnishes moreover an excellent example of Ventris' methods.

§ 42   Ventris found that in the E series an inscription belongs:

either to Class I,

which consists of words ending in
one of these signs: †

followed by ⫼ ℔ 𝟻 and the group ⑂ Ⓐ †

or to Class II,

which consists of words ending in
one of these signs: 𝔅

followed by ⚹ ℔ 𝟓 and the group ⑂ Ⓐ ⳗ

§ 43   Ventris now introduced an observation from the Knossos tablets in an attempt to find some meaning in this inflexional variation, especially that between - † and - ⳗ .   He saw that at Knossos
there are two distinct patterns of final signs which occur before
the MAN and the WOMAN ideogram respectively. The first pattern corresponds to the first words of 'Class I' at Pylos, the second to the
first words of 'Class II'.   It followed that the last word of the
'Class I' group must be the masculine, and the last word of the
'Class II' group must be the feminine, form of the noun.   It was
highly likely also that the noun preceding in 'Class II' was either
a personal name or, more probably, a 'department-name' .   Ventris
suggested, as a mere guess, that the sequence ⑂ Ⓐ † was a spelling of
do^welos 'slave' (contracted to δοῦλος in classical Greek): a guess
which later turned out to be correct, except that the word does not
in fact contain -w-.

§ 44   As a result of his extensive analysis of the Pylos E tablets (which may be regarded as the essential core of the whole decipherment), Ventris was able to express in still more precise terms
the inflexional characteristics of the language represented in the
Linear B texts.   He differentiated the declension of personal names
from that of vocabulary-words; he elucidated the nature of 'collective' affixes; with the help of ideograms, he separated many masculine from feminine words and, with the help of numerals, plurals
from singulars; finally, he suggested that three groups of endings
might be verbal, indicating differences of tense, mood, or aspect —
but, since verbs form a comparatively rare class in the Linear B
inscriptions, the analysis of verbal forms played only a small part
in the decipherment.   At this late stage of Ventris' work the capacity he had shown throughout for making inspired, but unverifiable,
guesses did not desert him; as an aside, he mentioned that some of
the endings he was dealing with at Pylos seemed to behave just like
the inflexion of Greek nouns in -os, which in Homer frequently have
a genitive singular ending in -oio.

§ 45   In short, Ventris now felt able to describe the general
characteristics of the language of the tablets.   But of course his
description, however internally consistent and however cogent in itself, remained purely theoretical until he could attach specific
phonetic values to the syllables.   He accordingly prepared a refinement of his phonetic grid: this 'second state' (dated 28th Sep-
tember 1951) incorporated the results of his grammatical analyses of
the Pylian inscriptions, but did not yet commit him to the actual
values.

§ 46   After the publication of the drawings and photographs of
the Knossos tablets in *Scripta Minoa* II (Oxford 1952), Ventris rap-
idly incorporated the new body of evidence and produced the 'third
state' of his grid, in which he did commit himself, tentatively, to
a number of phonetic correspondences (see facing page).

§ 47   Although Ventris himself seems to have been unaware of
the fact, he had in his hand by this stage all the materials for
achieving a successful decipherment.   It is true (as hostile cri-
tics of the decipherment have not failed to point out) that there
is no necessary connexion between the third state of the grid and
the arguments contained in Work Note 20, which marks the beginning
of the decipherment properly so called.   Up to and including the
construction of his third grid, Ventris had worked out as far as
possible a grammar of the underlying language by identifying the
different functions of the nouns and their inter-relationships in
recurring groups.   In addition, he had built up a frame-work of
verbal correspondences, not all of which he expected to be correct

Possible Values → Vowels ↓ Consonants	-i? -e? v1	-o? -e? v2	-e? -u? v3	v4	-a? -i? v5	vowel un-certain
Pure Vowel —	ᛒ				ⵌ	
j - ?			ⵂ		ⵀ	
s - ? v - ? o - ? c - ?	ⴼ	ⴼ	ʔ	ⴴ	ⴼ	
z - ? p - ?	ⵝ				ǂ	ⴹ
s - ?	ⵗ	ⵅ				
t - ?		ⵁ			ⵔ	
t - ?	⋔	ⵠ				
o - ? r - ?	ⵛ	ⵕ	ⵧ			
n - ?	ⵝ	ⵙ	ⵏ		ⵒ	
f - ?	ⵐ	ⵤ			⵬	
h - ? o - ?		ⵕ	ⵓ			
r - ? l - ?	ⵥ				ⵔ	
l - ?	ⵕ	✝	⵰		⵰	⵬
v - ? r - ?	⵬		ⴰ		⊕	
c - ?			ⵞ			
m - ?		⵮	⊖			ⵂ

but which at least gave the promise of transferring his syntactical
patterns from the plane of theory to that of demonstrable fact.

§ 48   In the twentieth and last of his Work Notes, Ventris asked
what would result if he assumed, for the moment, that elements of the
Greek language were present in the mass of inscriptional material he
had by this time so well organized.   Despite his feeling that the
language was somehow akin to Etruscan,   he occasionally thought the
coincidences with Greek usage very striking.   This must therefore
have been present in his mind all along.   He decided that a known
place-name must be sought first among the inscriptions and an attempt
made to associate it with the more likely sound-values.

§ 49   By this time Ventris had isolated a number of 'group-names'
at Knossos and Pylos. These formed an 'adjectival' variant by changing their last syllable to Ƕ and adding -ϙ or - ꓷ.   By analogy
with the Bronze Age accounts at Ugarit, it seemed likely that these
'group-names' were words for towns, the adjectives in -ϙ and - ꓷ being their ethnics. Ventris next asked whether this assumption could
be tested by applying the values suggested in his third grid to a
known place - name. One of the most likely candidates was Amnisos, a
Minoan site in the neighbourhood of Knossos, which had been excavated
in the 1930s.   If A....... did occur among the 'group-names' and if
the values (or at least some of the values) in the third grid were
correct, this place-name would be written in the form:

Υ̓....... Ψ̓.......

a   ni

Now one sign-group, and one only, contained this sequence, namely:

Υ̓   ᗐ   Υ   ᗮ

a   mi   ni   so

This word generated the 'adjectival' forms

ᗮ   ᗐ   Υ   ⩜   ϙ   Υ̓   ᗐ   Υ   ⩜   ꓷ

a   mi   ni   si jo   a   mi   ni   si ja

and also a form Υ ᗐ Υ Υ Υ, which could be seen as the Greek 'lative'
word a-mi-ni-so-de, 'Αμνισόνδε, 'to Amnisos'.

§ 50   In showing that a certain sequence of signs spelt *a-mi-ni-so,* Ventris did not thereby demonstrate the presence of even one Greek word in the Linear B texts, since the place-names in -σ(σ)ος, found both in Crete and on the mainland, had long been recognized as belonging to a pre-Greek substrate language.   But, as always, he saw the over-riding importance of inflexional variants; and, when he went on to identify two ethnics of Amnisos, he realized that he was dealing with formations of a Greek type.   His further suggestion that the group *a-mi-ni-so-* plus suffixed syllable represented Greek Ἀμνισόνδε, though a mere guess, was a very reasonable one, given the course of the argument so far, and was later proved correct.

§ 51   Some important consequences flowed from Ventris' identification of Ἀμνισός and its ethnics.   For example: since the ending -𐀰 seemed to represent -*so*, then other place-names ending in -σ(σ)ος should be identifiable in the texts.   So it proved:

𐀒 𐀜 𐀰   𐀶 𐀪 𐀰

ko no so   *tu li so*

'Knossos'   'Tylissos'

§ 52   In the course of his Work Note 20, Ventris proceeded to identify other Greek words purely from the contexts in which they appeared and (what is still more significant) to establish the presence of Greek types of inflexion.

§ 53 · Among the Greek words identified from their context were τόσος (with its inflexional variants) and κορίαννον.   Ventris observed that two totalling words, 𐀵𐀰 (masculine) and 𐀵𐀭 (feminine), are very common in the Linear B texts.   Since he had shown that 𐀰 stands for *so*, then:

𐀵𐀰 = *to-so*, standing for τόσον or τόσοι

𐀵𐀭 = *to-sa*, standing for τόσα or τόσαι

§ 54   A similar chain of reasoning led to the identification of κορίαννον.   The following variation in spelling occurs:

𐀒𐀪𐀊𐀙𐀺 at Knossos; but 𐀒𐀪𐀤𐀅𐀚 at Pylos

Reference to the grid showed that 𐀙𐀺 stood for *do no* and 𐀅𐀚 for *da na*.   Both forms appeared to contain a 'dead' syllable vowel-harmony.   Since it was reasonable to suspect that the 'consonantal' element represented by the signs 𐀪𐀤𐀅𐀊𐀰 was either *l* or *r* (because

the sounds *l, r,* and *n* were the most likely ones to be involved in
vowel-harmony), the commodity in question, which is measured in dry
units, would have the reading *ko-l/ri-ja-to-no,* that is, κορίαννον,
'coriander'.

§ 55   The two most important types of Greek inflexion established in Ventris' Work Note 20 were that of nouns in -εύς and that of
the perfect active participle:

§ 56   Ventris reasoned that if the ending - ⲅ , which was typical of ethnics and personal names, represented the *u*-element in the
Greek termination -εύς, then its 'genitive' suffix -⅄ might correspond to -*wo* in Greek -ῆϝος and its 'accusative' suffix -Ⴧ to -*wa* in
Greek -ῆϝα.   From these elements could be constructed the declension of Greek nouns with diphthongal stem, for example nominative
βασιλεύς, accusative βασιλῆϝα, and genitive βασιλῆϝος.   (Although
this line of reasoning was perfectly sound, it is now known that Ⴧ
in fact stands for *we,* not *wa,* and that the Linear B forms ending in
-*we* are not accusative but locative-dative; however, accusative forms
in -*wa,*-ᕬ, are found as well).

§ 57   Clear traces of Greek declension could be seen in the chariot tablets from Knossos.   In particular, two perfect active participles of the verb ἀραρίσκω ('equip, fit out') appeared:

ᵀ ᒻ ᵞ ᖯ   ᵀ ᒻ ᵞ ᕤ ᵀ

a   ra   ru ja   *a   ra   ru wo   a*

ἀραρυῖα   ἀραρϝόα

§ 58   These two types of inflexion, namely the declension of
diphthong-stems in -εύς and the variation in perfect participles
between feminine and neuter forms, when set beside the formation
of masculine and feminine ethnics already discussed, add up to a
constellation of forms which are not only characteristic of Greek
but found only in Greek; and the existence of a nucleus of Greek
words and forms is thereby made out.

§ 59   So much for Ventris' earliest identification of Greek
forms in the Linear B texts.   It remained to apply his suggestions,
in a systematic way, to the whole corpus.   This examination Ventris
carried out in 1952-1953, in collaboration with Chadwick.   Their
joint work, published in 1953, contains a translation of considerable parts of the Linear B texts, based upon the fourth and final
stage of Ventris' grid.

§ 60   The validity of Ventris' decipherment has subsequently been
confirmed, at least in its broad outlines, by the discovery of further inscriptions at Pylos and elsewhere.   His theory not only explained the linguistic phenomena known to him but successfully met
the test of any scientific hypothesis, in that it enabled him to pre-
dict with accuracy the behaviour of words in inscriptions discovered
later.   The work of analysis has gone on without interruption since
Ventris' death in 1956 and has resulted in the modern grid of sound-
values (p. 38).

§ 61   When so much is said, it cannot be claimed that we are in
a position to 'read' the Linear B texts as we can, for example, many
of the Egyptian Hieroglyphic inscriptions.   Many items of vocabulary, and among them some which are vital to our full understanding of
the texts, cannot be reconciled with any words known in later Greek.
The explanation may be that such words are indeed Greek but that they
went out of use before the historical period or that the Linear B
texts contain elements of a language, or languages, other than Greek.
These two explanations are not, of course, mutually exclusive.   Proper names too present great difficulties of interpretation, princi-
pally because of the ambiguity of the writing-system.   These problems can hardly be solved by repeated examination of texts already
known; and it is to be hoped that the discovery of new inscriptions,
perhaps setting in different contexts these perplexing names and
items of vocabulary, will one day suggest a solution.

                                   ***

Development of the Linear B script: S. Marinatos *Minos* 4 (1956)
13-16; F. Schachermeyr *Saeculum* 10 (1959) 66-71; M.W.M. Pope *KX* 16
(1963) 310-319; E. Grumach *Kadmos* 4 (1965) 45-57; J.T. Hooker *Europa*
132-142, *The origin of the Linear B script* (Salamanca 1979); J.-P.
Olivier *SMEA* 20 (1979) 43-52; A. Heubeck *SMEA* 23 (1982) 195-217.   The
question of 'double writing': W. Nahm *Kadmos* 9 (1970) 1-21.
    Preliminaries to a decipherment: A.E. Cowley in *Essays in Aegean
archaeology presented to Sir A. Evans* (ed. S. Casson)(Oxford 1927)
5-7; A.J. Evans *The Palace of Minos at Knossos* IV (London 1935) 666-
763; A.E. Kober *AJA* 49 (1945) 143-151, 50 (1946) 268-276, 52 (1948)
91-99, *AO* 17/1 (1949) 386-398; T.B. Jones *TAPA* 78 (1947) 430-431.
    Ventris' decipherment and its consequences: M.G.F. Ventris *Work
notes on Minoan language research* 1-20 (28th Jan. 1951-1st June
1952)(privately distributed); Ventris and J. Chadwick *JHS* 73 (1953)
84-103; J. Friedrich *Entzifferung verschollener Schriften und Spra-
chen* (Berlin 1966[2]) 109-119; J. Chadwick *The decipherment of Linear
B* (Cambridge 1967[2]); M.W.M. Pope *The story of decipherment* (London
1975) 146-179.

Principles of decipherment applied to Ventris' theory: E. Sittig *Minos* 3 (1954) 10-19; J. Friedrich *Minos* 4 (1956) 6-10; A.P. Treweek *BICS* 4 (1957) 10-26; S. Luria *Minoica* 209-225; E. Risch *Anthropos* 53 (1958) 143-160; A. Heubeck *Gymnasium* 66 (1959) 494-501; F. Schachermeyr *Saeculum* 10 (1959) 48-72; H.D. Ephron *Minos* 7 (1961) 63-100.

Criticisms of Ventris' decipherment: A.J. Beattie *JHS* 76 (1956) 1-17, *MIO* 6 (1958) 33-104; E. Grumach *OLZ* 52 (1957) 293-342; S. Levin *The Linear B decipherment controversy re-examined* (New York 1964); J.E. Henle *Minoica* 192-196, *BJRL* 48 (1965) 69-80; D.C.C. Young *Arion* 4 (1965) 512-542; H. Geiss *Klio* 48 (1967) 5-51; F.R. Richards *Europa* 257-276; W. Ekschmitt *Die Kontroverse um Linear B* (Munich 1969).

4   THE LINEAR B INSCRIPTIONS

Types of inscriptions

§ 62   Linear B inscriptions are found on four classes of objects: clay tablets, clay labels, clay sealings, and clay vases.

§ 63   The same method of writing was used for inscriptions on
tablets, on labels, and on sealings.   The scribe took a sharp-
pointed stylus and scratched the signs on a lump of soft clay.   The
incised pieces of clay were then left to dry in the sun.   It is evident from this procedure and from indications in the texts, which
sometimes speak of 'this year' and 'last year', that the Linear B
tablets from each palace constitute the records of a single year
and that the practice was to pulp down the tablets and use them
again from year to year.   In every case, these clay documents owe
their preservation to the extensive fires which periodically attack-
ed the Bronze Age sites of the Aegean.   Some of the tablets were so
blackened or damaged by the fires as to be illegible; but there remains a sufficient amount of material from Knossos and Pylos for the
general nature of the 'palatial' archives of those two sites to be
deduced.   The much smaller numbers of tablets from Mycenae and
Thebes and the minute quantity from Tiryns show that these palaces
possessed records very similar to those from Pylos and Knossos.

§ 64   The clay tablets, which furnish the great bulk of the inscriptions, are of two principal shapes: the so-called 'palm-leaf'
type (Pl. 3) and the 'page' type (Pll. 1, 2).   The 'page' type is
especially appropriate to long lists of personnel etc., the 'palm-
leaf' type to individual transactions and assessments.   Linear B
tablets vary greatly in size.   'Page' tablets reach a maximum
height of about $9\frac{1}{2}$ inches and a maximum width of about $4\frac{1}{2}$ inches;
'palm-leaf' tablets may be as long as seven inches and as wide as
$1\frac{1}{2}$ inches.

§ 65   The circumstances of finding at Knossos and Pylos indicate
that some tablets, at least, were stored in clay or wooden boxes and
secured by a sealing (Pl. 6); the few inscribed sealings which have
survived refer to the subject-matter of the tablets in the box.   The
twenty-three clay labels found at Pylos (e.g. Pl. 4) were originally
pressed into the material of wicker-work boxes;   like the sealings,
they bear inscriptions indicating the contents of the respective file
of tablets.

§ 66   Unlike tablets, sealings, and labels, the inscribed vases
(e.g. Pl. 5) do not belong to the 'archives' of the palaces.   Inscriptions were painted, not incised, on their surface: inscriptions
which refer, apparently, to the place of origin of the contents. The
largest number of vase-inscriptions (more than sixty) come from
Thebes, and the vessels themselves are, for the most part, large
stirrup-jars.   Other well-preserved inscriptions in Linear B are
found on vessels at Eleusis, Orchomenos, Mycenae, and Tiryns on the
mainland and at Knossos and Chania in Crete.

The classification of the Linear B inscriptions

§ 67   Whatever system the Linear B clerks used to organize their
archives, modern study of the inscriptions and of the scribal hands
has enabled the texts to be divided into classes according to the
subjects with which they deal (capital letter). Many classes are sub-
divided in order to show different arrangements of the contents
(small letter).   This designation is preceded by letters to indicate the place of origin of the inscription and is followed by the
inventory-number allotted by the excavators.

§ 68   The abbreviations used for the find-places of the inscriptions are: EL Eleusis, KH Chania, KN Knossos, MY Mycenae, OR Orchomenos, PY Pylos, TH Thebes, TI Tiryns.

§ 69   The following classes of Linear B inscriptions are recog-
nized in modern editions:
Personnel tablets: KN Ag, Ai, Ak, Am, Ap, As, B; MY Au; PY Aa, Ab,
    Ac, Ad, Ae, An, Aq.
Tablets dealing with livestock: KN Ca, Ce, Ch, Co, C; PY Cc, Cn, Cr;
    TI Cb.
Sheep tablets: KN Da, Db, Dc, Dd, De, Df, Dg, Dh, Dk, Dl, Dm, Dn,
    Do, Dp, Dq, Dv, D.
Grain tablets: KN E; MY Eu; PY Ea, Eb, Ed, En, Eo, Ep, Eq, Er, Es;
    TI Ef.
Tablets recording rations, offerings, and the allocation of olive
    oil: KN Fh, Fp, Fs, F, Ga, Gg, Gm, Gv, G; MY Fo, Fu, Ge, Go; PY
    Fa, Fg, Fn, Fr, Gn.
Tablets showing assessment or allocation of metals: PY Ja, Jn, Jo.
Vase tablets: KN K.
Cloth tablets: KN Lc, Ld, Le, Ln, L; PY La.
Tablets showing miscellaneous assessments or allocations: KN Mc, M,
    Nc, Np, Oa, Od, Og, Pp; MY Oe, Oi; PY Ma, Mb, Mn, Na, Ng, Nn, Ob,
    On, Pa, Pn, Qa; TH Of.
Tablets recording weapons: KN Ra, R.

Chariot and armour tablets: KN Sc, Sd,Se, Sf,Sg, Sk,So, Sp; PY Sa,Sh.
Utensil tablets: PY Ta, Tn.
Tablets showing miscellaneous provisions: KN Uc, Uf, U; MY Ue, Ui;
    PY Ua, Ub, Un; TH Ug.
Tablets giving lists without ideograms: KN Vc, Vd,V; MY V; PY Va, Vn.
Labels: KN Wb; PY Wa.
Sealings: KN Ws; MY Wt; PY Wr.
Fragmentary tablets: KN Xd, Xe, X; MY X; PY Xa, Xn.
Inscriptions on vases: EL Z; KH Z; KN Z;MY Z; OR Z;PY Za; TH Z; TI Z.

§ 70   Thus a Linear B inscription is referred to, for example,
as KN As 1516 or PY Fn 50.   When an inscription has been put together by joining fragments, it is denominated in the following manner:
KN L 7400 + 7402 + 8250.

The elements of the Linear B script

§ 71   The principal elements of the script are (1) syllabograms,
(2) ideograms,(3) signs for weights and measures,(4) numerical signs.

§ 72   (1) The syllabograms are set out on p. 38, together with
the arbitrary numbers which have been assigned to them and also th e
phonetic equivalents where these are securely established.

§ 73   Most often the syllabograms are put one after the other so
as to form recognizable words of the kind identified by Ventris in
the course of his decipherment.   But they can also be used in two
other ways: singly (§ 74) or as constituents of a monogram (§ 75).

§ 74   When a syllabogram is used in isolation, its function is
either the ligature or adjunct of an ideogram (a function which is
examined in §§ 77 - 78) *or* the abbreviation of a word.   As appears
from the following list, it is only rarely that the word thus abbre-
viated can be identified with certainty:
a: acts as ideogram, followed by numerals (meaning unknown)(PY).
a₂: acts as ideogram, followed by numerals (meaning unknown)(PY).
ai: abbreviation of *ai-ka-na-jo* (PY).
da: followed by numerals, especially in the KN and PY A tablets; it
    may represent the 'supervisor' of a work-force (cf. *ta*)(§ 201).
de: abbreviation of δεσμά? (MY)
di: acts as ideogram, followed by numerals (meaning unknown)(PY).
du: acts as ideogram, followed by numerals (meaning unknown)(PY).
e: (i) followed by numerals (meaning unknown)(KN, PY);
    (ii) abbreviation of *e-ne-me-na* (MY);
    (iii) abbreviation of *e-ra-pe-ja* or *e-ra-pi-ja* (PY).
ka: acts as ideogram, followed by numeral 1 (meaning unknown)(PY).

LINEAR B SYLLABOGRAMS

*08 a	*38 e	*28 i	*61 o	*10 u	*25 a₂	*43 ai	*85 au	*18	*83
*01 da	*45 de	*07 di	*14 do	*51 du	*71 dwe	*90 dwo		*19	*86
*57 ja	*46 je		*36 jo					*22	*89
*77 ka	*44 ke	*67 ki	*70 ko	*81 ku				*34	
*80 ma	*13 me	*73 mi	*15 mo	*23 mu				*35	
*06 na	*24 ne	*30 ni	*52 no	*55 nu	*48 nwa			*47	
*03 pa	*72 pe	*39 pi	*11 po	*50 pu	*29 pu₂	*62 pte		*49	
*16 qa	*78 qe	*21 qi	*32 qo					*56	
*60 ra	*27 re	*53 ri	*02 ro	*26 ru	*76 ra₂	*33 ra₃	*68 ro₂	*63	
*31 sa	*09 se	*41 si	*12 so	*58 su				*64	
*59 ta	*04 te	*37 ti	*05 to	*69 tu	*66 ta₂	*87 twe	*91 two	*65	
*54 wa	*75 we	*40 wi	*42 wo					*79	
*17 za	*74 ze		*20 zo					*82	

ki: acts as ideogram (meaning unknown)(KN).
ko: (i) abbreviation of *ko-wo* (KN);
    (ii) abbreviation of *ko-ri-a₂-da-na* (KN, MY, PY);
    (iii) abbreviation of *ko-ru-to* (PY).
ku: abbreviation of *ku-mi-no* (MY).
ma: abbreviation of *ma-ra-tu-wo* (KN, MY, PY).
me: acts as ideogram, followed by numerals (meaning unknown)(PY).
mi: abbreviation of *mi-ta* (MY).
mo: abbreviation of μόνϝος (vs. *ze* ii)(KN, PY).
mu: acts as ideogram (meaning unknown)(KN).
ni: acts as FIG ideogram (abbreviation of νικύλεον?)(KN, MY, PY).
o: (i) acts as ideogram (meaning unknown)(PY);
    (ii) abbreviation of *o-pa-wo-ta* (PY);
    (iii) abbreviation of *o-pe-ro* (most frequently)(KN, PY).
pa: (i) followed by numerals (meaning unknown)(KN, PY);
    (ii) abbreviation of *pa-ra-ja* or *pa-ra-jo* (KN);
    (iii) abbreviation of *pa-ra-wa-jo* (PY).
pe: (i) acts as ideogram (meaning unknown)(KN, MY, PY);
    (ii) abbreviation of *pe-ru-si-nu-wo* (KN).
po: followed by numerals (meaning unknown)(KN).
qo: followed by numeral 1 (meaning unknown)(KN).
ra: followed by numeral 1 (meaning unknown)(PY).
re: acts as ideogram (meaning unknown)(MY).
ri: acts as ideogram of weighed commodity (meaning unknown)(PY).
sa: (i) acts as ideogram for FLAX (KN, PY);
    (ii) abbreviation of *sa-sa-ma* (MY).
se: probably abbreviation of *se-to-i-ja* (KN).
ta: followed by numerals in KN and PY A tablets; it apparently represents the 'supervisor' of a work-force (cf. *da*).
u: followed by numeral 1 (meaning unknown)(PY).
we: abbreviation of ϝέταλον? (KN, PY).
wi: acts as ideogram (meaning unknown)(PY).
wo: acts as ideogram (meaning unknown)(PY).
ze: (i) acts as ideogram, apparently indicating amount of land (PY);
    (ii) abbreviation of ζεῦγος (vs. *mo*)(KN, PY).

§ 75   Two or three syllabograms are occasionally written as a single sign, or 'monogram', which then represents a word in its own right.   The following monograms are known:

KAPO   *ka + po:* καρποί 'fruits'

KANAKO *ka + na + ko:* κνᾶκος 'safflower'

AREPA *a + re + pa:* ἄλειφαρ 'ointment' (§ 289)

MERI   *me + ri:* μέλι 'honey'

TURO$_2$ *tu + ro$_2$:* τυροί 'cheeses'

§ 76 (2) The ideograms (or, more strictly, logograms) were in origin pictorial representations of persons, animals, or objects. Some of the Linear B ideograms are careful, and even detailed, drawings of objects; but many have degenerated into schematic sketches whose meaning cannot be made out if there is no satisfactory context. The commonest ideograms, with the numbers now assigned them, are illustrated on pages 42 and 43.

§ 77 Sometimes two ideograms are joined in a 'ligature': thus GOLD + DISH forms one sign in PY Tn 316 vs. 6. It is quite common for an ideogram to be ligatured with a syllabogram, for instance:
a: (i) ligatured with the OLIVE ideogram (KN);
 (ii) ligatured with the OIL ideogram (PY).
ko: ligatured with SKIN (PY).
o: ligatured with the BARLEY ideogram (KN, MY, PY).
pa: (i) ligatured with the CLOTH ideogram (KN);
 (ii) ligatured with the OIL ideogram (PY);
 (iii) ligatured with the CYPERUS ideogram (PY).
po: (i) ligatured with *211 (KN);
 (ii) ligatured with the OIL ideogram (PY).
qa: ligatured with the CYPERUS ideogram (KN).
ri: ligatured with the TUNIC ideogram (KN).
si: ligatured with the OX and PIG ideograms (PY).
ta: ligatured with the SHEEP ideogram (PY).
te: ligatured with the CLOTH ideogram (KN, PY) and with the WHEEL ideogram (PY).

§ 78 A syllabogram may be superimposed upon an ideogram to form a 'syllabic adjunct'. The commonest adjuncts are:

a: adjunct to the AMPHORA ideogram (KN).
ai: adjunct to the GOAT ideogram (KN).
de: adjunct to the WOMAN ideogram (KN).
di: (i) adjunct to the WOMAN ideogram (KN);
     (ii) adjunct to various ideograms representing vessels (KN).
e: adjunct to *177 (KN).
ka: (i) adjunct to STIRRUP-JAR (KN);
      (ii) adjunct to the PIG ideogram (PY).
ke: (i) adjunct to a vessel ideogram (KN);
      (ii) adjunct to FLAX (PY);
      (iii) adjunct to *189 (PY).
ki: (i) adjunct to the SHEEP and GOAT ideograms (KN);
      (ii) adjunct to TUNIC (KN).
ko: adjunct to the CLOTH ideogram (KN).
ku: (i) adjunct to the CLOTH ideogram (KN);
      (ii) adjunct to the CYPERUS ideogram (KN, MY).
me: adjunct to ideograms representing children (KN).
mi: adjunct to the CLOTH ideogram (KN).
ne: adjunct to women, children, and animals (abbreviation of *ne-wo* =
      νέϝος?)(KN).
pa: adjunct to women (KN).
pe: adjunct to the CLOTH, TUNIC, MAN, and WOMAN ideograms (KN).
po: adjunct to the CLOTH and MAN ideograms (KN).
pu: adjunct to the CLOTH ideogram (KN, PY).
qe: adjunct to the CORSLET ideogram (KN).
re: adjunct to the CLOTH ideogram (KN).
sa: adjunct to the SHEEP and GOAT ideograms (KN).
se: adjunct to *168 (KN).
su: adjunct to TREE (KN).
ta: adjunct to the OX ideogram (KN).
te: (i) adjunct to the MAN ideogram (KN);
      (ii) adjunct to the OIL ideogram (KN).
ti: adjunct to the OLIVE ideogram (KN, MY).
tu: adjunct to the WOMAN ideogram (abbreviation of *tu-ka-te* = θυγά-
      τηρ?)(KN).
u: adjunct to *212 (KN).
we: (i) adjunct to the OX ideogram (KN);
      (ii) adjunct to the OIL ideogram (MY, PY);
      (iii) adjunct to *166 (KN, PY).
wi: adjunct to *152 (PY).
za: adjunct to the SHEEP and WOMAN ideograms (KN).
zo: adjunct to the CLOTH ideogram (KN).

§ 79   (3) The signs for weights and measures are transliterated
arbitrarily by means of capital letters.   They are shown here in
the order which the Linear B scribes adopted, with the larger quantities preceding the smaller (p. 44):

LINEAR B IDEOGRAMS

*100 MAN (VIR)	*121 BARLEY (HORDEUM)	*145 WOOL (LANA)
*102 WOMAN (MULIER)	*122 OLIVE (OLIVA)	*151 HORN (CORNU)
*104 DEER (CERVUS)	*125 CYPERUS (CYPEROS)	*153
*105 HORSE (EQUUS)	*129 FLOUR (FARINA)	*155 RECEP-TACLE
*106ᶠ EWE (OVISᶠ)	*130 OIL (OLEUM)	*158
*106ᵐ RAM (OVISᵐ)	*131 WINE (VINUM)	*159 CLOTH (TELA)
*107 GOAT (CAPER)	*140 BRONZE (AES)	*162 TUNIC (TUNICA)
*108 PIG (SUS)	*141 GOLD (AURUM)	*164
*109 OX (BOS)	*142	*167
*120 WHEAT (GRANUM)	*144 CROCUS (CROCUS)	*168

LINEAR B IDEOGRAMS,
continued

*173 MOON (LUNA)	*209 AMPHORA	*230 SPEAR (HASTA)
*200 PAN	*212 URN	*231 ARROW (SAGITTA)
*201 TRIPOD	*213 DISH	*232
*202 JAR	*214 CONTAINER	*233 DAGGER (PUGIO)
*203 PITHOS	*215 TWO HANDLED GOBLET	*240 WHEELED CHARIOT (BIGAE)
*204 JUG	*216 CUP	*241 WHEEL-LESS CHARIOT (CURRUS)
*205 JUGLET	*218 ONE-HANDLED GOBLET	*242 CHARIOT (CAPSUS)
*206 HYDRIA	*227 RHYTON	*243 WHEEL (ROTA)
*207 TRIPOD HYDRIA	*228 PAN	*254 JAVELIN (JACLUM)
*208 BOWL	*229 LADLE	*257

Dry measure:	T	T
	◁	V
	⌐	Z
Liquid measure:	৭)	S
	◁	V
	⌐	Z
Weight:	△↑△	L
	₹	M
	♯	N
	₹	P
	♀	Q

Apart from L, which represents 'unity', each of these signs stands for a fractional quantity. 'Unity' itself is usually shown simply by the appropriate ideogram, followed by a numeral; thus 平⎮ T⫶◁ ⫶ stands for 1 large measure of WHEAT, 5 measures of the second largest size, and 4 of the third largest.

§ 80   (4) Numerals are expressed according to a decimal system, and are written from left to right in descending order as follows:

-φ- 10000   -φ- 1000   ο 100   - 10   ⎮ 1

So, for example, 607 is written ⹃⹃ ⫶⫶⫶ , and 2630 is written ⫶φ 88 ⹃ .
(No fractions are written in the extant Linear B inscriptions).

Writing-habits

§ 81   Like Linear A, the Linear B script was written from left to right; but in matters of detail there is little similarity bet- ween the two systems. The appearance of Linear B texts is, on the whole, neater and more orderly than those written in Linear A. On Linear B tablets of the 'page' type (§ 64), scribes regularly sep- arated different items by means of horizontal lines.   A part, or even the whole, of one side of a tablet was sometimes ruled with- out ever being inscribed (e.g. KN V 1526). Texts were often divi-

ded into 'paragraphs' by leaving blank lines (e.g. PY An 657, Er 312,
Un 718).   The Linear B scribes rarely followed the Linear A practice of carrying over a word from one line to the next, but when
space was short they finished a word in small characters above a
line of writing (e.g. PY Jn 829.2, Tn 316 vs.3).   Many, but not all,
scribes used a word-divider: this nearly always consists of a small
vertical stroke (on PY Cn 40.14 a horizontal one).   On a few tablets
(for example the Vd set at Knossos) the word-groups are separated
into compartments by tall vertical lines.   If necessary, an inscription was continued on the reverse of the tablet (e.g. PY Tn 316) or
on the edge (e.g. KN Sd 4404).   Variation in the size of the characters is a common feature of the Linear B tablets; sometimes (as on
PY Tn 316) it is obvious that a word is written in large characters
because it refers to the whole inscription, but in other cases the
reason for the variation in size cannot now be ascertained.   A
check-mark in the form of a small cross, ×, is found on a few inscriptions (e.g. KN V 280, PY An 594).   Some tablets show clear
traces of an earlier inscription which has been partially erased to
make room for the corrected version: that applies, for instance, to
most members of the Un set at Pylos.   In their lighter moments, one
or two scribes drew a sketch or doodle on the reverse side of the
tablet (e.g. MY Oe 106, PY Cn 1287).

§ 82   Study of scribal hands in the great archives of Knossos
and Pylos has now reached an advanced stage: forty-five different
hands have been recognized at Pylos, and sixty-six at Knossos. Extensive research into scribal differences has facilitated the joining of many inscribed fragments.

***

The structure of the Linear B script: A. Sacconi PP 31 (1976) 48-
65.
    The Linear B archives: J. Chadwick RF 90 (1962) 337-358, SM 11-
21; J.T. Hooker Kadmos 3 (1965) 114-121; C.G. Thomas PP 25 (1970)
301-311.
    Find-places of the tablets.   Knossos: L.R. Palmer and J. Board-
man On the Knossos tablets (Oxford 1963).   Pylos: E.L. Bennett MS
241-252; A. Sacconi SMEA 2 (1967) 94-102.   Thebes: T.G. Spyropoulos and J. Chadwick The Thebes tablets II (Salamanca 1975).
    Scribal hands.   General: E.L. Bennett Hesperia 35 (1966) 295-
309.   Knossos: J.-P. Olivier Les scribes de Cnossos (Rome 1967).
Mycenae: E.L. Bennett in The Mycenae tablets II (Philadelphia 1958)
89-95.   Pylos: E.L. Bennett Athenaeum 46 (1958) 328-333.

Knossos tablets and sealings. *Corpus:* A.J. Evans *Scripta Minoa*
II (ed. J.L. Myres)(Oxford 1952). Transliteration: J. Chadwick,
J.T. Killen, J.-P. Olivier *The Knossos tablets* (Cambridge 1971[4]).
Sealings: J.-P. Olivier *Minos* 9 (1968) 173-183. Joins: J.-P. Olivier *KX* 17 (1963) 252-260, *ABSA* 62 (1967) 325-336, *KX* 20 (1966) 249-
253; J.T. Killen and J.-P. Olivier *PCCMS* 49-92, *BCH* 92 (1968) 115-
141; L. Godart, J.T. Killen, J.-P. Olivier *Minos* 10 (1969) 151-165;
L. Godart and J.-P. Olivier *SMEA* 15 (1972) 33-49. New texts: J.
Chadwick *ABSA* 57 (1962) 46-73; J. Chadwick and J.T. Killen *ABSA* 58
(1963) 68-88; J.-P. Olivier *ABSA* 62 (1967) 267-323; J. Sakellarakis
and J.-P. Olivier *AAA* 5 (1972) 298-292; J. Bennet and J.A. Macgil-
livray *Kadmos* 21 (1982) 30-32.
    Mycenae tablets and sealings. *Corpora: The Mycenae tablets* II
(ed. E.L. Bennett)(Philadelphia 1958); *The Mycenae tablets* III (ed.
J. Chadwick)(Philadelphia 1963); J.-P. Olivier *The Mycenae tablets*
IV (Leiden 1969); A. Sacconi *Corpus delle iscrizioni in lineare B
di Micene* (Rome 1974). Epigraphical commentary: J.-P. Olivier
Kadmos 8 (1969) 46-53. Sealings: J. Chadwick *Eranos* 57 (1959) 1-5.
New text: G.E. Mylonas *Kadmos* 9 (1970) 48-50.
    Pylos tablets, sealings, and labels. Provisional publications:
E.L. Bennett *The Pylos tablets* (Princeton 1955); M.L. Lang *AJA* 62
(1958) 181-191, 63 (1959) 128-137, 64 (1960) 160-164, 65 (1961) 158-
163, 66 (1962) 149-152, 67 (1963) 160-162, 69 (1965) 98-101. The Fr
tablets: E.L. Bennett *The olive oil tablets of Pylos* (Salamanca
1958). Labels: J. Chadwick *BICS* 5 (1958) 1-5. Transliteration of
all known inscriptions: E.L. Bennett and J.-P. Olivier *The Pylos
tablets transcribed* I-II (Rome 1973, 1976).
    Thebes tablets. *Corpora:* J.Chadwick *Minos* 10 (1969) 115-137;
T.G. Spyropoulos and J.Chadwick *The Thebes tablets* II (Salamanca
1975); L. Godart and A. Sacconi *Les tablettes en linéaire B de
Thèbes* (Rome 1978). Commentary: J.-P. Olivier *AAA* 4 (1971) 269-272.
    Tiryns tablets. *Corpus:* L. Godart and J.-P. Olivier *Tiryns* VIII
(Mainz 1975) 37-53. Additional fragments: U. Naumann, L. Godart,
J.-P. Olivier *BCH* 101 (1977) 229-234; L. Godart, J.T. Killen, J.-P.
Olivier *AA* (1979) 450-458.
    Vase-inscriptions. *Corpora:* J. Raison *Les vases à inscriptions
peintes de l'âge mycénien* (Rome 1968); A. Sacconi *Corpus delle
iscrizioni vascolari in lineare B* (Rome 1974). Commentary: L.
Godart *PP* 31 (1976) 118-122. Chania: E. Hallager *OpAth* 11 (1975)
64-86. Knossos: M.R. Popham *Kadmos* 8 (1969) 43-45. Thebes: J.
Chadwick *ZA* 8 (1958) 237-239. General: C. Consani *SSL* 20 (1980) 55-
114; H.W. Catling, J.F. Cherry, R.E. Jones, J.T. Killen *ABSA* 75 (1980)
49-115.
    Indexes and lexicons: A. Morpurgo *Mycenaeae Graecitatis lexicon*
(Rome 1963); J. Chadwick and L. Baumbach *Glotta* 41 (1963) 157-271;
M. Doria *Indice retrogrado delle iscrizioni in lineare B di Pilo e
di Micene* (Trieste 1964); M. Lejeune *Index inverse du grec mycénien*

(Paris 1964); L. Baumbach *Glotta* 49 (1971) 151-190; J.-P. Olivier, L. Godart, C. Seydel, C. Sourvinou *Index généraux du linéaire B* (Rome 1973).

Syllabograms. Origin of the syllabic values: V. Georgiev *Athenaeum* 46 (1958) 415-430. Rare signs. General: M. Lejeune *AM* I 73-98. *17, *20, *74, *79: M.D. Petruševski *CM* 259-265. *35, *47: M. Doria *AM* II 36-46. *52: J.-P. Olivier *SM* 71-73. *65: A. Heubeck *SMEA* 13 (1971) 147-155. *66, *91: M. Doria *Kadmos* 3 (1964) 64-71; M. Lejeune *Mémoires* II 327-337. *82: M. Doria *AM* II 46-51. *85: M.D. Petruševski and P.H. Ilievski *ZA* 8 (1958) 265-278; M. Lejeune *Mémoires* III 179-199. *90: E. Risch *Minos* 5 (1957) 34. Monogram: A. Sacconi *Kadmos* 11 (1972) 22-26. Abbreviations. General: H. Geiss *AR* II 504-506, *Abbreviations and adjuncts in the Knossos tablets* (Berlin/Amsterdam 1970). *da, pa, ta, ze, *171:* F.R. Adrados *Emerita* 29 (1961) 287-296. *di, pa, pe, re, za:* J.T. Killen *AM* II 433-440. *ko:* H. Geiss *Europa* 113-119. *sa:* T.G. Spyropoulos *AE* (1963) 154-162. *tu:* J.T. Killen *ZA* 16 (1966) 207-212. *we, wi:* A. Sacconi *SMEA* 3 (1967) 97-134. *ze* in PY Aq: A. Sacconi *PP* 29 (1974) 182-189.

Ideograms. General: J. Sundwall *EM* 35-37; A.M. Frenkian *SC* 2 (1960) 303-307; E.L. Bennett *PCCMS* 11-25, *Minos* 8 (1967) 63-99, *AM* I 55-72; J.-P. Olivier *BCH* 93 (1969) 830-837; M. Lejeune *Mémoires* II 141-165; C. Sourvinou-Inwood *Minos* 13 (1972) 67-97; F. Vandenabeele and J.-P. Olivier *Les idéogrammes archéologiques du linéaire B* (Paris 1979). *102: J. Chadwick *Kadmos* 2 (1963) 124-126. *106: J.T. Killen *PP* 17 (1962) 26-31. *106, *107, *108, *109: L. Godart *KX* 23 (1971) 89-94. *123: A. Sacconi *AM* II 18-32. *124: J.L. Melena *Minos* 13 (1972) 52. *124, *125: A. Sacconi *CM* 347-351. *134, *190: P.H. Ilievski *ZA* 15 (1966) 271-280. *142: L. Baumbach *AC(CT)* 14 (1971) 7-8; J.L. Melena *Minos* 13 (1972) 44. *145: J.T. Killen *Hermathena* 96 (1962) 38-72. *146: M. Lejeune *Mémoires* II 313-325. *146, *160: Y. Duhoux *Minos* 15 (1974) 116-122. *146, *150, *152, *153, *154, *165, *166, *167: A. Sacconi *SMEA* 3 (1967) 97-134. *165, *166: Y. Duhoux *Minos* 15 (1974) 122-132. *166, *167: A. Sacconi *AntCret* I 202-204. *168: Y. Duhoux *Kadmos* 14 (1975) 117-120. *169: J. Manessy-Guitton, N. Weill, M. Lejeune *REG* 89 (1976) 183-215, 596-598. *181: Y. Duhoux *Kadmos* 14 (1975) 121-124. *249: J.-P. Olivier *Kadmos* 4 (1965) 58-63.

Adjuncts and ligatures. General: J. Sundwall *Minos* 4 (1956) 43-49; E. Grumach *BJRL* 45 (1962) 40-57. *pa, pe, se, za:* J.T. Killen *Eranos* 61 (1963) 69-93. *te:* J.T. Killen *BICS* 13 (1966) 109. *u:* A. Sacconi *SMEA* 3 (1967) 105-108.

Weights and measures. General: E.L. Bennett *AJA* 54 (1950) 204-222; J. Sundwall *Minos* 3 (1954) 107-110; N.F. Parise *PP* 19 (1964) 5-21; A. Sacconi *Kadmos* 10 (1971) 135-149. Units of capacity: M.L. Lang *AJA* 68 (1964) 99-105. Square measure: Y. Duhoux *Kadmos* 13 (1974) 27-38.

5   THE LANGUAGE OF THE LINEAR B TEXTS

The spelling rules

§ 83   The signs of the Linear B script to which syllabic values may be assigned with reasonable confidence are seventy-three in number, namely:

a	e	i	o	u	a_2	ai	au
da	de	di	do	du	dwe	dwo	
ja	je		jo				
ka	ke	ki	ko	ku			
ma	me	mi	mo	mu			
na	ne	ni	no	nu	nwa		
pa	pe	pi	po	pu	pu_2	pte	
qa	qe	qi	qo				
ra	re·	ri	ro	ru	ra_2	ra_3	ro_2
sa	se	si	so	su			
ta	te	ti	to	tu	ta_2	twe	two
wa	we	wi	wo				
za	ze		zo				

§ 84   It will be observed that each sign represents an open syllable, namely a syllable consisting *either* of a vowel *or* of consonant + vowel *or* of consonant + consonant + vowel.   When a syllable comprises vowel + consonant or consonant + vowel + consonant, the consonant which closes the syllable is usually ignored by the Linear B scribes: e.g. *a-ku-ro* = ἄργυρος, *a-mo-ta* = ἄρμοτα, *a-pi* = ἀμφί, *e-ko* = ἔγχος, *ka-ko* = χαλκός, *pa-te* = πάντες.   But when a syllable consists of the sequence consonant + consonant + vowel, the usual practice is to express it as two syllables, the first containing an 'empty' or 'dead' vowel, which receives the colouring of the vowel in the following syllable: e.g. *a-mi-ni-so* = 'Αμνισός, *du-ru-to-mo* = δρυτόμος, *ko-no-so* = Κνωσός, *ku-ru-so* = χρυσός, *ku-su* = ξύν, *po-ro-* = προ-.   The spelling *qi-si-pe-e* for ξίφεε is evidently anomalous.

§ 85   Although all five simple vowels are represented in the syllabary, the only diphthongs to have special signs are *ai* and *au;* and the syllabic sign for *ai* is used only rarely, most often the diphthong αι being represented simply by *a*.   Of the other diphthongs some, such as ευ, have to be indicated by two signs, e.g. *qa-si-re-u* = βασιλεύς; some, such as οι, are written with the simple vowel, e.g. *o-no* = ὄνοι.   The script does not distinguish long from short vowels: a defect it shares with the earliest known Attic alphabet of classical Greek, which uses one sign for both short and long *e* and one for both short and long *o*.   On the other hand, the Linear B syllabary provides equivalents which do not seem to be strictly necessary for a rendering of the Greek language.   This is true especially of the signs transliterated a_2 and ra_2: signs which may mark the association of the *a*-vowel with a 'glide' sound (*aj, rja*) or with an aspirate (*ha, rha*).   With this possible exception, aspiration or the lack of it is not marked anywhere in the system.   Apart from the dentals (*da* etc., *ta* etc.), the script does not distinguish between voiced and voiceless stops.   The failure to mark aspiration or the length of vowels, combined with the fact (noted in § 54) that there is only one set of signs for the *r* and the *l* series, can lead to serious ambiguity: for example, the sign conventionally transliterated *ke* can, in theory, represent any one of the six syllables κε, κη, χε, χη, γε, or γη; similarly, *pe* stands not only for πε but also for πη, φε, φη, βε, and βη; while the sign transliterated *re* spells λε and λη as well as ρε and ρη.

§ 86   Further ambiguities are apparent when it is considered exactly how the script renders Greek words.   The two sounds *s* and *n* are not written at the end of a word: a practice which effectively obscures the case-endings of *a*-stem and *o*-stem nouns and adjectives: thus *to-so* stands not only for τόσος, masculine singular nominative, but also for τόσον, masculine singular accusative.   In addition, *s* is normally not written when it precedes a stop: e.g. *e-ka-ra* = ἐσχάρα, *pa-ka-na* = φάσγανα, *pe-mo* = σπέρμο.   The word ϝάναξ is represented by the spelling *wa-na-ka,* in which -σ- has been ignored and -κ- expanded by means of a 'dead' vowel (see further § 116).

§ 87   it is a widespread, but not invariable, practice of the Linear B scribes to insert a 'glide' when *i* or *u* is followed by a vowel.   The 'glide' assumes the colouring of the preceding vowel, appearing as *j* when that vowel is *i* and as *w* when it is *u:*

a-ni-ja	ἀνίαι		
i-je-re-u	ἱερεύς	*ku-wa-no*	κύϝανος
i-jo-te	ἰόντες	*tu-we-a*	θύϝεα
po-ti-ni-ja	πότνια		

Sometimes *i-e-re-u* is found instead of *i-je-re-u*. Another possible example of a 'glide' which is sometimes written and sometimes omitted is seen in the alternation between the prefixes *o-* and *jo-* (§ 130).[1]

Phonology

§ 88   So far as the sounds represented by Linear B are concerned, the decipherment of the script has enabled us to catch glimpses (if no more) of a much earlier stage in the development of the Greek language than was previously possible. Four important features call for comment:

§ 89   The Linear B scribes fairly consistently use the *w*-series to indicate the presence of the 'digamma' or 'vau'.   This sound, pronounced like English *w* or *v*, had disappeared from some dialects by the beginning of the historical period; but in others it was still written (ϝ), and in any case it is known to have been present in a number of Greek words, partly on the evidence of cognate words in other Indo-European languages, partly because the assumption of its presence enables us to account for the scansion of many Homeric verses.

§ 90   Firmly established examples of words containing digamma in the Linear B texts are: *di-wo* = Διϝός 'of Zeus'; *ko-wo* = κόρϝος 'son, boy'; *ne-wo* = νέϝος 'new'; *-wi-de* = -ϝίδε '(he) saw'; *ra-wo-* = λᾱϝο- 'people'; *wa-na-ka* = ϝάναξ 'lord'; *wa-tu* = ϝάστυ 'town'; *we-to* = ϝέτος 'year'.

§ 91   Spellings such as these cause no surprise.   It could have been predicted that all of the words in question still contained the digamma in the Late Bronze Age.

§ 92   The presence of a digamma in the comparative adjective μείων was, however, unexpected.   In historical Greek, this word retains no trace of a digamma; yet the Linear B spelling varies between *me-u-jo* and *me-wi-jo,* both spellings pointing clearly to the original presence of digamma between the vowels.

[1] Alphabetic Greek too occasionally indicated in writing the glide-sound of the spoken language: E. Schwyzer *Griechische Grammatik* I (Munich 1953) 202.

§ 93   The digamma in μείων, though unpredictable, does not actually conflict with any later witness.   The spelling *e-ne-ka,* on the
other hand, is impossible to reconcile with the traditional etymology of this word.   Before Ventris' decipherment, ἕνεκα was usually
analysed into the elements ἐν and ϝεκα, the second being the stem of
(ϝ)ἑκων 'willing'.   Confronted by the Linear B spelling,which shows
no trace of the expected digamma, *either* we must say that the traditional derivation is erroneous (and indeed it is not easy to see how
ἕνεκα, in its attested meaning, could ever have arisen from the juxtaposition of ἐν and *ϝεκα), *or* we must invent a spelling rule for
Linear B to account for this one instance and assume that, in certain circumstances, *w* was not rendered in the script if it was in immediate contact with *n.* If the first choice is made, the 'diphthong'
in Homeric εἵνεκα will be seen not as Ionic vowel-lengthening before
ν + ϝ but as a case of 'metrical' lengthening.[1]

§ 94   With another word also the Mycenaean evidence has shown
the traditional etymology to be false.   The god's name which is
spelt Ποσειδῶν in Attic and Ποσειδάων in Homer was usually seen as
the reflexion of an original form with digamma, namely Ποσειδάϝων:
an etymology which seemed unassailable in view of the occurrence of
Ποτειδάϝονι and Ποτειδάϝονος in the Doric dialect of Corinthia.[2]   But
the name is spelt *po-se-da-o* in the Linear B tablets at Pylos.   This
spelling disposes of the accepted etymology and makes it necessary
to regard the Corinthian forms as innovations, in which the digamma
was introduced by analogy.

§ 95   (2) A class of sounds which had changed into others by
the classical period but which must have existed at earlier stages
of Greek consists of 'labio-velars' (velar sounds pronounced with
rounding of the lips).   From the evidence of other Indo-European
languages, for example Latin, it has long been established that some
of the *b, d, p, ph, t,* and *th* sounds of classical Greek had descend-
ed from labio-velars.   A long list of correspondences could be made
to show that Latin either retained the labio-velar or developed it
in a direction different from that taken by Greek.   For example:

---

[1]   Cf. W.F. Wyatt *Metrical lengthening in Homer* (Rome 1969) 88-
89.

[2]   F. Bechtel *Die griechischen Dialekte* II (Berlin 1923) 218.

Developments of I-E *k^w: Developments of I-E *g^w:

quis?	τίς;		venio	βαίνω
-que	τε		vivus	βίος

quo?	ποῖ;
sequor	ἕπομαι
linquo	λείπω

§ 96   From these comparisons, and many others like them that
could be made, we can deduce that generally in Greek: (i) the labio-
velar *k^w develops into the unvoiced labial π before the back vowels
o and ω and into the unvoiced dental τ before the front vowels ε and
ι; (ii) the labio-velar *g^w develops into the voiced labial β, but
into the voiced dental δ before ε (e.g. ἀ-δελφός from *g^welbh-). Before the decipherment of the Linear B script, it was completely unknown when the change from labio-velars to these other sounds had
taken place.   The discovery that the script had a separate series
of signs (conventionally transliterated qa, qe, qi, qo) to represent
the labio-velars shows that these were still pronounced as labio-
velars in Mycenaean times or, at the very least, that they were regarded as different in origin from the sounds represented by the labial and dental series.   Clear examples are: e-qe-ta = ἐπέτᾱς
(< *ἐκ^{w}έτᾱς); mo-qo-so = Μόψος (< *Μόκ^{w}σος); qa-si-re-u = βασιλεύς
(< *γ^{w}ασιλεύς); -qe = τε (< *κ^{w}ε).

§ 97   There are two exceptions to the general principle that
labio-velars were still represented as such in the Linear B script:
(i) as in later Greek, when a labio-velar is in contact with u, it
becomes a simple velar, e.g. e-u-ke-to = εὔχετοι (not e-u-qe-to);
(ii) occasionally, when two labio-velars are present in the same
word, one of them is dissimilated, for instance two different spellings of what is evidently the same word appear in the Pylos tablets:
qe-re-qo-ta-o and pe-re-qo-ta.

§ 98   As with the digamma, so with the labio-velar series the
decipherment has produced some unexpected spellings.   For example,
the temporal conjunction ὅτε used to be analysed as neuter pronoun
ὅ + 'generalizing' τε (as found in ὥστε etc.).   The discovery of
o-te at Pylos (§§ 160, 234), which can hardly represent anything
other than ὅτε, suggests that neither part of the analysis is correct, since ὅ would probably have been written jo in Linear B, while
(as we saw in § 96) τε appears as -qe.

§ 99   The Linear B spelling i-qo for ἵππος is anomalous.   The
-ππ- of ἵππος is derived not from the Indo-European labio-velar *k^w,
which would have produced *ἵπος, but from two separate sounds k + w.

Though linguistically indefensible, the Linear B spelling may indicate that in Mycenaean times the descendants of $*k^w$ and of $*k + *w$
were pronounced in so similar a fashion that the same series of
graphic signs could serve for both of them.

§ 100   (3) The script possessed a series of signs conventionally
rendered *za, ze, zo*.   These signs represent stops which were originally 'palatalized', that is, pronounced with a palatalized glide:
kja, gja, dja, and so on for the other vowels.   We cannot, of
course, tell whether these sounds were still pronounced as palatals
in the Mycenaean period.   As will be seen from the following examples, the sounds represented by the Linear B *z*-series often resulted in classical ζ: *ka-zo-e* = κάκχο(ν)ες (classical κακίονες); *me-zo-
e* = μέγγο(ν)ες (classical μείζονες); *to-pe-za* = τόρπεδϳα (dialectal
†τόρπεζα, Attic τράπεζα); *za-we-te* = κϳάϝετες (Ionic σῆτες).

§ 101   (4) The most important innovation, in contrast to the ar-
chaisms already noted, is seen in the treatment of original *ti*, e-
specially at the end of a word.   The original sequence τι was retained intact in West Greek dialects, but in East Greek it became
σι.   Before the decipherment of Linear B, it was unknown when
this change took place in the East Greek dialects.   Since the
script everywhere shows final -*si*, never final -*ti*, the change must
have taken place at least as early as 1400.   Very clear examples
come in the third person of verbs:

     sing. *di-do-si* = δίδονσι (> δίδουσι)(West Greek δίδοντι);
     plur. *e-e-si* = ἐενσί (> εἰσί)(West Greek ἐντί);
     plur. *e-ko-si* = ἔχονσι (> ἔχουσι)(West Greek ἔχοντι);
     sing. *pa-si* = φᾱσί (West Greek φᾱτί).

§ 102   Two non-verbal forms also give evidence of a change from *t*
to *s*: (i) *po-si* = ποσί, which is not actually attested in historical
Greek but which may be inferred from East Greek (Arcadian) πός (vs.
West Greek ποτί); (ii) *po-se-da-o* = Ποσειδάων (vs. West Greek Ποτει-
δάν).

Morphology

§ 103   (1) The declension of nouns in vowel-stems is well attested
in the Linear B texts.   In most respects, they are declined exactly
as would have been expected, within the spelling rules already established.   Some clear examples of the case-forms are first
given; and those which give rise to special difficulty or are of special interest are discussed afterwards:

a-stems: feminine

sing.:	nominative	ko-wa	κόρϝᾱ
	accusative	ki-ri-ta	κρῑθάν
	genitive	ko-to-na	κτοίνᾱς
	dative		
	instrumental		

| dual: | nominative | to-pe-zo | {τορπέζω? τορπέζοι? |

plur.:	nominative	a-ni-ja	ἀνίαι
	accusative	ai-ka-sa-ma	αἰξμάνς
	genitive	ko-to-na-o	κτοινάων
	dative		
	instrumental	a-ni-ja-pi	ἀνίᾱφι

o-stems: masculine   neuter

sing.:	nominative	ko-wo	κόρϝος	e-ra₃-wo	ἔλαιϝον
	accusative	do-so-mo	δοσμόν	ri-no	λίνον
	genitive	te-o-jo	θεοῖο		
	dative	da-mo	δάμωι		
	instrumental	ka-ko	χαλκῶι		

| dual: | nominative | po-ro | πώλω | | |

plur.:	nominative	i-qo	ἵπποι	pa-ka-na	φάσγανα
	accusative	si-a₂-ro	σίαλονς	o-na-ta	ὄνᾱτα
	genitive	a-ne-mo	ἀνέμων		
	dative	do-e-ro-i	δοέλο-ι		
	instrumental	de-so-mo	δεσμοῖς		

§ 104 (i) The genitive singular of o-stems usually ends in -o-jo, a form of great interest, showing that the Indo-European ending *-osyo had developed to -oyo in Mycenaean Greek. (This archaic genitive singular in -οιο is common in Homer, who also uses forms in -oo and in -ου). Spellings such as du-ni-jo, si-ri-jo, and te-o, instead of du-ni-jo-jo, si-ri-jo-jo, and te-o-jo respectively, may arise from scribal error or may reflect the existence of an 'ablative' genitive ending in -o.

§ 105 (ii) In the plural, separate forms are used for the dative and the instrumental. So far as o-stems are concerned, the instrumental plural ending is -o, which can represent nothing but -οις. The dative plural ending is -o-i; but this is not easy to interpret, and even now there is no consensus of oponion as to its Greek equivalent. It is known that among the Greek dialects both -οις and -οισι are used for the dative and the instrumental indifferently, and there can

be little doubt that the ending spelt -o-i in Linear B became -οισι
in later times; but -o-i cannot itself represent -οισι, nor is it
satisfactory to suppose that it represents -οις.   Although it is
often supposed that -o-i is simply a spelling of -οιηι, this theory
gives rise to historical problems: in particular,it is not easy to
imagine why the postulated -h- was replaced by -σ-.

§ 106 (iii) The ending -pi in the plural of a-stems is the same
suffix which is found in Homer (-φι) and which descends from Indo-
European *-bhis.   But its use is more restricted in Mycenaean Greek
than in Homer.   While Homer often attaches -φι to nouns in the singular, the Linear B scribes use it mostly with plurals, and with
plurals of a-stem or consonant-stem nouns.   Mycenaean is, however,
similar to Homeric Greek in that it uses -pi not only in a strictly
'instrumental' sense but also as an ablative or locative.

§ 107 (iv) A surprising form is found in the dual of the feminine, e.g. to-pe-zo 'two tables'.   Two different views have been
taken of this formation.   Either original *-αι has been changed to
-ω by analogy with the ending of the masculine dual (Hesiod's καλυψαμένω at Erga 198 is quoted in support of this view); or the Linear B -o stands not for -ω but for -οι, which is postulated as the
original ending of the dual.

§ 108 Examples of the declension of masculine a-stems are furn-
ished by the following forms:

sing.:	nominative	e-qe-ta	ἐπέτᾱς
	genitive	su-qo-ta-o	συβώτᾱο
	dative	ra-wa-ke-ta	λᾱϝᾱγέτᾱι
dual:	nominative	e-qe-ta-e	ἐπέταε
plur.:	nominative	e-qe-ta	ἐπέται
	genitive	e-re-ta-o	ἐρετᾱ́ων
	dative	e-qe-ta-i	ἐπέτα-ι

In this declension, it is remarkable that not only the genitive plural but also the genitive singular ends in -a-o: a fact which casts
serious doubt on the traditional view that the -ου ending of the genitive singular in later Greek (e.g. Attic νεανίου) was formed on the
model of the -οο of the o-stem genitive.   It is worth noting, further, that this declension has borrowed a dual ending -e from the consonant stems.

§ 109 (2) The importance of Greek nouns in -ευς for the decipherment of Linear B has already been pointed out (§ 56), and only the outlines of the declension are presented here:

sing.:	nominative	i-je-re-u	ἱερεύς
	genitive	i-je-re-wo	ἱερῆϝος
dual:	nominative	a-(pi-)po-re-we	ἀμ(φι)φορῆϝε
plur.:	nominative	ka-ke-we	χαλκῆϝες
	dative	ka-ke-u-si	χαλκεῦσι
	instrumental	ku-te-re-u-pi	†Κυθηρεῦφι?

§ 110 Among examples of other diphthong-stems, the most important are two oblique cases of Ζεύς: di-wo = Διϝός (genitive); di-we = Διϝεί (dative).

§ 111 The dative singular i-je-we appears to be a heteroclite form of the word for 'son', (υ)ἱός; but the whole question of the representation of words for 'son' in Linear B is very complex.

§ 112 qo-o must represent some form of βοῦς, showing the expected spelling with a labio-velar (it is known that βοῦς is derived from a stem beginning with $*g^{w}o-$). Mycenaean qo-o may stand for nominative singular $g^{w}\bar{o}s$ or accusative plural $g^{w}\bar{o}ns$ (which likewise became βοῦς in Attic as the result of regular sound-changes). The spelling in Linear B with doubled o is inexplicable; it may be taken either as a scribal error or as an isolated representation of vowel-length or as an avoidance of spelling a word as a monosyllable in case it was confused with an ideographic sign.

§ 113 (3) Neuters in both -ος and -ας are represented by some certain examples, which in the dual and plural show the uncontracted forms that would have been expected:

sing.:	nominative	te-me-no	τέμενος	di-pa	δέπας?[1]
	accusative	we-to	ϝέτος		
	dative	we-te-i	ϝέτει		
dual:	nominative	qi-si-pe-e	ξίφεε	ke-ra-e	κέραε
plur.:	nominative			ke-ra-a	κέραα
	accusative	tu-we-a	θύϝεα		
	instrumental	pa-we-pi	φάρϝεσφι		

[1] For the i/e variation see § 167.

§ 114 (4) The extant forms do not allow the construction of the full declension of stems in liquids and nasals, but the following forms suffice to show that the type was declined along predictable lines:

sing.:	nominative	*ma-te*	μᾱ́τηρ	*po-me*	ποιμήν
	genitive			*po-me-no*	ποιμένος
	dative			*po-me-ne*	ποιμένει
plur.:	nominative			*po-me-ne*	ποιμένες
	dative	*pi-ri-e-te-si* .....-σι			

Only one observation need be made on this table.   The dative singular most often ends in *-e*, as *po-me-ne* does here;   but examples of dative singular in *-i* are found as well, especially with the name of Poseidon, which varies between *po-se-da-o-ne* and *po-se-da-on-i*.   The same variation is found in the declension of stems ending in a stop. The Indo-European dative/locative singular ending is *-ei*, which is replaced by -ι generally in historical Greek, although traces of a dative in -ει are still found (e.g. ἐχεῖ, Διϝείφιλος).   The two Linear B spellings may therefore represent the old and the new form respectively.

§ 115 (5) The following table represents the principal types of masculine nouns (except *wa-na-ka*) whose stem ends in a stop:

sing.:	nominative	*ti-ri-po*	τρίπως	*e-re-pa*	ἐλέφας
	genitive			*e-re-pa-to*	ἐλέφαντος
	dative	*po-de*	ποδεί	*e-re-pa-te*	ἐλεφάντει
dual:	nominative	*ti-ri-po-de*	τρίποδε		
plur.:	nominative	*du-ma-te*	...-τες		
	instrumental	*po-pi*	πό(π)φι		

In the instrumental plural *po-pi*, the ending of the stem ποδ- meaning 'foot' has been assimilated to the stop of the ending -φι.

§ 116 Following are the attested forms of *wa-na-ka*:

sing.:	nominative	*wa-na-ka*	ϝάναξ
	genitive	*wa-na-ka-to*	ϝάνακτος
	dative	*wa-na-ka-te* or *wa-na-ke-te*	ϝανάκτει

wa-na-ka-to and *wa-na-ka-te* exhibit anomalous spellings.   According to the usual practice (§ 84), the vowel of the 'dead' syllable is brought into harmony with the following vowel, so that **wa-na-ko-to* and *wa-na-ke-te* respectively would have been predicted. It is likely that the scribes modelled the whole declension on the nominative *wa-na-ka* (§ 86); and the same explanation probably holds good for the spelling of the adjective *wa-na-ka-te-ro* (§ 142).

§ 117   Neuter nouns are represented by the following:

sing.:   nominative *pe-ma* σπέρμα/*pe-mo* σπέρμο   *a-mo*   ἄρμο

dual: nominative   *a-mo-te* ἄρμοτε

plur.:   nominative   *a-mo-ta* ἄρμοτα
          dative   *a-mo-si* ἄρμοσι

The variation between *pe-ma* and *pe-mo* can hardly be explained, except on the hypothesis that different dialects have left traces in our inscriptions (§ 167).   In later Greek, of course, only σπέρμα and ἄρμα respectively are found.

§ 118   (6) Four comparative adjectives are found in our texts, namely *me-zo* 'larger', *me-u-jo/me-wi-jo* 'smaller', *a-ro$_2$* 'better, superior', and *ka-zo* 'worse, inferior')(*a-ro$_2$* and *ka-zo* are not actually attested, but their existence may be inferred):

		masculine/feminine		neuter	
sing.:	nominative	*me-zo*	μέζων/-ως?		
dual:	nominative	*me-zo-e*	μέζοε	*me-zo-e*	μέζοε
plur.:	nominative	*me-zo-e*	μέζοες	*me-zo-a$_2$*	μέζοha?
sing.:	nominative	{*me-u-jo* / *me-wi-jo*}	μειων/-ως?	*me-wi-jo*	μειον
dual:	nominative	*me-wi-jo-e*	μειοε		
plur.:	nominative	{*me-u-jo-e* / *me-wi-jo-e*}	μειοες	*me-u-jo-a$_2$*	μειοha?
sing.:	genitive	*a-ro$_2$-jo*	ἀριοος?		
plur.:	nominative	*a-ro$_2$-e*	ἀριοες	*a-ro$_2$-a*	ἀριοha?
plur.:	nominative	*ka-zo-e*	κακιοες		

§ 119   Although the extant texts show the use of -τερος in the formation of adjectives (§ 142), this suffix does not function as a comparative termination.   The Mycenaean comparative is formed with the suffix *-yo(s)-*, which in later Greek produces the declension in -ίων, -ίονος, e.g. ἡδίων and Ionic μέζων.[1]   The latter is formed

---

[1]   The -ει- of Attic μείζων was introduced by analogy with other comparatives such as μείων and χείρων.

from the stem μεγ- 'large' and the comparative suffix -yω; the sound
produced by the coalescence of *g* and *y* being spelt *z*, as in the Mycenaean comparative *ka-zo*.   Unlike later Greek, Mycenaean shows no
trace of -*n*- in the declension; so it must remain unclear whether the
nominative singular *me-zo* represents μέζων or μέζως.

§ 120   The table in § 118 gives the probable equivalents of *a-ro₂*-
jo etc.: Mycenaean presents a form ἀρίων (or ἀρίως), which in later
Greek is re-fashioned as ἀρείων. (The variation between *me-u-jo* and
me-wi-jo is purely scribal: compare *di-u-jo* ~ *di-wi-jo*).

§ 121   (7) Only two personal pronouns are certainly attested: -*mi*
= μιν (3rd singular accusative masculine/feminine) and *pe-i* = σφεις
(Arcadian 3rd plural dative masculine/feminine).

§ 122   (8) Some words are formed with the demonstrative stem *to-*:
to-so = τόσ(σ)ος 'so much';
to-so-de = τοσ(σ)όσδε (with emphatic suffix), same meaning;
to-so-ne = τοσ(σ)όνε (with deictic suffix?), same meaning;
to-to, nominative sing. neuter (perhaps from an original *todtod*);
to-e and *tome*, dative sing. (?) of the demonstrative pronoun;
to-jo = τοῖο, genitive sing. of the demonstrative pronoun.

§ 123   (9) Six only of the cardinal numerals are unambiguously attested:
1: *e-me*, dative: an archaic form reflecting Greek ἐμεί (with the
    stem which was orignially *sem-*, still seen in Latin *semel*); by
    historical times the *m* had been replaced by *n*, as in ἐνί.
2: *dwo*, accusative; *du-wo-u-pi*, instrumental.   These forms may re-
    present an original variation (Indo-European *dwō* ~ *duwō*).
3: *ti-ri-si* = τρισί; *ti-ri-* = τρι- in compounds.
4: *qe-to-ro-* in compounds: the form faithfully reflects the origin-
    al labio-velar at the beginning (cf. Latin *quattuor*). The third
    syllable shows that in the Mycenaean dialect an original syllabic
    r had developed to *ro*, whereas in Attic it became *ar* (τέτταρες)
    (cf. Mycenaean *to-pe-za* = τόρπεζα vs. Attic τράπεζα).
6: *we-* in the compound *we-pe-za* (ϝέϰ-πεζα).
9: *e-ne-wo-* = ἐννεϝο- in compounds.

§ 124   (10) The Linear B inscriptions, by their very nature, contain only a limited range of verbal forms.   There are no occurrences
of the first or second person or of the subjunctive, optative, or im-
perative.   The only tenses certainly used are the present, future,
aorist, and perfect.   But, even within the compass of the available
evidence, there are some verbal forms which give valuable information
about the state of the Greek language in the Late Bronze Age (§ 125).

§ 125   List of well-attested verbal forms:

(Attic
present)

ἀγείρω	a-ke-re = ἀγείρει (3 sing. act. pres.).	
ἀραρίσκω	a-ra-ru-ja = ἀραρυῖα (perf. act. part. fem. sing.);	
	a-ra-ru-wo-a = ἀραρυϝόα (perf. act. part. neut. plur.).	
δέω	de-de-me-no = δεδεμένος (perf. pass. part. masc. sing.).	
δέχομαι	de-ka-sa-to = δέξατο (3 sing. mid. aor.).	
δίδωμι	di-do-si = δίδονσι (3 plur. act. pres.);	
	di-do-to = δίδονται (3 plur. pass. pres.);	
	do-se = δώσει (3 sing. act. fut.);	
	do-so-si = δώσονσι (3 plur. act. fut.);	
	-do-ke = -δῶκε (3 sing. act. aor.);	
	de-do-me-na = δεδομένα (perf. pass. part. neut. plur.).	
εἰμί	e-e-si = ἔενσι (3 plur. pres.);	
	e-o = ἐών (pres. part. masc. sing.).	
εὔχομαι	e-u-ke-to = εὔχετοι (3 sing. mid. pres.).	
ἔχω	e-ke = ἔχει (3 sing. act. pres.);	
	e-ko-si = ἔχονσι (3 plur. act. pres.);	
	e-ko = ἔχων (pres. part. masc. sing.);	
	e-ko-te = ἔχοντες (pres. part. masc. plur.);	
	e-ke-e = ἔχεεν (pres. act. inf.).	
ὁράω	-wi-de = -ϝίδε (3 sing. act. aor).	
τίθημι	te-ke = θῆκε (3 sing. act. aor.).	
φημί	pa-si = φᾶσί (3 sing. act. pres.).	

§ 126   As we would expect, active infinitives and participles are not yet contracted: thus the participle e-o stands for ἐών (Homeric; later ὤν) and the infinitive e-ke-e spells ἔχεεν (later ἔχειν).

§ 127   A suggestion first made before the decipherment finds support in the medio-passive forms e-u-ke-to and di-do-to. It has long been known that in the Arcadian dialect of historical times the medio-passive ending was -τοι/-ντοι, in contrast to the -ται/-νται of other dialects.   This -τοι was assumed to be the result of a secondary development from -ται in that dialect alone, until in 1952 Ruipérez suggested that Greek had inherited -τοι from Indo-European and that Arcadian had preserved this feature, while the remaining dialects had introduced -ται by analogy with other medio-passive endings.

§ 128   In two areas the decipherment has produced verbal forms which are surprising and which could not have been predicted:

(i) The perfect participle (with intransitive meaning) ending in -u-ja represents the feminine form in -υῖα. As was seen in § 57,

this is one of the striking correspondences which persuaded Ventris
that the language he was dealing with contained at least some elements of Greek.   But the neuter plural *a-ra-ru-wo-a*, while it too
is recognizably Greek, differs in an important respect from the
classical formation, for it ends in -όα, not -ότα.   The Mycenaean
form shows that the -τ- which appears in the declension in historical times was introduced after the end of the Bronze Age.

(ii) The augment presents one of the standing problems in the morphology of the Indo-European verb.   The facts are clear, but an explanation of them still escapes us.   The verbal augment in historic tenses is found in only a small number of languages, including
Greek, Avestan, and Vedic.   In Avestan and Vedic, as in Greek, the
augment is not an indispensable part of the verb; it seems possible
to include it or to omit it at will, especially for metrical reasons.
Before Ventris' decipherment, it might have been thought that the
augment was an integral part of the Greek verbal system but that the
literary or poetical language used by Homer tolerated its omission.
The Mycenaean evidence shows that such a view is incorrect.   The
forms displayed in our inscriptions show that the augment is usually
omitted: in fact, there is only one occurrence of a historic verb
which possibly contains an augment, namely *a-pe-do-ke* (ἀπέδωκε?),
and even this is written elsewhere without augment: *a-pu-do-ke* (ἀπύδωκε).   So it is impossible to assert any longer that the omission
of the augment is a purely poetical phenomenon, since it is the normal procedure in these highly prosaic texts.   It seems that the alternation between augmented and augmentless forms, previously thought
to be characteristic of Homer's language, represents a feature of
Common Greek.

  § 129 (11) The following adverb-prepositions known from classical Greek appear in Mycenaean:

a-pi = ἀμφί 'on both sides', especially in compounds, e.g. *a-pi-e-ke*
= ἀμφιέχει.
a-pu = ἀπύ 'off, away', the Aeolic/Arcado-Cypriot form (Attic ἀπό).
e-ne-ka = ἕνεκα (with genitive)(§§ 93, 203).
e-n- = ἐν (only in the compound *e-ne-e-si* = ἐνέενσι).
e-pi (ἐπί), and more commonly *o-pi* (ὀπί), are found both in compound
and as independent words; ὀπί occurs sporadically in later Greek.
ku-su (ξύν) and *me-ta* (μετά), with dative, 'together with'.
pa-ro with dative is used like later παρά.   Its sense is probably
'from'; but it may mean 'at' in some contexts.
pe-da with accusative, '(motion) to': πεδά is found in Aeolic and
in some Doric dialects.
pe-ri- and *po-ro-* represent περι- and προ- respectively (only in
compound).

po-si corresponds in meaning to πρός. Its function is that of an adverb, 'upon'.
u-po (ὑπό) is used as an adverb, 'beneath'.

§ 130 (12) Prefixes and suffixes. Some twenty Linear B inscriptions begin with proclitic *o-* or *jo-*: in all but one, the *o-* or *jo-* is spelt as part of the first word. Nearly always the word prefixed by *o-/jo-* is a main verb; or, to put it more accurately, the presence of *o-/jo-* brings the main verb to the beginning of the sentence. The variation between *o-* and *jo-* is purely scribal: the two forms do not differ in meaning. They are most often explained as spellings of a relative (ὡς or ὅ) or demonstrative (ὧς); but in fact the Mycenaean usage is not closely paralleled by anything in later Greek. Whatever the correct explanation, the function of *o-/jo-* is plain enough: it serves as an introductory particle, not only of one inscription but sometimes of a whole set of texts (§§ 207, 229).

§ 131 Three words seem to be extensions of 'introductory' *o-*: *o-a₂*, *o-da-a₂*, and *o-de-qa-a₂*. Of these, the first and third occur once only and appear to be mere variants of *o-da-a₂*. The function of all three is that of introducing a new 'paragraph' within the body of an inscription.

§ 132 The negatives *o-u-* (οὐ-) and *o-u-ki-* (οὐκι-) are written as part of the following word. *o-u-qe* (οὔτε) is also found.

§ 133 Among the Mycenaean suffixes, *-de* (spelt as part of the preceding word) functions very much as in later Greek. It is used: (i) as the adversative particle δέ; (ii) as the deictic suffix (in *to-so-de* etc.); (iii) as the 'allative' suffix -δε indicating place 'to which'. The allative use of the *-de* suffix is widespread in the Linear B texts. Much rarer, though of reasonably certain occurrence, is the adverbial suffix -*te* (-θεν), indicating place 'from which', e.g. *a-po-te-ro-te* = ἀμφοτέρωθεν.

§ 134 *-qe*, written as part of the preceding word, is used like τε in later Greek as a copulative particle to connect words or sentences; on occasion, *-qe....-qe....* is found, corresponding to τε.... τε.... (For *o-u-qe*, see § 132). In the E tablets from Pylos, *-qe* is attached to *e-ke* (ἔχει) and to *e-ko-si* (ἔχουσι) in circumstances which make its interpretation as a copula impossible. Furthermore, the presence of *-qe* in these texts disturbs the word-order without bringing about any perceptible change of meaning. These facts suggest that in the E series *-qe* represents a particle different from τε as it is used in later times.

Word-formation

§ 135 Only the salient points will be noted here; the subject is
dealt with further in §§ 142-151.

§ 136 (1) Nouns in *-e-u* and *-e-ja*. Nouns (particularly personal
names) in *-e-u* (-εύς) are plentiful in the Linear B texts, and sometimes their feminine counterparts are found:

i-je-re-u = ἱερεύς 'priest': *i-je-re-ja* = ἱέρεια 'priestess'
ke-ra-me-u = κεραμεύς 'potter': *ke-ra-me-ja* = Κεράμεια 'female pot-
                                                     ter', as personal name

The opposition between these masculine and feminine forms is a typi-
cally Greek feature; the absence of *-w-* before *-ja* in Linear B can
perhaps be explained by supposing that in the ending *-εϝya /*-ηϝya
the group *-ϝy-* developed to *-yy-*.

§ 137 (2) Agent-nouns.   Agent-nouns in both *-τηρ* and *-τᾱς* are
represented in the Linear B documents.

§ 138 Of the fifteen or so Mycenaean nouns ending in *-te* (-τηρ),
only very few are susceptible of interpretation so far as their stem
is concerned: e.g. *i-ja-te* = ἱᾱτήρ 'doctor'. The official title *ko-
re-te* certainly belomgs to this class; but no convincing explanation
has yet been found for the *ko-re-* element.   The feminine equivalent
is represented by some plural nouns ending in *-i-ra₂*, for example *a-
ke-ti-ra₂* and *ra-pi-ti-ra₂*.

§ 139 Examples of the second type, ending in *-ta* (-τᾱς, Attic-
Ionic -της), are: *ai-ki-pa-ta* = αἰγι-... 'goatherd'; *e-qe-ta* = ἐπέτᾱς
'follower'; *e-re-ta* = ἐρέτᾱς 'rower'; *ku-na-ke-ta-i* = κυνᾱγέτᾱι (dative) 'hunter'; *qo-u-qo-ta* = βουβότᾱς 'cowherd'; *ra-wa-ke-ta* = λᾱϝᾱγέτᾱς 'leader of the people'; *su-qo-ta* = συβώτᾱς 'swineherd'; *to-ko-
so-ta* τοξότᾱς 'bowman'.

§ 140 (3) Nouns in *-i-ko*. It is unfortunate that the ending *-i-
ko*, which is found in some twenty Mycenaean words, could stand equally well for *-ικός*, *-ίσκος*, or *-ιχος*. A fairly certain example of the
last is seen in the personal name *ma-ni-ko* = Μάνιχος?   In *ti-ri-po-
di-ko*, however, the ending probably represents the diminutive *-ισκ-*:
τριποδίσκοι 'small tripods'.   It remains uncertain whether *-ικός* is
ever found: for instance, there is nothing to tell whether the woman's name *ta-ra-mi-ka* spells θαλαμικᾱ́ or θαλαμίσκᾱ.

§ 141 (4) Adjectives with the suffix *-we/-we-sa*. Mycenaean inherited the suffix *-ϝεντ, and attached it directly to the stem of a

noun so as to produce an adjective meaning 'provided with': in later
Greek, the ending *-ϝεντ-ς was simplified to -εις. The feminine ending was originally *-wnt-yə/*-wet-yə, which by the Mycenaean period had
become -ϝεσσα, spelt in Linear B as -we-sa. The suffix -ϝεντς/-ϝεσσα
is seen in four important classes of tablets (in most cases the stem
to which it is attached being difficult, or impossible, to identify):

(i) Neuter words describing e-ra₃-wo (ἔλαιϝον 'olive oil'): e-ti-we,
ku-pa-ro-we, pa-ko-we, wo-do-we. The following correspondences have
been suggested for the last three words respectively: κυπαρόϝεν
'mixed with cyperus'; σφακόϝεν 'mixed with sage';   ϝορδόϝεν 'rose-
scented'. (PY Fr). (For e-ti-we cf. E.P. Hamp ZA 32 [1982] 33-34).

(ii) Neuter plural adjectives describing a-mo-ta (ἅρμοτα 'wheels'):
o-da-ku-we-ta, with its variants o-da-ke-we-ta and o-da-tu-we-ta
(the stem of ὁδούς with the -ϝεντ suffix?);   te-mi-dwe-ta (perhaps
τερμίδϝεντα, referring to the edge of the wheel). (KN So).

(iii) Feminine singular adjectives in -we-sa (-ϝεσσα) describing i-
qi-ja (ἱππία): mi-to-we-sa (μιλτόϝεσσα 'painted red'?); wo-ra-we-sa
(with unknown stem). (KN Sd).

(iv) Feminine singular adjectives describing:
    (a) e-ka-ra (ἐσχάρα 'hearth'): au-de-we-sa, i-to-we-sa, pe-de-we-
        sa (πέδϝεσσα 'equipped with feet');
    (b) qe-ra-na (a type of jug): ko-ro-no-we-sa, to-qi-de-we-sa (τορ-
        πίδϝεσσα 'equipped with spirals');
    (c) to-pe-za (τόρπεζα 'table'): pi-ti-ro₂-we-sa.   (PY Ta).

§ 142 (5) Adjectives with the suffix -te-ro.   Although the Mycenaean suffix -te-ro (-τερος) does not, as in later Greek, indicate
the comparative, it is used to form an adjective from a noun (presumably with some 'contrasting' force, as in the later ἀρίστερος).
The only clear example, but a very important one, is wa-na-ka-te-ro,
ϝανάκτερος, in which the suffix is added directly to the stem wanak-
(cf. § 188).

§ 143 (6) Verbal adjectives in -te-o/-te-jo.   A word which has
the appearance and function of a verbal adjective is found in two distinct forms in the Mycenaean documents.   At Pylos it is written
qe-te-jo in the neuter singular and qe-te-a₂ (= qe-te-ja?) in the plural; but at Knossos its singular is qe-te-o and its plural qe-te-a.
The qe- element may be identical with a stem which appears, for instance, in ἔ-τει-σα 'I paid'.   In Aeolic dialects the stem is spelt
with π: this spelling shows that originally the stem was *kʷei-, for
which the Linear B equivalent would be qe-. The formal identification of qe-te-(j)o as a verbal adjective corresponding to the later

Greek †τειτέον would be impeccable, were it not for a morphological difficulty.   The -τέος of the verbal adjective in classical Greek can have originated only in *-τέϝος.   The ending -te-jo is sometimes connected with Hesiod's φατειός at *Theogony* 310, an adjective formed from φημί; but the connexion may be illusory, since the ending of φα-τειός is explicable as an example of metrical lengthening.[1]   It is, therefore, unlikely that qe-te-(j)o represents a verbal adjective of the precise kind found in later Greek: if it is a verbal adjective, it is of a type which did not survive.   But the meaning of the word can be established with some confidence.   In KN Fh 348.2, qe-te-o is used in opposition to o-no.   Although the exact meaning of o-no is unknown. a comparison of its occurrences at ·Knossos, Pylos, and Myc-enae shows that it signifies something like 'payment'.   Hence qe-te-(j)o should mean roughly 'lack of payment' or 'to be paid'.[2]

§ 144   (7) Adjectives of material.   These adjectives may have one of three endings in Mycenaean Greek: -e-jo, representing an archaic -ειος; a later -e-o (-εος); -i-jo, which recalls the termination -ιος of similar adjectives in Aeolic.   The alternation between -ειος and -εος is found in Homer as well, although there the former type may arise from metrical lengthening.   Sometimes all three possible forms are attested in Mycenaean, for example:
stem φοινιϰ-: po-ni-ke-ja, po-ni-ke-a, po-ni-ki-ja;
stem ϝριν-:   wi-ri-ne-jo, wi-ri-ne-o, wi-ri-ni-jo.

§ 145   (8) Patronymics, ethnics, and other adjectives in -i-jo and -we-jo. It is of interest that the patronymic suffix is -i-jo (-ιος); we may compare Homeric Τελαμώνιος Αἴας and the use of the patronymic suffixes -ειος and -αιος in Lesbian.   A number of proper names, to-gether with patronymics in -i-jo, are found in o-ka tablets at Pylos (§ 232), for example: a-re-ku-tu-ru-wo e-te-wo-ke-re-we-i-jo 'A. the son of e-te-wo-ke-re-we';   di-ko-na-ro a-da-ra-ti-jo 'D. the son of a-da-ra-to'.

§ 146   Many ethnics in -(i)-jo/-(i)-ja are known, corresponding to the later Greek -ιος/-ιᾱ: a-mi-ni-si-jo 'man of Amnisos'; di-ka-ta-jo 'man of Dikte';   ko-no-si-jo 'man of Knossos';   pa-i-ti-jo 'man of Phaistos';   pa-ki-ja-ni-ja 'woman of Pakijana';   ro-u-si-jo 'man of Lousos?';   tu-ri-si-jo 'man of Tylissos'.

§ 147   Three further types correspond closely to later adjectives:

[1] Cf. H. Troxler *Sprache und Wortschatz Hesiods* (Zürich 1964) 50.

[2] M. Lejeune *Mémoires* II 287-312.   By a different line of rea-soning, M. Gérard-Rousseau arrives at a meaning 'estimated': *Les men-tions religieuses dans les tablettes mycéniennes* (Rome 1968) 195-197.

(i) from the noun *ko-re-te* (-τηρ), *ko-re-te-ri-jo* (-τέριος);   (ii)
from the noun *ra-wa-ke-ta* (-τᾱς), *ra-wa-ke-si-jo* (-γέσιος);   (iii)
from the noun *i-je-re-u* (-εύς), *i-je-re-wi-jo* (-ήϝιος).

§ 148   In addition, Mycenaean shows two forms which have no later
parallel, namely *wa-na-se-wi-ja* (ϝανασσηϝία, a derivative of *wa-na-
sa* = ϝάνασσα) and *po-ti-ni-ja-we-jo* (also spelt *po-ti-ni-ja-wi-jo* and
po-ti-ni-ja-we-i-jo),which is connected in some way with *po-ti-ni-ja*
= πότνια. The word cannot be formed directly from *po-ti-ni-ja*, since
in that case an adjective such as *po-ti-ni-ja-jo* would have been expected (cf. *di-u-ja-jo* from *di-u-ja*);nor is a form ποτνιεύς a likely
starting-point, because then only the spelling with *-wi-jo* is explicable, not the spelling with *-we-jo*.   No satisfactory explanation of
the second form has yet been advanced.   It has been suggested that
it comes from an (unattested) noun *po-ti-ni-ja-wo* meaning 'domain of
Potnia' (Lejeune) or 'one who prays to Potnia' (Ruijgh) or, from a
quite different point of view, that the *-we-jo* represents an Indo-
European suffix analogous to the *-meyo- seen in Homeric ἀνδρόμεος
(Risch)(cf. § 182).

§ 149   (9) Alpha privative.   Negative compounds are formed with
the prefix *a(n)-* (< *n̥-), just as in later Greek:

(i)   *a-e-ti-to* 'without *eti*';
(ii)   *a-ki-ti-to* 'without *kit*';
(iii)   *a-na-i-ta, a-na-i-to, a-na-ta* 'without ornament?';
(iv)   *a-na-mo-to* (ἀνάρμοστοι) 'not fitted out?';
(v)   *a-na-pu-ke* (ἀνάμπυκες) 'without head-bands';
(vi)   *a-no-we, a-no-wo-to* (ἀνῶϝες, ἀνώϝοτος) 'earless'.

The form *a-e-ti-to* (i) is found in opposition to *e-ti-we* in descriptions of oil: we cannot tell why the word was so spelt,and not *a-ne-
ti-to*.   The three forms mentioned under (iii) are in opposition to
a-ja-me-na, which appears to mean 'fitted out';contrary to the usual
practice of later Greek, *a-na-i-ta* and *a-na-ta* are apparently adjectives of three terminations.

§ 150   (10) The compound noun *ko-to-no-o-ko*.   As may be seen from
the compound personal names, the usual Mycenaean practice is to jux-
tapose the two elements of a compound without the intervention of a
vowel.   But in the case of one word, *ko-to-no-o-ko*, Mycenaean fore-
shadows the practice of later Greek by inserting an *o*-vowel between
the first element and the second: *ko-to-no-o-ko* = κτοιν-ό-hοχος 'holder of a κτοίνᾱ'.   The meaning of the word is discussed further at §
273.   (The 'expected' form *ko-to-no-ko* occurs at PY Eb 173.1).

Personal names

§ 151 Personal names form the largest class of words in the Linear B inscriptions, and they offer many instructive examples of word-formation.   The context in which they are found, however, is rarely sufficient to enable us to analyse them convincingly in Greek terms. Although only the most hardened sceptic would deny the probability that, for example, e-u-me-de is a spelling of the Greek name Εὐμήδης, very few of the Linear B personal names are so perspicuous as that. In consequence, the Greek 'equivalents' suggested in the following outline should be treated with even more reserve than usual.   Selected names are arranged under (1) simple nouns; and (2) compounds.

§ 152 Simple names

(i) Names in -e-u (-εύς):   a-ke-u = 'Αλκεύς? (from ἀλκή); di-wi-je-u = Διϝιεύς (from Ζεύς, Διϝός); do-ro-me-u = Δρομεύς (from δρόμος); ka-ke-u = Χαλκεύς (from χαλκός); ku-ke-re-u = Κυκλεύς (from κύκλος); po-ro-te-u = Πρωτεύς (from πρῶτος).

(ii) Feminines from names in -e-u: i-do-me-ne-ja = 'Ιδομένεια (fem. of 'Ιδομενεύς); ke-ra-me-ja = Κεράμεια (fem. of Κεραμεύς).

(iii) Common nouns: e-ru-to-ro = 'Ερυθρός; ka-ra-u-ko = Γλαῦκος; ko-so-u-to = Ξοῦθος; po-ri-wo = Πόλιϝος.

(iv) Participles: e-u-ko-me-no = †Εὐχόμενος; ku-ru-me-no = Κλύμενος.

(v) Verbal adjective: a-nu-to = "Ανυτος.

(vi) Agent-nouns in -τᾱς and -τωρ: e-pi-ja-ta = 'Επιhάλτᾱς; o-pe-ta = 'Οφέλτᾱς; a-ko-to = "Ακτωρ; e-ko-to = "Εκτωρ; ka-to = Κάστωρ.

(vii) Ethnics in -τᾱς: e-ko-me-ne-ta-o = 'Ερχομενάτᾱο; ma-ri-ta = Μαλίτᾱς.

(viii) Names in -τᾱς formed from nouns: e-u-me-ta = Εὐμήτᾱς; o-re-ta = 'Ορέστᾱς; tu-we-ta = Θυϝέστᾱι.

(ix) Names in -a-ro (-αλος or -αρος): ko-ka-ro = Κώκαλος; pe-ta-ro = Πέταλος.

(x) Names in -e-ro (-ελος), -i-ro (-ιλος), -u-ro (-υλος): ko-tu-ro₂ = Κότυλος; ku-pe-se-ro = Κύψελος; na-wi-ro = †Νᾱϝιλος?

(xi) Names in -o (-ων): ai-to = Αἴθων; de-u-ka-ri-jo = Δευκαλίων; di-wo = Δίϝων; i-ja-wo-ne = 'Ιάϝονες; ma-ka-wo = Μαχάϝων.

(xii) Names in -a-no (-ᾱνος) and -i-no (-ῑνος): e-ki-no = Ἐχῖνος; ku-ra-no = Κύλλᾱνος.

(xiii) Non-Greek personal names in -so (-σος or -σσος): i-wa-so; ka-ra-pa-so; ke-ra-so; mo-qo-so = Μόψος; pu-ra-so; qa-da-so; qa-nu-wa-so; qa-ra-i-so; re-u-ka-so; ru-na-so; tu-qa-ni-ja-so.

§ 153 Compound names

(i) Arranged by first element:
   (α) with adverb/preposition as first element:
      a-pi- (ἀμφι-): a-pi-a₂-ro = Ἀμφίαλος; a-pi-me-de = Ἀμφιμήδης.
      e-ri- (ἐρι-): e-ri-ke-re-we = †Ἐρικλέϝης?
      e-u- (εὐ-): e-u-da-mo = Εὔδᾱμος; e-u-me-de = Εὐμήδης;e-u-me-ne
                 = Εὐμένης; e-u-me-ta = Εὐμήτᾱς.
      e-u-ru- (εὐρυ-): e-u-ru-da-mo = Εὐρύδᾱμος.
      me-t- (μετ-): me-to-qe-u = †Μετωπεύς?
      o-pi- (ὀπι-): o-pi-ri-mi-ni-jo = †Ὀπιλίμνιος?
      pa- (παν-): pa-di-jo = Πανδίων?
      pe-ri- (περι-): pe-ri-me-de = Περιμήδης.
      po-ru- (πολυ-): po-ru-ka-to = †Πολύκαστος?
   (β) with noun-stem as first element:
      a-k- (ἀκτ-): a-ka-ta-jo = Ἀκταῖος.
      a-k- (ἀλκ-): a-ka-ma-no = Ἀλκμάνωρ.
      ai-ki- (αἰγι-): ai-ki-po = †Αἰγίπως.
      da-i- (δᾱι-): da-i-qo-ta = Δᾱιφόντᾱς.
      na-u-si- (ναυσι-): na-u-si-ke-re-[= Ναυσικλε-[
      pi-r- (φιλ-): pi-ro-we-ko = Φιλόϝεργος.
      qo-u- (βου-): qo-u-qo-ta = Βουβότᾱι.
      ra-wo- (λᾱϝο-): ra-wo-do-ko = Λᾱϝόδοκος.
      wa-tu- (ϝάστυ-): wa-tu-o-ko = Ϝαστύοχος.
      wi-pi- (ϝιφι-): wi-pi-no-o = Ϝῑφίνοος.
      wo-no- (ϝοινο-): wo-no-qo-so = Ϝοῖνοψ.
   (γ) with verbal stem as first element:
      a-k- (ἀγ- or ἀρχ-): a-ke-ra-wo = Ἀρχέλᾱϝος?
      e-ke- (ἐχε-): e-ke-da-mo = Ἐχέδᾱμος; e-ke-me-de = Ἐχεμήδης.
      ma-na-si- (μνᾱσι-): ma-na-si-we-ko = Μνᾱσίϝεργος.

(ii) Arranged by second element:
     -a-no (-ᾱνωρ): a-ka-ma-no = Ἀλκμάνωρ
     -da-mo (-δαμος): e-ke-da-mo = Ἐχέδᾱμος; e-u-da-mo = Εὔδᾱμος;
                 e-u-ru-da-mo = Εὐρύδᾱμος.
     -do-ko (-δοκος): ra-wo-do-ko = Λᾱϝόδοκος.
     -do-ro (-δωρος): a-pi-do-ro = Ἀμφίδωρος.
     -ke-re-we (-κλέϝης): e-ri-ke-re-we = †Ἐρικλέϝης?
     -me-de (-μήδης): a-pi-me-de = Ἀμφιμήδης; e-ke-me-de = Ἐχεμή-
              δης; e-u-me-de = Εὐμήδης.

-me-ne (-μένης): e-u-me-ne = Εὐμένης.
-o-ko (-οχος): wa-tu-o-ko = Ϝαστύοχος.
-o-qo (-οψ or -ωψ): ai-ti-jo-qo = Αἰθίοψ; wo-no-qo-so = Ϝοῖνοψ.
-po-ro-wo (-πλοϝος): e-u-po-ro-wo = Εὔπλοϝος.
-qo-ta (-βοτᾱς): qo-u-qo-ta = Βουβόται.
-qo-ta (-φοντᾱς): da-i-qo-ta = Δαϊφόντᾱς.
-ra-wo (-λᾶϝος or -λᾶϝων): a-ke-ra-wo = ᾿Αρχέλᾱϝος?
-to-wo (-θοϝος): pe-ri-to-wo = Περίθοϝος.
-wa-ta (-ϝᾱτᾱς)(names of which the first element is a place-
        name): ka-ra-do-wa-ta = ⁺Χαραδοϝᾱτᾱς?; ne-de-wa-ta =
        ⁺Νεδϝᾱτᾱς?; pi-sa-wa-ta = ⁺Πισϝᾱτᾱς?
-we (-ϝευς): ai-ta-ro-we = ⁺Αἰθαλόϝευς?; ko-ma-we = ⁺Κομάϝευς?
-we-ko (-ϝεργος): pi-ro-we-ko = Φιλόϝεργος.

Place-names

§ 154 The Mycenaean texts furnish rich evidence for the place-
names of Bronze Age Greece.   The Knossos tablets contain about one
hundred words which are certainly or probably place-names, and the
Pylos tablets rather more than 160.   In 1964, a list of place-names
from the reign of Amenhopis III was found at Egyptian Thebes: a list
which is dated to the early fourteenth century and which is, therefore, roughly contemporary with the Linear B tablets from Knossos.
Most of the names in the Egyptian list cannot be identified, but a few
undoubtedly refer to sites in the Aegean area: Amnisos, Knossos, Kydonia, and Mycenae are the best attested.   No other contemporary reference to Aegean places is known from the Bronze Age.

§ 155 Most of the place-names mentioned in the Linear B tablets
are formed with the same suffixes which are used for this purpose in
classical Greek.   Especially at Knossos, a number of the names are
non-Greek or consist of Greek suffixes attached to non-Greek stems.

§ 156 Pylos, but not Knossos, yields examples of compounds of a
purely Greek type:
a₂-ka-a₂-ki-ri-jo   =   a₂-ka-ra + ἄγριος
e-u-de-we-ro   =   ⁺Εὐδείϝελος?
ke-i-ja-ka-ra-na   =   ke-i-ja + κρᾱνᾱ ('spring')
ma-to-(ro-)pu-ro   =   ⁺Μᾱτρόπυλος
o-re-mo-a-ke-re-u   =   o-re-mo + ἀγρεύς

§ 157 At Pylos, again, a place is sometimes indicated by a personal name in the genitive followed by the word wo-wo, which may represent *ϝόρϝος (classical ὅρος) 'boundary', so 'land, territory':
ke-ra-ti-jo-jo wo-wo; me-ka-o wo-wo; re-qa-se-wo wo-wo; u-po-di-no
wo-wo.

§ 158 Neuter plural compounds ending in *-wo-wi-ja* (*ϝόρϝια) are: *ko-ro-jo-wo-wi-ja* and *ru-ke-wo-wo-wi-ja*.

§ 159 The following list gives examples of the principal types of place-names:

(i) Names (mostly non-Greek) in *-so* (-σος or -σσος) and *-to* (-νθος):

KN	*a-mi-ni-so*	=	Ἀμνισός
KN	*ko-no-so*	=	Κνωσ(σ)ός
PY	*ko-ri-to*	=	Κόρινθος
PY	*kuJ-pa-ri-so*	=	Κυπαρισσός
PY	*o-ru-ma-to*	=	Ὀρύμανθος
KN	*ra-su-to*	=	†Λάσυνθος?
PY	*ro-u-so*	=	Λουσός?
KN	*tu-ri-so*	=	Τυλισ(σ)ός

(ii) Names in *-e-u* (-εύς)(all at Pylos):
a-ne-u-te; a-pa-re-u-pi; a-po-ne-we; da-we-u-pi; e-ni-pa-te-we; ku-te-re-u-pi; te-re-ne-we; wo-no-qe-we; wo-qo-we.

(iii) Name in *-e-jo* (-εῖον):
KN *da-da-re-jo-de* = Δαιδαλεῖόνδε.

(iv) Names in *-a-jo/-a-ja* (-αιος/-αιᾱ):
KN *ra-ja*   PY *u-ka-jo*

(v) Names in *-i-jo/-i-ja* (-ιος/-ιᾱ) and *-u-wa* (-υϝᾱ):

KN	*a-ka-wi-ja-de*	= Ἀχαιϝιᾶνδε?
PY	*a-ṣ(i-j)a-ti-ja*	
PY	*e-wi-te-wi-jo*	(ethnic from man's name *e-wi-te-u*)
PY	*ke-i-jo*	(ethnic from place-name *ke-e*)
KN	*ku-do-ni-ja*	= Κυδωνίᾱ
PY	*ri-jo*	= Ῥίον
KN	*se-to-i-ja*	
PY	*te-/ti-mi-ti-ja*	(cf. *ti-mi-to-a-ke-e*, § 215)
PY	*u-pa-/po-ra-ki-ri-ja*	(neuter plur. in -άκρια)

(vi) Names in *-a-n-* (-ᾱν-)(cf. Ἕλλᾱνες):
KN *u-ta-no*   PY *pa-ki-ja-na*

(vii) Names in *-o* (-ων)(all at Pylos):
a-ka-si-jo-ne; e-ko-so-no; pe-re-u-ro-na-de = Πλευρῶνάδε.

(viii) Names in *-wo/-wa* (-ϝος/-ϝᾱ)(only at Pylos):
a-ke-re-wa; ke-re-ti-wo; ro-o-wa; sa-ma-ri-wa (cf. *sa-ma-ra*).

(ix) Names in -wo-t-/-we(-t)- (-ϝοντ-/-ϝεντ-):
  PY ne-do-wo-te   = †Νεδϝόντει?
  PY sa-ri-nu-wo-te and se-ri-no-(wo-)te = †Σελινοϝόντει?

(x) Names in -ro/-ra (-λος/-λᾱ or -ρος/-ρᾱ):
  PY pu-ro   = Πύλος
  KN qa-ra
  PY sa-ma-ra

(xi) Names with -u- suffix:
  KN si-ja-du-we   PY ko-tu-we

(xii) Names formed from neuter stems in -ος/-ες (only at Pylos):
  e-ra-te-i   = †'Ελάτει?
  e-re-e/-i   = †'Ελέει? (cf. e-re-e-u)
  ke-e   (cf. ke-i-jo)
  ne-de-we   (cf. ne-do-wo-te?)

(xiii) Name in -a-to (-ᾱτος)(cf. Μίλᾱτος):
  PY e-ro-ma-to

(xiv) Names in -a-po/-a-pa (only at Pylos):
  e-wi-ri-po = "Εϝριπος; me-ta-pa = Μέταπα.

(xv) Names in -to-no (-θνος/-τνος)(only at Pylos):
  o-wi-to-no; pe-to-no.

(xvi) Unclassified names:
  KN a-pa-ta-wa   = †"Απταρϝα?
  PY a-pu₂-de
  KN da-*22-to
  KN di-ka-ta-de   = Δίκτᾱνδε
  PY e-ko-me-no   = †'Ερχόμενος
  KN e-ra-de
  PY ka-ra-do-ro   = Χάραδρος
  KN ku-ta-(i-)to   = †Κύταιστος?
  KN ma-ri
  KN pa-i-to   = Φαιστός
  PY pi-*82
  KN qa-mo
  KN ra-to   = Λᾱτώ
  KN ri-jo-no
  KN su-ri-mo
  KN ti-ri-to
  PY u-wa-si
  KN wa-to   (also at Thebes)
  PY wo-wo-u-de

Syntax

§ 160   Since most of the Linear B inscriptions consist of simple
lists, they yield little information about the syntax of Mycenaean.
Only two series, the Ta and E tablets from Pylos, contain elements of
even a moderately complex syntactic structure.   Thus the only known
example of a temporal clause introduced by *o-te* (ὅτε) is found on Ta
711.1 (§ 234).   Again, Ta 641.1 (§ 241) exhibits a feature familiar
in later Greek, the accusative of respect.   But the same tablet displays two examples of syntactic incongruence, of a kind which would
be expected in lists which are not conceived as sentences, but have
been built up piece-meal:
(i) Whatever view is taken of line 1 (§ 239), it is clear that strict
rules of syntax have not been applied: either singular words, *ai-ke-u*
and *we-ke,* stand in apposition to the dual *ti-ri-po-de* or *ti-ri-po-de*
must be regarded as a nominative of rubric (i.e. a nominative uncon-
nected grammatically with the rest and merely denoting the subject-
matter of the text), while the word-group beginning *ai-ke-u* forms a
descriptive phrase.
(ii) In line 2 (§ 243), the dual *me-zo-e* qualifies the singular noun
di-pa; but, in view of the dual numbers recorded elsewhere in this
text, *me-zo-e* may arise from scribal error rather than from syntactic incongruence.

§ 161   The peculiar behaviour of the particle *-qe* in the E series
has been noted (§ 134).   It does not seem possible to explain this
behaviour in terms of Greek as it is known at present.   The same
series, however, contains a statement which is transparently Greek in
respect of its syntax, containing as it does two sentences joined by
the particle *-de,* each of which contains a verb of speaking followed
by an accusative and infinitive (PY Ep 704.5-6):
e-ri-ta i-je-re-ja e-ke e-u-ke-to-qe e-to-ni-jo e-ke-e te-o
'Ερίθα ἱέρεια ἔχει εὔχετοί τε ἐτώνιον? ἔχεεν θεόν
da-mo-de-mi pa-si...o-na-to e-ke-e
δᾶμος δέ μίν φᾶσι...ὄνᾱτον ἔχεεν

§ 162   PY Es 644.1-13 shows the form *we-te-i-we-te-i*.   This is a
reduplicated dative of *we-to* = ϝέτος 'year' and is used in the sense
of 'annually'   The formation finds parallels in later Greek and elsewhere in Indo-European.

The Mycenaean dialect

§ 163   The evidence presented so far is sufficient to prove that
a certain number of words in the Linear B texts belong to the Greek
language: a proof which rests on phonological and, above all, on mor-

phological and syntactic grounds.   The question now arises whether,
given this information about Mycenaean words on the one hand and on
the other hand our extensive knowledge of the Greek dialects in historical times, we can assign Mycenaean a place among the dialects.
We found it possible (§§ 101-102) to deduce from the verbal ending *-si*
and other assibilated morphemes that Mycenaean undoubtedly belongs
to East Greek, not to West Greek.   Other features suggest that Mycenaean has a special connexion with the Arcado-Cypriot dialect of
East Greek.   The middle ending *-to* = -τοι (§ 127) provides a link
with Arcadian; and this is an encouraging link, since the Mycenaean
communities of mainland Greece would, *prima facie,* be expected to
have used a dialect close to that spoken in the interior of the Pel-
oponnese in historical times. And if *pa-ro* does mean 'from', it is
notable for taking the dative case: among the historical dialects,
only Arcadian and Cypriot use the dative with words meaning 'from'.

§ 164 Other characteristic features of Mycenaean, however, appear
in Aeolic as well as in Arcado-Cypriot: such are the form *a-pu* = ἀπύ
(vs. Attic-Ionic ἀπό) and the development of original syllabic *ṛ to
ro or *or,* not to *ra/ar,* as in Attic-Ionic.   A further connexion with
Aeolic, but not with Arcadian, is provided by a well-marked feature
of Mycenaean, namely 'its use of patronymics in *-i-jo* (-ιος)(§ 145).

§ 165 In short, it can be stated that Mycenaean does not correspond exactly to any one historical Greek dialect; nor would a close
correspondence be expected, in view of the long time which elapsed
between the latest Linear B inscriptions and the first appearance of
alphabetic Greek; especially since in the interim there were several
far-reaching migrations of Greek-speakers, involving considerable over-
laps between one dialect-group and another. The connexions are clo-
sest with Arcadian, as Ventris and Chadwick saw soon after the decipherment of the script, but the correspondences with Aeolic cannot be
overlooked.   The latter may suggest that some of the features which
later became associated with Aeolic were in the Bronze Age more widely spread among the East Greek dialects.[1]

§ 166   Finally, it is necessary to mention a curious feature of
the Linear B texts because of its possible implications for the dialectal affinities of Mycenaean.   Apart from occasional anomalies of
spelling which appear here and there in the texts and which seem to
arise from scribal errors or local differences which are not significant for the dialect, it is possible to isolate a number of varia-

[1] The Mycenaean evidence is not, in itself, sufficient to confirm
the suggestion of E. Risch *MH* 12 (1955) 61-76 that in the Bronze Age
the Arcado-Cypriot group formed part of the South Greek speech-area,
which included also the ancestors of the Attic-Ionic group.

tions which suggest that there were real dialect -differences within Mycenaean itself:

(i) The dative-locative of consonant-stem nouns nearly always ends in -e; but five times in -i: e.g. po-se-da-o-ne/po-se-da-o-ni (§ 114).

(ii) Certain words appear both in a short and in a long form — e.g. ku-ta-to beside ku-ta-i-to (KN); wo-ko-de (TH) vs. wo-i-ko-de (KN).

(iii) The word for 'seed, grain' is most often pe-mo (σπέρμο), but on two Pylos tablets and four Knossos tablets it is spelt pe-ma (σπέρμα).

(iv) Some words, especially those with a stem corresponding to later Greek θεμ-, display an alternation between e and i: thus, against several occurrences of ti-mi-to and ti-mi-ti-ja, we can set te-mi-ti-ja. This fact is interesting because of the Mycenaean spelling of a word for a receptacle: di-pa is to be equated with Homeric δέπας and, apparently, with nothing else, despite the difference in the vowel.

§ 167 The difference between pe-mo and pe-ma and that between po-se-da-o-ne and po-se-da-o-ni are perhaps explicable if the Linear B texts are written not in a single monolithic 'Mycenaean' dialect but in at least two dialects.   These are sometimes called 'normal' and 'special' Mycenaean respectively.   As for the i/e alternation seen in the Linear B spelling of θέμις and δέπας, this seems to occur most frequently in non-Greek stems; it may, therefore, reflect the uncertainty of writers called upon to transcribe sounds for which they had no precise notation.

***

The Mycenaean language: E. Vilborg A tentative grammar of Mycenaean Greek (Gothenburg 1960); Interpretation 36-64; S. Luria Klio 42 (1964) 5-60; C.J. Ruijgh Études sur la grammaire et le vocabulaire du grec mycénien (Amsterdam 1967); O.J.L Szemerényi AR II 715-725; O. Panagl Orbis 20 (1971) 207-219, ZA 25 (1975) 422-431; E. Risch DI 107-117, QU 23 (1976) 7-28; J. Chadwick Current trends in linguistics XI (ed. T.A. Seboek)(The Hague/Paris 1973) 537-568; Documents 67-105, 395-405; R. Schmitt Einführung in die gr. Dialekte (Darmstadt 1977).

Spelling rules. General: M. Lejeune Mémoires I 321-330, III 89-104, BSL 71 (1976) 195-197; M. Doria AIV 119 (1960-1961) 709-743, 120 (1961-1962) 643-675; F.W. Householder MS 71-76; C. Consani SCO 31 (1981) 205-225.   Language for which Linear B was designed: L. Stephens and J.S. Justeson TAPA 108 (1978) 271-284.   Scribal errors: P.H. Ilievski ZA 15 (1965) 45-59.   w: M. Doria Minos 8 (1963) 21-36; A. Morpurgo Davies AM II 80-121.   Consonant-groups: R.S.P. Beekes Mnemosyne 24 (1971) 337-357.   qi-si-pe-e: A. Heubeck Minos 6 (1958) 55-60.   Diphthongs: A. Bartoněk Minos 8 (1963) 51-61.   a₂: C. Milani Aevum 32 (1958) 101-138; E.P. Hamp Glotta 38 (1960) 190-194. a₃ (ai):

J. Chadwick *The Thebes tablets* II (Salamanca 1975) 97.   *pte* and *ra₂*:
M. Lejeune *BSL* 71 (1976) 198-206.   *ro₂, ra₂, ta₂*: A. Heubeck *CM* 239-
257. Dentals: G.R. Hart *Kadmos* 12 (1973) 95-97.   Non-representation
of *s*: K. Strunk *IF* 66 (1961) 155-170; R. Viredaz *SMEA* 23 (1982) 301-
322. *j*: C. Gallavotti *PP* 15 (1960) 260-281; F.W. Householder *Glotta*
39 (1960) 179-190; L. Deroy *Kadmos* 13 (1974) 9-26.
    Phonology. General: M. Lejeune *Phonétique historique du mycénien et
du grec ancien* (Paris 1972); G. Caracausi *Formazione e struttura fono-
logica del miceneo* (Palermo 1973). Digamma: P. Chantraine *RP* 36 (1962)
15-22; A. Heubeck *Sprache* 9 (1963) 193-202; V. Georgiev *PCCMS* 104-124;
C. Camera *SMEA* 13 (1971) 123-138.   Poseidon: A. Heubeck *IF* 64 (1959)
229-240; C.J. Ruijgh *REG* 80 (1967) 6-16. Labio-velars: C. Gallavotti
Athenaeum 46 (1958) 369-382; M. Lejeune *Mémoires* I 285-317, *SMEA* 20
(1979) 53-68; A. Heubeck *IF* 65 (1960) 254-262; O.J.L. Szemerényi *SMEA*
1 (1966) 29-52; R. Arena *SMEA* 8 (1969) 7-27; Y.-M. Charrue *RPL* 3
(1972) 77-95.   *z*: H. Mühlestein *MH* 12 (1955) 119-131; J. Chadwick *EM*
83-91; A. Bartoněk *SPFFBU* E9 (1964) 89-102; G.R. Hart *PCCMS* 125-134;
A. Heubeck *Kadmos* 10 (1971) 113-124; *Mémoires* II 95-129; M.D. Petruševski *ZA* (1979) 21-24.   Sonants: C.J. Ruijgh *Mnemosyne* 14 (1961)
193-216; A. Morpurgo Davies *AR* II 791-814; F. Bader *Minos* 10 (1969)
7-63; V. Georgiev *AM* II 361-379; A. Heubeck ib. 55-79; J.J. Moralejo
Álvarez *Emerita* 41 (1973) 409-426. Palatalization: C. Gallavotti *PP*
15 (1960) 260-281; E. Risch *CM* 267-281.
    Morphology. General: C.J. Ruijgh *SMEA* 20 (1979) 69-89.   Dative
and instrumental: P.H. Ilievski *SMEA* 12 (1970) 88-116; A. Morpurgo
Davies *PP* 19 (1964) 346-354, *PCCMS* 191-202; A. Moreschini Quattordio
SSL 11 (1971) 69-88; J.-L. Perpillou *BSL* 76 (1981) 231-240. Genitive
in *-o-jo*: A. López Eire *Tres cuestiones de dialectología griega* (Salamanca 1969); *Mémoires* III 11-20; M.S. Ruipérez *CM* 283-293.   Genitive
singular in *-o*: S. Luria *PP* 12 (1957) 322-324; J. Chadwick *PP* 13 (1958)
290-291; V. Pisani *PP* 14 (1959) 81-86; A. Morpurgo *RAL* 8 (1960) 33-61;
C. Gallavotti *PCCMS* 180-182; R. Lazzeroni *SSL* 8 (1968) 184-190. Plural
in *-a-i* and *-o-i*: D.M. Jones *Glotta* 37 (1958) 163-165; C.J. Ruijgh
Mnemosyne 11 (1958) 97-116; F.R. Adrados *Minos* 7 (1961) 49-61; K.H.
Schmidt *Glotta* 41 (1963) 8-9; C. Gallavotti *PCCMS* 182-185; O.J.L. Szemerényi ib. 222-225; M. Doria *AR* II 764-780; *Mémoires* III 253-266. *-pi*
(*-φι*): *Mémoires* I 157-184; I.M. Tronsky *Eirene* 1 (1960) 37-50; G.P.
Shipp *Essays in Mycenaean and Homeric Greek* (Melbourne 1961) 29-41;
A. Morpurgo Davies *Glotta* 47 (1969) 46-54; L. Deroy *AC* 45 (1976) 40-
74.   Dual: V. Pisani *PP* 14 (1959) 241-244; *Mémoires* II 47-62, III
275-283; O.J.L. Szemerényi *PCCMS* 217-222.   Genitive singular in
-a-o: H. Geiss *Glotta* 35 (1956) 142-144; O.J.L. Szemerényi ib. 195-
208. 'Son' in Mycenaean: D.J.N. Lee *Kadmos* 5 (1966) 25-43; A. Heubeck *SMEA* 13 (1971) 147-155; *Mémoires* II 387-390.   Accusative plural
in *-e* (*-ες*): E. Risch *BSL* 53 (1957-1958) 96-102.   Declension of
wa-na-ka: S. Luria *Glotta* 40 (1962) 161-162; O. Panagl *Kadmos* 10
(1971) 125-134. Comparative: O.J.L. Szemerényi *SM* 25-36.   Pronouns:

C. Milani *Aevum* 39 (1965) 405-440, *Kadmos* 4 (1965) 129-134; F. Bader *Minos* 14 (1973) 85-109.   *to-to:* M. Lejeune *RP* 53 (1979) 205-214. Medio-passive -τοι: M.S. Ruipérez *Emerita* 20 (1952) 8-31, *Minos* 9 (1968) 156-160.   Perfect participle: O.J.L. Szemerényi *SMEA* 2 (1967) 7-26; P. Chantraine *SMEA* 3 (1967) 19-27; M. Lejeune *Scritti in onore di G. Bonfante* I (Brescia 1976) 405-411.   Augment: M.D. Petruševski *ZA* 10 (1960) 324; H.M. Hoenigswald *MS* 179-182; R. Schmitt *ZVS* 81 (1967) 66-67; R. Bottin *SMEA* 10 (1969) 83-84; H.J. Blumenthal *IF* 79 (1974) 69-70.   *o-pi:* J.T. Killen *AR* II 636-643; L. Deroy *ZA* 25 (1975) 366-368, 26 (1976) 265-300; W. Burkert *MH* 38 (1981) 196; E.P. Hamp *MSS* 40 (1981) 39-60.   *pa-ro:* F.W. Householder *Glotta* 38 (1959) 1-10.   *-de:* E. Risch *SL* 833-838; *Mémoires* II 251-265.   *o-/jo-:* J.T. Hooker *IF* 73 (1968) 72-80; E. Risch *AR* II 686-698; F. Bader *Minos* 15 (1974) 164-194; M. Lejeune *BSL* 71 (1976) 199-202.   *o-da-a₂:* E.D. Floyd *IF* 83 (1978) 262-289; E.P. Hamp *IF* 86 (1981) 190; J. Taillardat *RP* 55 (1981) 33-35.   *o-de-qa-a₂:* C. Milani *Kadmos* 4 (1965) 134-137. *-qe:* J.T. Hooker *Glotta* 43 (1965) 256-261.   *-te:* P. Ilievski *ZA* 9 (1959) 105-128.

Word-formation.   *-e-u/-e-ja:* O.J.L. Szemerényi *MX* 159-181; D.M. Jones *Glotta* 37 (1958) 163; H.B. Rosén *Lingua* 7 (1957-1958) 367-376; M.S. Ruipérez *PCCMS* 211-216; H. Humbach *MSS* 24 (1968) 47-51; E.P. Hamp *SMEA* 11 (1970) 61-62; J.-L. Perpillou *Les substantifs grecs en -ευς* (Paris 1973); A. Christol *BSL* 70 (1975) 137-161.   Agent-nouns: P. Chantraine *EM* 99-104 (feminines in -τρια); *Mémoires* II 197-224 (masculines in -τηρ); O.J.L. Szemerényi *AM* II 301-317 (the ra-wa-ke-ta type).   Nouns in *-i-ko:* P. Chantraine *PCCMS* 161-179.   Adjectives in *-we/-we-sa:* *Mémoires* II 11-33.   *o-da-ke-we-ta:* A. Heubeck *DI* 127-128.   Adjectives in *-te-ro:* M. Wittwer *Glotta* 47 (1970) 69-71; *Mémoires* II 267-283.   Verbal adjectives in *-te-(j)o:* L. Deroy *Kratylos* 10 (1965) 189-190.   *-eos/-eios:* E. Benveniste *Origines de la formation des noms en indo-européen* (Paris 1962) 71-72; J.W. Poultney *Language* 43 (1967) 875.   Adjectives of material in *-e-jo:* E. Risch *SGIIL* 309-318.   Patronymics in *-i-jo:* N. van Brock *RP* 34 (1960) 222-225; A. Sacconi *RAL* 16 (1961) 275-297; J.M. Aitchison *Glotta* 42 (1964) 132-138; O. Masson *Glotta* 43 (1965) 217-221; P. Wathelet *Les traits éoliens dans la langue de l'épopée grecque* (Rome 1970) 351-353.   Ethnics in *-i-jo:* E. Risch *MH* 14 (1957) 70-74.   *u-pi-ja-ki-ri-jo:* A. Heubeck *BN* 13 (1962) 146-147.   *po-ti-ni-ja-we-jo:* C.J. Ruijgh *SMEA* 4 (1967) 40-52; *Mémoires* II 359-364; E. Risch *AM* II 294-300.   Alpha privative: A.C. Moorhouse *Studies in the Greek negatives* (Cardiff 1959) 47; *Mémoires* II 35-45.   *a-no-we* and *a-no-wo-to:* O.J.L. Szemerényi *SMEA* 3 (1967) 59-61.   *ko-to-no-o-ko* etc.: F. Bader *AM* II 141-196; *Mémoires* III 171-177.

Personal names.   General: O. Landau *Mykenisch-griechische Personennamen* (Gothenburg 1958); T. Milewski *LP* 8 (1960) 146-182; M. Lindgren *The people of Pylos* (Uppsala 1973).   Particular names: A. Heubeck *BN* 8 (1957) 28-35, 268-278, *IF* 64 (1958-1959) 119-135, *BN* 11

(1960) 1-10, *Kadmos* 1 (1962) 59-64, *SMEA* 4 (1967) 35-39; L.R. Palmer
Eranos 54 (1956) 1-13; H. Mühlestein *MH* 22 (1965) 155-165; C. Milani
RIL 103 (1969) 640-646; O. Masson *AM* II 281-293.   Mycenaean and
classical names: O. Masson *SMEA* 2 (1967) 27-40.   Names in -e-u: M.F.
Galiano *AM* II 207-260; M. Doria *Studi Triestini in onore di L.A.*
Stella (Trieste 1975) 107-133.   ko-pe-re-u and ku-ke-re-u: P. Chan-
traine *AM* II 199-202.   Names in -me-no: *Mémoires* III 29-37.   de-ki-
si-wo: O. Masson *Glotta* 39 (1961) 111-112.   ai-wa: H. Mühlestein
SMEA 2 (1967) 41-52.   Personal names formed from military terms:
F. Ferluga *ZA* 25 (1975) 381-387.   Personal names formed from place-
names: F. Gschnitzer *DI* 90-106.   Personal names giving rise to
vocabulary words: P.H. Ilievski *CM* 135-146.   Names in -u-ro: P.H.
Ilievski *AM* II 262-280.   Names in -wo: C.J. Ruijgh *Minos* 9 (1968)
109-155.   Non-Greek names: R.D. Barnett *JHS* 73 (1953) 140-143; A.
Scherer *FF* 39 (1965) 57-60; K.D. Ktistopoulos *Europa* 191-193; P.
Chantraine *AR* II 574-577; J.C. Billigmeier *Minos* 10 (1969) 177-183;
P.H. Ilievski *ZA* 25 (1975) 413-421.   Names in -a-no: H. Mühlestein
Athenaeum 46 (1958) 361-365, *MH* 15 (1958) 223-225; A. Heubeck *AM* II
67-69.   Names in e-ri-: R. Gusmani *SMEA* 6 (1968) 20.   Names in e-u-:
F. Bader *Études de composition nominale en mycénien* I (Rome 1969) 22-
24.   Names containing ra-wo: A. Heubeck *Studi linguistici in onore di*
V. Pisani II (Brescia 1969) 535-544.   wo-no-qo-so: M. Doria *PP* 15
(1960) 47-50, 16 (1961) 212-215; S. Luria *PP* 16 (1961) 54-62; M.D.
Petruševski *ZA* 11 (1962) 250.

        Place-names.   Greek place-names: H. Krahe *Sprache und Vorzeit*
(Heidelberg 1954) 144-148; D.J. Georgacas *Names* 7 (1959) 65-83; E.
Risch *MH* 22 (1965) 193-205.   List of Amenhopis III: E. Edel *Die*
Ortsnamenlisten aus dem Totentempel Amenhopis III. (Bonn 1966).   My-
cenaean place-names: V. Georgiev *LB* 9 (1964) 5-39; M.D. Petruševski
Neue Beiträge zur Geschichte der alten Welt I (Berlin 1964) 163-172;
M. Doria *Problemi di toponomastica micenea* (Trieste 1971).   Pylos
place-names: E.G. Turner *BICS* 1 (1954) 17-20; M. Doria *VII Congresso*
Internazionale di Scienze Onomastiche (Florence 1961) 417-440; F.
Kiechle *Kadmos* 1 (1962) 98-116; G. Lucchini *SMEA* 13 (1971) 59-62;
A.P. Sainer *SMEA* 17 (1976) 17-63.   Names in -a-na: S. Luria *Eunomia* 1
(1957) 45-49; M.D. Petruševski *ZA* 9 (1959) 84; L. Deroy and M. Gérard
Le cadastre mycénien de Pylos (Rome 1965) 168-179.   Names in -to-no:
M.D. Petruševski *Klio* 58 (1976) 289-294.   Names in -wa: M.S. Ruipérez
EM 118-120; J. Chadwick *TPS* (1969) 97.   Names in -wo-: A. Heubeck *BN*
12 (1961) 95-96; L. Deroy *AR* II 578-579; M. Lejeune *BSL* 64 (1969) 43-
56.   Names in -wo-t-/-we-t-: A. Heubeck *SMEA* 17 (1976) 127-136. a-pu₂:
Mémoires II 338-355.   ai-ko-ra-i-ja: K.D. Georgoulis *Platon* 16 (1964)
325-328.   e-ko-me-no: G. Pugliese Carratelli *SCO* 7 (1958) 45.
ma-to-ro-pu-ro: A. Heubeck *Kadmos* 1 (1962) 61-62.   o-na-ka-ra[:
W. Merlingen *Sprache* 8 (1962) 263.   pa-ki-ja-na/-ne: R. Guglielmino
SMEA 23 (1982) 141-193.   pi-*82: L.R. Palmer *Minos* 4 (1956) 132; C.
Gallavotti *PP* 12 (1957) 248-249; M. Doria *Athenaeum* 46 (1958) 389-398;

J. Chadwick *Minos* 9 (1968) 64. *qe-re-me-e:* A. Heubeck *Kadmos* 1 (1962)
59-60. *ro-o-wa:* H. Mühlestein *SM* 115.   Knossos place-names: P.
Meriggi *AGI* 39 (1954) 83-91; G.R. Hart *Mnemosyne* 18 (1965) 1-28; V.
Georgiev *2ICretStud* II 40-43; L. Godart *BICS* 17 (1970) 159-161; L.R.
Palmer *Kadmos* 11 (1972) 31-46; J. Chadwick *3ICretStud* I 39-45; A.L.
Wilson *Minos* 16 (1977) 67-125; M.V. Cremona, D. Marcozzi, E. Scafa,
M. Sinatra *La toponomastica cretese nei documenti in lineare B di
Cnosso* (Rome 1978).
    Syntax.   Parataxis: Y. Duhoux *AR* II 781-785. Hypotaxis: F. Bader
CM 295-311.   Word-order: F. Bader *Minos* 14 (1973) 85-109; Y. Duhoux
Minos 14 (1973) 123-163; O. Panagl *ZVS* 87 (1973) 199-206, *CM* 313-322.
Acc. + inf.: M.D. Petruševski *ZA* 9 (1959) 56.   *we-te-i-we-te-i:*
O. Masson *ZA* 15 (1966) 257-266; W. Dressler *IBK* 14 (1968) 39-47.
    The Mycenaean dialect.   General: W.C. Cowgill *Ancient Indo-
European dialects* (Berkeley/Los Angeles 1966) 77-95; A. Bartoněk *SM*
37-51, *AM* II 329-360; M. Doria *La posizione dialettale del miceneo*
(Trieste 1968); *Mémoires* III 215-222; M.S. Ruipérez *AM* I 136-169;
F.R. Adrados *Emerita* 44 (1976) 65-113; E. Risch *SMEA* 20 (1979) 91-
111; J.L. García Ramón *EC* 24 (1980) 5-31.   Arcado-Cypriot con-
nexions: F.R. Adrados *IF* 62 (1956) 240-248.   Aeolic connexions: H.
Mühlestein *EM* 93-97; A. Tovar *MX* 188-193, *MS* 141-146; C. Gallavotti
RF 86 (1958) 113-133, *SMEA* 5 (1968) 42-55.   Mycenaean seen as part
of a South Greek continuum: E. Risch *EM* 167-172, 249-258; A. Heubeck
Glotta 39 (1961) 159-172.   Mycenaean and central Greek: G. Dunkel
Kadmos 20 (1981) 132-142.   Mycenaean seen as a *koine:* N.S. Grinbaum
VY 8 (1959/6) 78-86; V. Georgiev *MS* 125-139; A. Bartoněk *PCCMS* 95-
103.   Connexions between the Mycenaean and the Homeric language:
C.J. Ruijgh *L'élément achéen dans la langue épique* (Assen 1957) 11-
18, 89-97; J. Chadwick *Minoica* 116-122; P. Chantraine *Athenaeum* 46
(1958) 314-327; D.J.N. Lee *BICS* 6 (1959) 6-21; V. Georgiev *Klio* 38
(1960) 69-74, *Minoica und Homer* (Berlin 1961) 10-19, *PCCMS* 104-124;
G.P. Shipp *Essays in Mycenaean and Homeric Greek* (Melbourne 1961) 1-
28; F.R. Adrados *Emerita* 44 (1976) 100-106, *Glotta* 59 (1981) 13-27.
Dialectal peculiarities of Mycenaean: M. Doria *RAL* 18 (1963) 507-
525; E. Risch *BSL* 53 (1957-1958) 96-102.   Dialectal differences
within Mycenaean: E. Risch *PCCMS* 150-157; G. Nagy *AR* II 663-679; A.
Heubeck *SGIIL* 97-101.   The *i/e* alternation: N.E. Collinge *BICS* 4
(1957) 55-59; D.A. Hester *Minos* 6 (1958) 24-36; A. Heubeck *IF* 65
(1960) 252-254; S. Luria *Klio* 42 (1964) 33-35; C. Milani *Aevum* 41
(1967) 225-231.   Possible Doric features: J. Chadwick *PP* 31 (1976)
111-114; J.J. Moralejo Álvarez *Emerita* 45 (1977) 243-267.

PART TWO

1   KNOSSOS SWORD TABLETS: THE Ra SET

pi-ri-je-te in Ra 1548: A.M. Biraschi *PP* 33 (1978) 281-287.

***

§ 168   KN Ra 1540 = *Documents* no. 261 = *Interpretation* no. 246

to—sa   pa-ka-na   SWORD 50

This fragmentary inscription is placed first because of the extreme
simplicity of its structure and because of the unimpeachably Greek
character of the two phonetic words, τόσ(σ)α φάσγανα.   The tablet
forms one of a small archive in the Corridor of the Sword Tablets,
to the south-west of the Central Court of the Knossian palace: an
archive recognized by its excavator as containing SWORD tablets from
the realistic drawing of the ideogram, A.J. Evans *ABSA* 8 (1901-1902)
94-95.

§ 169   Since a very early type of written record in Crete consist-
ed of two parts only, an ideogram and a numeral, our tablet represents the next stage, in which a third, phonetic, component is added.
Although the ideogram appears simply to repeat the 'message' already
sufficiently conveyed by the phonetic part and thus to be redundant,
the appearance is illusory.   In the history of writing, the ideographic representation comes first, the phonetic representation afterwards, and sometimes long afterwards; but in Linear B, as in many
other scripts of the Mediterranean Bronze Age, the ideograms did not
die out but continued, in co-existence with the phonetic signs: cf.
W. Nahm *Kadmos* 9 (1970) 1-21.

§ 170   The shape of the ideogram in Ra 1540 is worth attention.
Different shapes of weapons are depicted within the Ra set.   Since
each of them is quite carefully drawn and since the whole archive
was written by one and the same scribe, it is a reasonably secure
conclusion that different weapons are being shown.   Despite the

time-honoured description of these weapons as 'swords', their shape
makes it more likely that they should be regarded as daggers: cf. J.
Boardman *On the Knossos tablets* (Oxford 1963) *79-80;* A.M. Snodgrass
Kadmos 4 (1965) 107-109.   If that is so, the Greek word φάσγανον
seems to have meant originally 'dagger', the word ξίφος (found in
Linear B in the form *qi-si-pe-e*) being reserved for 'sword'.

§ 171 A slightly more complex member of the set is:
KN Ra 1548 = *Documents* no. 262 = *Interpretation* no. 245

ku — ka-ro   pi-ri-je-te pa-ka-na a-ra-ru-wo-a SWORD 3

It will be noticed that the 'sword' here is different in shape from
that shown on Ra 1540.   The words of the inscription fall into two
groups, which are not connected by any finite verb:
ku-ka-ro pi-ri-je-te   *pa-ka-na a-ra-ru-wo-a de-so-mo*
Κύκαλος? ....-τηρ   φάσγανα ἀραρυϝόα   δεσμοῖς
Kykalos? the ....   'swords' fitted   with bands(?)
ku-ka-ro is a man's name which recurs on the Knossos sheep-tablet Da
1238.   *pi-ri-je-te* is presumably an agent-word in -τηρ, which describes the man *ku-ka-ro:* it is impossible that *pi-ri-je-te* contains
the stem of πρίω, since that verb means 'saw', and 'swordsmith', not
'sawyer', is the meaning required here.   (A plural *pi-ri-je-te-re*
is found at PY An 207.5 in a list of craftsmen).   *a-ra-ru-wo-a* is
neuter plural of the perfect participle of ἀραρίσκω 'fit': it represents ἀραρϝόα, the -u- in the Linear B spelling arising under the
influence of the neighbouring -w-.   *de-so-mo* represents an instrumental plural δεσμοῖς 'things which bind', but it is hard to be more
specific; perhaps the *de-so-mo* are bands of metal or leather attached to the weapon?

2   SHEEP AND WOOL TABLETS FROM PYLOS AND KNOSSOS: PY Cn AND KN D

PY Cn.   General studies: M. Doria *Interpretazioni di testi micenei*
II (Trieste 1958); M.L. Lang *PCCMS* 250-259; G.F. Polyakova *VDI* 118
(1971) 3-26.   *wo-no-we:* P.H. Ilievski *ŽA* 17 (1967) 23-31.

KN D.   General studies: J.T. Killen *ABSA* 59 (1964) 1-15.   The ideograms *106, *107, *108, *109:* L. Godart *KX* 23 (1971) 89-94.   Adjuncts: J.T. Killen *Eranos* 61 (1963) 69-93; Godart op. cit. 90.   The
ideogram *145:* L. Deroy *AC* 29 (1960) 312-314 ('bundle'); J.T. Killen
Hermathena 96 (1962) 38-72 (always 'wool'); M. Lejeune *Mémoires* II
164-165 (two forms to be distinguished, that shown on the D tablets
representing 'wool'); L.Y. and C.W. Beck *AJA* 82 (1978) 213-215 (always 'wool').   Dm tablets: G. Pugliese Carratelli *PP* 9 (1954) 220-
221; L. Deroy *SMEA* 10 (1969) 48-53; L. Godart, J.T. Killen, J.-P.
Olivier *Minos* 10 (1969) 154-156; M. Lejeune *Mémoires* II 364-367.   Dn
tablets: J.-P. Olivier *SMEA* 2 (1967) 71-93, *Minos* 13 (1972) 22-28.
Dp 997: J.T. Killen *PP* 17 (1962) 26-31, 18 (1963) 447-450 (*po-ka* =
'fleece').

***

The Pylos Cn tablets

   § 172 Forty-one tablets make up the Cn set.   With the exception
of Cn 3 (which records the presence of single oxen or bulls, perhaps
destined for some ritual operation) and Cn 608 (in which very small
numbers of pigs are assigned to the 'nine' towns of the state, §
215), these texts constitute a census of sheep, pigs, and goats, the
people who own them and herd them, and sometimes also the places in
which they are herded.   The structure of an important group is exemplified by:

PY Cn 40

wa-no-jo wo-wo pa-ro ne-ti-ja-no-re pa-ra-jo   RAM 140

wa-no-jo wo-wo pa-ro po-so-pe-re-i wo-ne-we   RAM 75

wa-no-jo wo-wo pa-ro zo-wi-jo a-ko-so-ta-o   RAM 70

wa-no-jo wo-wo po-ro pa-ru-qo-ta we-da-ne-wo   RAM 60

e-ko-me-no pa-ro pa-ta pa-ra-jo   RAM 80

e-ko-me-no pa-ro [ ] ma-te-we we-da-ne-wo   RAM 70

a-ne-u-te pa-ro ma-ri-ti-wi-jo a-ko-so-ta-o   RAM 83

ma-ro-pi pa-ro ro-ko pa-ra-jo   RAM 150

ma-ro-pi pa-ro ka-da-ro we-da-ne-wo   RAM 85

ma-ro pa-ro tu-ri-ta a-ke-o-jo   RAM 80

re-pe-u-ri-jo pa-ro e-zo-wo a[-ko-so-]ta-o   RAM 82

ma-ro pa-ro ma-u-ti-jo a-ko-so-ta-o   EWE 60

a-ne-u-te pa-ro ka-ta-wa a-ko-so-ta(-o)   EWE 80

a-te-re-wi-ja pa-ro e-wi-te-we a-ke-o-jo   EWE 70

Each line of the foregoing text contains five elements arranged in
the following order:
(1) a place-name in the dative case;
(2) *pa-ro* and a personal name in the dative;
(3) a personal name in the genitive;
(4) the SHEEP ideogram (RAM in lines 1-11, EWE in lines 12-14);
(5) a numeral.

§ 173 (1) Although, in theory, most of the place-names could be
either nominative or dative, the presence of the dative-locative
ending -*i* in *ma-ro-pi*, lines 8 and 9, suggests that they are all in
the dative.   (It is not known whether *ma-ro* in lines 10 and 12 denotes the same place which is called *ma-ro-pi* in the other entries).
a-ne-u-te too (lines 7 and 13) may contain a dative ending: -*te* =
-τει.   *wa-no-jo wo-wo* in lines 1-4 is a compound place-name, consisting of a genitive singular, ending in -*o-jo* = -οιο, and a dative
singular *wo-wo* = ϝόρϝωι 'boundary' (ϝόρϝος > Attic ὅρος, after loss
of the digammas); the first part *wa-no-jo* is obscure, being possibly
a personal or a geographical name.[1]

§ 174 (2) The meaning of *pa-ro* + dative is uncertain in this
context; it is more likely to mean 'at (the place of), apud, chez'
(like the later Greek παρά + dative) than 'from'.   The men 'at'
whom the flocks are situated would then naturally be the shepherds.

§ 175 (3) Similarly, the last word in each line (which is always
in the genitive) probably gives the name of the 'owner' of the flock.
It is not clear whether a direct relationship obtains between the man
named in (2) and the man named in (3): thus, it is possible that (2)
is the 'local representative' or even the servant of (3).

⁂

The Knossos D tablets

§ 176 The D tablets at Knossos number about 1100.   They come
from the East Wing of the palace, and most of them were written by
the same scribe (Olivier's 'Hand 117').   The Da set record numbers
of RAMS at named places; Db numbers of RAMS and EWES; Dc RAMS, some
of which are further particularized by adjuncts placed alongside the
ideogram; Dd, De, and Df RAMS and EWES with adjuncts; Dk and Dl RAMS,
EWES, and WOOL; Dm RAMS classified as *ai-mi-re-we* or *e-ka-ra-e-we*.
Dn is probably a totalling set.

[1] Compare the structure of English place-names beginning Mark-
(Old English *mearc* 'boundary').

§ 177 The ideograms which appear in this series are: EWE (OVIS^f), RAM (OVIS^m), and WOOL (LANA). (On Dl 463, § 182, an ideogram which appears to be the EWE sign is used; but, in the given context, this must be taken as RAM). In his paper at *ABSA* 59, Killen showed that the RAM ideogram depicts not only entire but also castrated beasts: an observation which at once explains the large proportion of rams to ewes in each flock and makes it likely that our tablets constitute a census of actual flocks within the Knossian domain. The amounts of wool recorded in the Dk and Dl sets would then represent the produce of the flocks specified. Where the *o*-sign is attached to a SHEEP or WOOL ideogram, it presumably stands for a word beginning with *o*- (probably *o-pe-ro* 'deficit') and signifies a number of beasts or an amount of wool which the census-takers expected to be present but which was not present. If this is a correct account of the matter, the large numbers of sheep mentioned on the D tablets suggest that the production of wool was one of the most important industries of Minoan Crete, at least in the fifteenth century.

§ 178 Most of the D inscriptions, except those belonging to the Dn set, share a similar structure. They consist of a group of large signs on the left of the tablet and two rows of smaller signs, usually ruled off from each other, on the right. The function of the respective sign-groups may be deduced, at least partially, from an inscription simple in structure, KN Da 1156 + 7236:

we-we-si-jo RAM 100

a - re - ke - se - u

pa-i-to

The word in large characters at the left may confidently be taken as a personal name in view of the ending *-e-u* (-εύς), while *pa-i-to* in the lower register at the right can hardly be anything other than the place-name Φαιστός. To judge from its ending, the word *we-we-si-jo* before the RAM ideogram appears to be another personal name (perhaps formed from an ethnic in -ιος).

§ 179 So far, it is impossible to assert with great confidence what were the respective functions of the persons named. But the problem may be clarified by reference to another tablet, KN Db 1159:

du - ta-so

Here in the upper register we have the genitive of the word which
appeared in the nominative on Da 1156.   And in tablet after tablet
the scribe writes the nominative we-we-si-jo or the genitive we-we-
si-jo-jo indifferently (so, on other tablets, his practice varies
between the nominative u-ta-jo and the genitive u-ta-jo-jo); but the
fact that he writes the genitive at all suggests that in this position on the tablet we expect to find the name of the owner of the
flocks which are specified immediately afterwards.   If that is so,
it is most likely that the name in large characters at the left is
that of the shepherd charged with managing the flock and rendering
an account of it.[1]   This likelihood is confirmed by the fact that
many different personal names in large characters are associated
with the same man we-we-si-jo.   As well as a-re-ke-se-u and du-ta-
so, already mentioned, we have:
the 'shepherds' a-ni-ja-to, a-nu-ko, a-qe-mo, da-i-qo-ta, ku-tu-qa-
no, o-ki-ro, and wi-se-jo at the 'place' pa-i-to (Φαιστός);
a 'shepherd' a-te-mo at the 'place' ku-ta-to;
the 'shepherds' au-ta₂ and da-ja-ro at the 'place' di-ro;
a 'shepherd' da-ja-ro at the 'place' ru-ki-to (Λύκτος);
the 'shepherds' da-ta-ja-ro, ko-ro, and su-di-ni-ko at the 'place'
da-*22-to;
a 'shepherd' ma-di at the 'place' e-ko-so;
the 'shepherds' wi-jo-ka-de and wo-*82-ni-jo at the 'place' da-wo.

§ 180 we-we-si-jo(-jo) is thus most frequently connected with
Phaistos.   It seems likely that the other places mentioned in connexion with him are not far distant from Phaistos.   At any rate, a
probable link between pa-i-to and da-wo is established by their oc-
curring together as a pair on this totalling tablet:

---

1   Some tablets (e.g. Db 1097, 1099, 1105 + 1446) have no entry
in the 'owner's' place.   Palmer infers (Interpretation 178) that the
owner is in fact the king; but the inference is unwarranted, since
it is possible for the 'shepherd' to be the 'owner' as well.

KN Dn 1094 + 1311 = *Documents* no. 79 = *Interpretation* no. 66

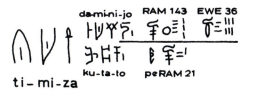

§ 181 Another 'owner', namely *da-mi-ni-jo,* is named on KN Df
1121 + 7689:

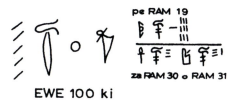

Here twenty-one of the RAMS are specified as *pe;* this, according to
Killen, is an abbreviation of *pe-ru-si-nu-wo* 'last year's', and his
interpretation is corroborated by the interesting text KN Do 927:

This inscription distinguishes *pe* rams from *za* rams; and a satisfactory opposition is achieved by taking *za* as the abbreviation of **za-
we-te-jo* — cf. the adverb *za-we-te* 'this year' (§ 100). *ki* ewes
are interpreted by Killen as immature beasts of either sex.

§ 182 So far we have observed the distribution of sheep by sex and age and the mention of sheep as 'missing' or 'owing'. Two sets of tablets, Dk and Dl, add information about the wool which has been obtained from the sheep. There is no serious objection to the assumption that *145 stands for WOOL on these tablets; although elsewhere this meaning gives rise to some difficulty. There follow two examples of tablets giving numbers of SHEEP and amounts of WOOL:

KN Dl 946

po-ti-ni-ja-we-jo   EWE 70 WOOL 7

ke - u - sa

si-ja-du-we   o   ki RAM 70   o   WOOL 7

KN Dl 463

EWE   56   ki EWE? 5   WOOL 5   M 1

mi — ti   ku - ta-to   o EWE 35   o ki EWE? 45   o   WOOL 20 M 2

By analogy with other D tablets, we might deduce that ke-u-sa and mi-ti are the names of shepherds who are in charge of flocks at the places si-ja-du-we and ku-ta-to respectively.   Dl 463 exhibits no 'owner's' name; so, as was suggested above, perhaps the shepherd himself is the 'owner'.   On Dl 946, in place of the 'owner's' name, we have the word po-ti-ni-ja-we-jo (also on seven other tablets of this set).   The word is connected, in some way, with po-ti-ni-ja 'mistress'.   The inference has usually been made that the flocks in question 'belong' to the πότνια (whether that word means 'goddess' or 'queen').   If that is true, the precise form of the word po-ti-ni-ja-we-jo is inexplicable (cf. § 148).

§ 183 The probable interpretation of the Dl tablets is as follows.   The upper register on the right states the number of ewes
and young rams, and also the amount of wool which these yielded, actually found by the inspector.   The lower register expresses the
deficit of ewes and young rams and the consequent short-fall of wool,
compared with what was expected.   The wool is shown as units of the
WOOL ideogram, and sometimes also by fractions (M).   Comparison
with texts of the Dk set establishes the ratio between M and one
unit of WOOL as 1:3 (*Interpretation* 179).

§ 184 The Dl tablets therefore differ in an important respect
from those of the Da-Df sets.   Whenever the latter refer to 'missing' sheep, these are always fewer than the sheep actually present.
Where (as in the Da set) a flock is said to consist of 100 or 80 or
60 or 50 sheep, this figure may be taken to represent the notional
strength of the flock.   But tablets like Dl 946 and Dl 463 show the
actual state of affairs: their upper register expressing what the
census-taker really found, the lower what he regarded as missing,
so that in these cases the 'notional' strength would be arrived at
by adding together the numbers of the upper and the lower register.

3   KNOSSOS CLOTH AND WOOL TABLETS: THE L SERIES

The archive in general: G. Björck *Eranos* 52 (1954) 271-275; J.L. Melena *Studies on some Mycenaean inscriptions from Knossos dealing
with textiles* (Salamanca 1975).   Lc: J.T. Killen *BICS* 13 (1966)
105-109, *Hermathena* 118 (1974) 82-90.   Ld: J.T. Killen *CM* 151-181.

***

§ 185   The L tablets contain inventories of cloths.   The CLOTH
ideogram, *159,* is represented by these variants:

§ 186   Another ideogram, *164,* also depicts a kind of cloth.   It
is found only twice, in the following forms:

(L 520)   (L 698)

§ 187   The different forms of *159 are not mere scribal variants,
but reflect different shapes or sizes of cloth.   This fact is indicated by the occurrence of two types in separate entries on the same
tablet Lc 526 (§ 190) and also by the variation between the 'two-
pronged' and the 'three-pronged' form on the following tablets:

KN Ld 572

pa-we-a   pe-ne-we-ta   a-ro-a *158 1

e-qe-si-ja   re-u-ko-nu-ka CLOTH 25

KN Ld 571 = *Documents* no. 214 = *Interpretation* no. 182

pa-we-a   pe-ne-we-ta   a-ro$_2$-a *158 1

e-qe-si-ja   re-u-ko-nu-ka CLOTH 25

§ 188 Ld 571 and 572 were written by the same scribe, and they
convey exactly the same information, except for the number of
'prongs' on the CLOTH ideogram.   The sign-group in large characters
at the left is readily equated with φάρϝεα, the plural of a word
which appears in later Greek as φᾶρος or φάρος.   The original meaning of this word seems to be 'something made of cloth', and Mycenaean *pa-we-a* may be understood as 'pieces of cloth' of a particular
variety.   The remaining four words, written in smaller characters,
are all neuter plural adjectives, describing the pieces of cloth.
Of these words, *pe-ne-we-ta* cannot be equated plausibly with anything in Greek.   *a-ro$_2$-a* may be understood as the comparative of
the stem *ar-*, which appears in the later Greek comparative ἀρείων
(§§ 118-120); so it means 'better, of superior quality'.   *e-qe-si-ja*
is an adjective derived from the noun *e-qe-ta* (ἑπέτᾱς); it is a word
parallel in function to *wa-na-ka-te-ra* in Lc 525 (§ 190).   The
fourth word *re-u-ko-nu-ka* is a spelling of a Greek word λευκόνυχα,
which would mean '(decorated with) white ὄνυχες'.   The analysis is,
apparently, impeccable, but we cannot tell for certain what manner
of decoration is implied by such a description.   In later Greek the
word ὄνυξ has two principal meanings: (i) animal's 'hoof' or bird's
'claw' or the human 'nail'; (ii) 'onyx'.   It is possible to believe
that meaning (ii) had already developed in Mycenaean times and that
the cloths in question were decorated in a manner which recalled the

appearance of onyx.   They could be designated either 'white', as on
the two foregoing tablets, or 'variegated', as on Ld 598, where *po-
ki-ro-nu-ka* (ποικιλόνυχα) is contrasted with *re-u-ko-nu-ka* as a description of cloths.   On the other hand, meaning (i) might be considered to fit the context better: in that case, the adjective probably refers to a decorative motif consisting of hooks or claws.

§ 189   The ideogram *158* is of unknown signification.   It is always followed by the numeral 1, no matter how many pieces of cloth
are associated with it.   This fact has given rise to Björck's interpretation 'container of cloths' (which suits the context well)
and to Furumark's interpretation 'hat' (which suits the shape of the
ideogram).   But all is speculative.

***

§ 190   The following tablets resemble each other in structure:

KN Lc 525 = *Documents* no. 209 = *Interpretation* no. 178

se – to -i - ja

KN Lc 526 = *Documents* no. 210

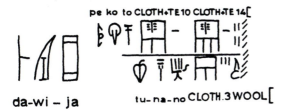

da-wi – ja

The words spelt in large characters at the left of these two tablets
are the names of places in which the wool was worked.   On the complete tablets of the Lc set, a fairly constant ratio is observed between CLOTH + *TE* and WOOL (1:7); it is therefore probable that this
set records consignments of wool which are to be made into pieces of
cloth.   *pe-ko-to* and *tu-na-no* are types of cloth about which nothing
is known except that they must be different from *pa-we-a,* since the
three terms form items of a list on Lc 535.   Nor is it evident in
what way the simple CLOTH ideogram differs in significance from CLOTH
+ *TE*.   The description *wa-na-ka-te-ra* has been mentioned already (§
188): it is a neuter plural adjective (and presumably, by analogy
with Ld 571 etc., the noun *pa-we-a* has to be understood), meaning
'intended for the *wanax*' or 'fit for the *wanax*'.

✲✲✲

§ 191 The following tablet relates textiles to bronze:

KN L 693 = *Documents* no. 222

Three items are here associated with amounts of BRONZE, the first
and third explicitly and the second by implication: (i) *ri-no*
re-po-to qe-te-o ki-to; (ii) *sa-pa;* (iii) *e-pi-ki-to-ni-ja.*   It
is easy to explain (i) and (iii) in terms of Greek. (i) is formally equivalent to λίνον λεπτόν, xʷειτέος χιτών 'fine linen,
kʷeiteos chiton'.   The meaning 'linen' seems fairly certain: C.
Milani *Aevum* 44 (1970) 303-305. *re-po-to* presents no difficulty
either; according to the spelling rules, it fits λεπτόν exactly.
The presence of χιτών is interesting, since it provides a clear
example of a Semitic loan-word in use in the Aegean as early as
the fourteenth century: E. Masson *Recherches sur les plus anciens*
emprunts sémitiques en grec (Paris 1967) 27-29.

§ 192 As for *qe-te-o*, the linguistic problems raised by the ending have been discussed already (§ 143).   In his treatment of L
693, Lejeune suggested that *qe-te-o* refers to all three items in the
list, not merely to *ki-to: Mémoires* II 302.   We may go farther and
relate the words *ri-no re-po-to* likewise to all the items; otherwise, it is hard to see why the name of the material and not the
name of the object should have been brought to the beginning of the
inscription.   If that is so, and since *ki-to* is known to be the
name of a garment, it follows that all three members of the list are
words for garments, even though the meaning of *sa-pa* is unknown. The
third item *e-pi-ki-to-ni-ja* must be a neuter plural meaning literal-
ly 'what is upon (ἐπί) the *ki-to*': namely, an over-garment such as a
cloak (compare the structure of *o-pi-a₂-ra* § 230 and *o-pi-i-ja-pi* §
304).   In later Greek, the term for such a cloak is χλαῖνα or χλαμύς, but these words are not found in the extant Mycenaean texts.

§ 193 The monuments tell us nothing of the wearing of a χιτών in
Late Minoan Crete, if that word is understood in its later Greek
sense of 'tunic'.   It is possible that χιτών denoted different garments at different stages of its history — equally possible that a
certain type of garment was in use in the Late Bronze Age but is not
shown on the surviving monuments: cf. H.L. Lorimer *Homer and the monuments* (London 1950) 360-362 and S. Marinatos *Kleidung Haar- und
Barttracht* (Archaeologia Homerica I)(Göttingen 1967) A 22-25.   The
frescoes and seals, from which our information comes, rarely depict
ordinary life: their concern is with the ceremonies of the palace,
for which participants wear a sort of short-sleeved jacket reaching
to the ground, or with men in rapid movement, who are equipped with
very short divided drawers.

§ 194 It remains to discuss the connexion between the garments
and the amounts of bronze.   Three suggestions have been made: (i)
the bronze refers to actual attachments of the garments (so that we
are, in fact, dealing with items of armour); (ii) the amounts of
bronze indicate the weight of the respective garments; (iii) the
value of the garments is measured by the bronze.   Of these suggestions, the third seems the most likely.   'Fine linen' is an improba-
ble fabric to which plates of armour would be attached, while the
amounts of bronze specified are too large to form an appropriate
counter-weight to the fine stuffs.

4   GROUPS OF WOMEN: THE PYLOS A SERIES

Aa and Ab: T.B.L. Webster *BICS* 1 (1954) 11-12.   Aa, Ab, Ad: E.L. Bennett *EM* 121-136; C. Milani *Aevum* 51 (1977) 89-111.   Ad 684: F.J. Tritsch *Minos* 5 (1957) 154-162.   Ae: M. Benavente *EC* 12 (1968) 307-309.   Status of the women: F.J. Tritsch *Minoica* 406-445; Ja.A. Lencman *Die Sklaverei im mykenischen und homerischen Griechenland* (tr. M. Bräuer-Pospelova)(Wiesbaden 1966) 153-169.   DA and TA: L.R. Palmer *Sprache* 5 (1959) 137-142; E.L. Bennett *Temple University Aegean Symposium* 2 (Philadelphia 1977) 16-18.   *ra-mi-ni-ja*: S.Hiller *ZA* 25 (1975) 388-412.

***

§ 195   The A tablets at Pylos comprise a number of important sets which differ greatly from one another, having in common only the fact that they record numbers of persons engaged in various activities.   It is convenient to begin with simple inscriptions which refer to numbers of women, boys, and girls:

PY Aa 85

a - ke - ti - ri - ja WOMAN 12   ko-wa 16   ko-wo 8   DA 1   TA 1

PY Aa 717 = *Documents* no. 7

ro-u-so   a-ke-ti-ri-ja WOMAN 32   ko-wa 18   ko-wo 8 DA 1 TA 1

PY Ad 666

pu-ro a-ke-ti-ra₂-o ko-wo MAN 20 ko-wo 7

PY Ab 189

WHEAT 6 T 7 TA DA

pu-ro ki-ni-di-ja WOMAN 20 ko-wa 10 ko-wo 10 NI 6 T 7

PY Ab 573

WHEAT 5 T 1 DA TA

pu-ro mi-ra-ti-ja WOMAN 16 ko-wa 3 ko-wo 7 NI 5 1

§ 196 The women whose numbers are recorded in the Aa set are not named, but they are usually described according to their occupation. The most probable explanation of the need for such records is that groups of women were assigned specific tasks. Only the numbers of women, their occupation, and (sometimes) their location were of interest to the scribes. Since the women of the Aa set are never named and since they are associated only with boys and girls, never with men, they are probably slaves organized into work-units.

§ 197 The Aa inscriptions contain some or all of the following elements: (i) a place-name; (ii) a noun in the nominative plural feminine, designating the occupation or status of the women; (iii) the WOMAN ideogram; (iv) a numeral; (v) varying numbers of *ko-wa* (κόρϝαι) 'girls' and *ko-wo* (κόρϝοι) 'boys', who are perhaps to be regarded as the daughters and sons of the women respectively; (vi) the phonetic sign *da*, often followed by the numeral 1; (vii) the phonetic sign *ta*, often followed by the numeral 1.

§ 198 The word *a-ke-ti-ri-ja* probably contains the stem found in ἀσκέω, so that it would mean 'decorators' or 'finishers' (J.T. Killen *CM* 165). The sign for WOMAN in this set does not fulfil quite the same function as the ideogram on KN Ra 1540, for example: there it simply repeats the phonetic spelling of the word, whereas here the WOMAN sign is preceded, not by a phonetic representation of the word 'woman', but by a feminine noun. Thus in the Aa inscriptions the WOMAN sign does not function as an ideogram in the strict sense, but is a determinative or classifier of a kind found in other Bronze Age scripts.

§ 199 The text of Aa 85 amounts to a very bald statement, namely that twelve 'decorators' form a group together with sixteen girls and eight boys. The name of the place of work must have been known to the scribe; perhaps it was mentioned on a sealing attached to this archive. In other tablets, the place is specified. Aa 717, for instance, states that thirty-two 'decorators' with eighteen girls and eight boys work at the place *ro-u-so*. This is known, from a number of other tablets, to be a place of interest to the scribes (e.g. PY Cn 328, Jn 829, Ma 365), but it is especially apt to compare Ad 666. The first word of this inscription, *pu-ro,* is manifestly a spelling of the place-name Πύλος, and so it is natural to look for a place-name in the corresponding position in the Aa texts. The word *a-ke-ti-ra₂-o* represents a genitive plural ἀσκη-τριῶν, and *a-ke-ti-ra₂-o ko-wo* must mean 'sons of the decorators'. The addition of seven *ko-wo* after the MAN ideogram is hard to account for. Were Ad 666 an isolated tablet, it could be suggested that the scribe had overlooked seven κόρϝοι and added them after the writing of the ideogram. But this cannot be the correct explanation, since at least nineteen other tablets in the Ad set have precisely the same structure, with varying numbers of *ko-wo* added after the ideogram. Once or twice in this set (e.g. at Ad 357) a number of men are marked as *o-pe-ro;* if (as is generally assumed) this word is ὄφελος 'deficit', we must conclude that the taker of the census expected to find a certain number of *ko-wo* in each group. This conclusion immediately leads to another, namely that the census-takers checked the actual numbers they found against the 'notional' strength recorded on some other document in their possession (cf. Tritsch *Minoica* 433-435). The most that can be said about the Ad set is that it records numbers of *ko-wo* who are in some way dependent upon, or connected with, the women mentioned in Aa. Nowhere is the occupation of these *ko-wo* stated, and the presumption is that they are as yet too young to form part of the work-force in their own right, for it seems inconceivable that adult able-bodied males in such circumstances would not have been allotted some task. And associated with some groups of these dependent *ko-wo* are other (perhaps independent) *ko-wo,* who are counted along with them for the purposes of the census.

§ 200 The Ab set presents the following points of interest. On
some, and perhaps on all, of the Ab tablets the word standing between the place-name and the WOMAN ideogram does not denote occupation but appears to be an ethnic. In Ab 189 *ki-ni-di-ja* = Κνίδιαι
'women of Knidos' and in Ab 573 *mi-ra-ti-ja* = Μιλᾱτιαι 'women of Miletos', a type of ethnic formation which is widespread in later
Greek: E. Risch *MH* 14 (1957) 63-66. It is a suspicious coincidence,
to say the least, that Knidos and Miletos are both the names of
coastal sites in south-western Anatolia, of which Miletos at least
is known to have been in close contact with the Mycenaeans. It is
therefore possible that the *ki-ni-di-ja* and the *mi-ra-ti-ja* were
slave-women who had been brought to Pylos from the respective places
indicated by their ethnics. It is impossible to surmise why some
groups of women are identified by occupation-words and others by
ethnics. It is almost as if, in the case of women from abroad,
their occupation was irrelevant to the census: irrelevant, or perhaps superfluous, if it can be assumed that women from certain
places were known to be especially apt for certain tasks.

§ 201 The Ab tablets not only contain the entries *ta* and *da* (as
in the Aa set) but also refer to amounts of WHEAT and *ni* (= 'figs').
The meaning of the WHEAT ideogram is fixed by its phonetic accom-
paniment on some Linear B texts (cf. *si-to* = σῖτος in the Pylos E
series); that of *ni* by its occurrence before *su-za* (*σῦκyαι) at KN F
841.5. Wheat and figs, then, were the commodities which served as
rations for the group of women in question. By correlating all the
occurrences of *ta* and *da,* at Knossos as well as at Pylos, Palmer was
able to show that *ta* accounted for the same amount of food as did
one (slave-)woman and that *da* accounted for 2½ times as much. The
most likely explanation of these facts is that advanced by Palmer
himself, namely that *ta* represents a female 'supervisor' of the
women and *da* a male 'supervisor': *Sprache* 5 (1959) 140-141.

§ 202 A completely different situation is envisaged in:

PY Ae 303 = *Documents* no. 27 = *Interpretation* no. 30

pu-ro i-je-re-ja do-e-ra e-ne-ka ku-ru-so-jo WOMAN 14 [

Ae 303 is one of the few Linear B texts which permit an immediate
transcription into Greek:

Πύλος· ἱερείᾱς δοέλαι ἔνεκα χρυσοῖο ἱεροῖο· WOMAN 14+
Pylos: slaves of the priestess on account of the sacred gold: 14+
women

§ 203 It may appear surprising, at first sight, that the women
of Ae 303 are expressly stated to be slaves, whereas the women in
the Aa and Ab tablets are not so described, even though they were
apparently slaves. The probable explanation is that different
types of 'slavery' are involved. On one level are women bound to
certain kinds of menial service. On another, and surely much higher, level are those described as 'slaves of the priestess'. Still
higher, presumably, are the 'slaves of the god' mentioned in the E
tablets. The expression 'slave of the priestess' recurs also in
one of these tablets, Eo 224.6. It is remarkable that in that
place the 'slave' is given a name (*e-ra-tá-ra*), that she is a land-
holder, and that she is included in a list together with the priestess herself (§ 269). Everything, in short, points to a much higher
position than would be occupied by menial workers: so high, indeed,
that the very expression 'slave of the priestess' is perhaps to be
regarded as an honorific title. (For the word *e-ne-ka*, see § 93).

§ 204 The picture which emerges from a study of Ae 303 is that
of a group or guild of priestesses (on the assumption that the
i-je-re-a was only *prima inter pares*), who are charged with the duty
of attending the sacred treasure.

5   THE ASSESSMENT AND DISTRIBUTION OF BRONZE: PY Jn

General studies: G. Pugliese Carratelli *SCO* 12 (1963) 242-253; M.S. Ruipérez *Minos* 8 (1963) 37-50; M.L. Lang *Hesperia* 35 (1966) 397-412; A. Morpurgo Davies *PP* 23 (1968) 220-222; A. Hurst *SMEA* 5 (1968) 92-96; M. Lejeune *Mémoires* II 167-195, III 113-133; S. Hiller *SMEA* 15 (1972) 51-72.   Names of the smiths: P. Attinger *ZA* 27 (1977) 55-75. *a-ke-te-re*: M. Lejeune *Mémoires* II 207-208.   *a-ta-ra-si-jo*: I. Tegyey *AC(D)* 4 (1968) 3-5.   *du-ma-te*: M. Lejeune *Mémoires* I 187-201. *ka-ko na-wi-jo*: A. Leukart, S. Hiller *CM* 183-195.   *ko-re-te* and *po-ro-ko-re-te*: M.S. Ruipérez *EM* 105-120; A. Heubeck *IF* 64 (1959) 132-135, *WJ* 4 (1978) 97-98; K. Murakawa *JCS* 7 (1959) 1-24; J. Taillardat *REG* 73 (1960) 1-5; M. Lejeune *Mémoires* II 214-215; J.T. Hooker *ZA* 26 (1976) 27-29.   *po-ti-ni-ja-we-jo*: C.J. Ruijgh *SMEA* 4 (1967) 40-52.   *qa-si-re-u*: J.L. O'Neil *ZA* 20 (1970) 11-14.   *ta-ra-si-ja*: Y. Duhoux *AVEM* 69-115.

***

§ 205   The Jn tablets are characterized by the presence of the BRONZE ideogram, which is often accompanied by the fractional amounts N, M, or L.   The extant tablets of the Jn set fall into two classes, which must be considered separately:
(1) Jn 829 and the fragmentary text Jn 881, which record the assessment of weights of BRONZE in various parts of the Pylian domain;
(2) All the other Jn texts, which record the distribution of weights of BRONZE to smiths for working.

The assessment of bronze

§ 206 PY Jn 829 = *Documents* no. 257 = *Interpretation* no. 173

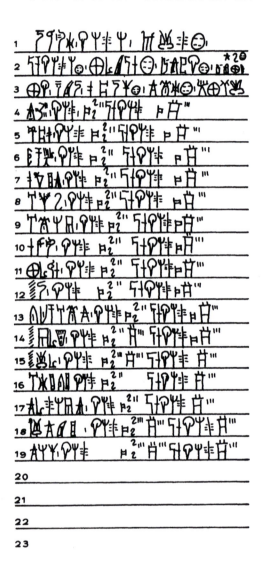

jo-do-so-si ko-re-te-re du-ma-te-qe

-e-we-qe
po-ro-ko-re-te-re-qe ka-ra-wi-po-ro-qe o-pi-su-ko-qe o-pi-ka-pe

ka-ko na-wi-jo pa-ta-jo-i-qe e-ke-si-qe ai-ka-sa-ma

pi-^{x}82 ko-re-te BRONZE M2 po-ro-ko-re-te BRONZE N3

me-ta-pa ko-re-te BRONZE M2 po-ro-ko-re-te BRONZE N3

pe-to-no ko-re-te BRONZE M2 po-ro-ko-re-te BRONZE N3

pa-ki-ja-pi ko-re-te BRONZE M 2 po-ro-ko-re-te BRONZE N3

a-pu$_2$-we ko-re-te BRONZE M2 po-ro-ko-re-te BRONZE N3

a-ke-re-wa ko-re-te BRONZE M2 po-ro-ko-re-te BRONZE N3

ro-u-so ko-re-te BRONZE M 2 po-ro-ko-re-te BRONZE N3

ka-ra-do-ro ko-re-te BRONZE M 2 po-ro-ko-re-te BRONZE N 3

ri-]jo ko-re-te BRONZE M 2 po-ro-ko-re-te BRONZE N3

ti-mi-to-a-ke-e ko-re-te BRONZE M2 po-ro-ko-re-te BRONZE N3

ra-]wa-ra-ta$_2$ ko-re-te BRONZE M2 N3 po-ro-ko-re-te BRONZE N3

sa-]ma-ra ko-re-te BRONZE M3 N3 po-ro-ko-re-te N 3

a-si-ja-ti-ja ko-re-te BRONZE M 2 po-ro-ko-re-te N 3

e-ra-te-re-wa-pi ko-re-te BRONZE M 2 po-ro-ko-re-te N 3

za-ma-e-wi-ja ko-re-te BRONZE M3 N3 po-ro-ko-re-te N 3

e-re-i ko-re-te BRONZE M3 N3 po-ro-ko-re-te N 3

§ 207   Jn 829 consists of two parts, a 'heading' (lines 1-3) and
a 'list' (lines 4-19).   The following facts suggest that it formed
the first of a closely connected group of texts all dealing with the
same subject.   While six classes of officials are mentioned in the
'heading', the contribution of only two classes is recorded in the
'list' on this tablet.   It is a reasonably secure inference that
the contribution of the remaining four classes was recorded on other
tablets.   Furthermore, the prefix *jo-* attached to the opening word
of line 1 indicates that, within the postulated group of Jn tablets
dealing with assessments, our text is the first (§ 130).

§ 208   We examine first the structure of the 'heading'.   After
the verb *do-so-si* (δώσονσι) 'will give' (probably with the imperati-
val force 'are to give' which is found in classical Greek) come the
six subjects, all in the nominative plural and all, except the
first, linked together by the copulative suffix *-qe* (τε):[1]   'the
ko-re-te-re and *du-ma-te* and *po-ro-ko-re-te-re* and *ka-ra-wi-po-ro*
and *o-pi-su-ko* and *o-pi-ka-pe-e-we*'.   These, then, are the six
classes of persons who are to give such-and-such.

§ 209   The first class consists of the *ko-re-te-re,* a word which
almost certainly represents a Greek agent-noun ending in -τηρες.
The stem *ko-re-,* however, cannot be equated with anything known in
Greek.   Whatever place the *ko-re-te-re* held in the Pylian state, it
was a reasonably important one.   Along with the *po-ro-ko-re-te-re,*
they recur on PY Jo 438, which records an assessment of GOLD in certain places, just as Jn 829 records an assessment of BRONZE.   Again
on the fragmentary tablet PY On 300 the *ko-re-te-re* are found in
named places.   From the way in which the *ko-re-te-re* and *po-ro-ko-
re-te-re* are mentioned in these texts, it is evident that in each
place there was only one *ko-re-te* and only one *po-ro-ko-re-te.*   They
were therefore local officials of some kind.   (A *ko-re-te-ri-jo*
ke-ke-me-no is mentioned at PY An 830.6.   Since *ko-re-te-ri-jo* is
an adjective formed from *ko-re-te* and since the feminine of *ke-ke-
me-no* is applied to a type of land-holding in the E tablets, § 260,
the whole phrase probably refers to the plot of a *ko-re-te* at a
given place.   At KN V 865, both a *ko-re-te* and a *po-ro-ko-re-te*
are recorded at the place *qa-ra*).   The exact relationship between a
ko-re-te and a *po-ro-ko-re-te* is impossible to determine because the
force of the prefix *po-ro-* is unknown.   This prefix is often explained by reference to Latin *pro,* so that a *po-ro-ko-re-te* is seen
as a kind of 'deputy *ko-re-te*'.   But it is unnecessary to go outside Greek to find a parallel to the form *po-ro-ko-re-te.*   Classical
πρό, both as an independent word and in compounds, means 'before, in
front (of)'.   Compounds with a noun denoting a person are rare, but

[1]   According to the usual practice of Linear B scribes: cf. PY Ta
714.1, 722.1.

πρόμαντις and πρόξενος are well attested.   In both words, the prefix has its customary meaning: a πρόμαντις is a seer in the public
eye, while a πρόξενος is recognized officially by the state.   Perhaps it would be right to interpret the Mycenaean term po-ro-ko-re-te
along similar lines, leaving open the possibility that po-ro- is the
spelling of some prefix other than προ-.

§ 210   The meaning of the word du-ma-te (du-ma-τες) and its connexion (if any) with da-ma-te (§ 267) cannot be ascertained.   Elsewhere it is sometimes found in the compound forms po-ro-du-ma-te
(PY Fn 50.7) and me-ri-du-ma-te (PY An 39.2, 424.3, 427.2, 594.2).

§ 211   The word ka-ra-wi-po-ro is usually understood as κλᾱϝιφόροι
and analysed as a compound of *κλᾱϝιδ- 'key'.   A priestly title
κλᾱικοφόρωι (formed from a stem *κλᾱϝικ-) is found in a Hellenistic
inscription from Messene: F. Bechtel Die griechischen Dialekte II
(Berlin 1923) 426.   The 'key-bearers' of Jn 829 (if that is what
they are) are likely to be women, since on PY Ep 704.7 the word
ka-ra-wi-po-ro is put in apposition to the woman's name ka-pa-ti-ja.
It is not impossible that in each place a priestess holding an honorific title should be held responsible for providing a quantity of
bronze.   At the same time, there always resides a danger in adopt-
ing such purely 'etymological' interpretations when the context is
not sufficient to fix the meaning precisely.

§ 212   No satisfactory sense can be assigned to the two remaining
words in the nominative plural, o-pi-su-ko and o-pi-ka-pe-e-we.   The
presence of the prefix o-pi- (ὀπι-) suggests that both are classes
of people 'in charge of' certain things; but to regard the first
class as 'supervisors of figs' (on the assumption that -su-ko is a
spelling of σῦκον) or the second as 'supervisors of hoeing or of
hulls' (on the assumption that -ka-pe represents the stem σκαφ-) is
only to confess our ignorance of the real meaning of these terms.

§ 213   The next two words of the 'heading', ka-ko na-wi-jo, form
the object of the verb do-so-si.   ka-ko represents the accusative
singular χαλκόν 'bronze', while na-wi-jo is an adjective (νάϝιον)
in agreement with it.   The question arises whether νάϝιον is formed
from the stem of ναῦς 'ship' or that of νᾱϝός 'temple'.[1]   Although
the second interpretation has received more widespread support, no
final judgment is possible.   Even if the meaning 'temple' is more

---

[1] The meaning 'temple' should not be pressed too closely. Since
independent 'temples' are not yet attested on the Greek mainland in
Mycenaean times, the word 'shrine' would perhaps be more apposite.
Herodotus 6.19.3 uses νηός 'shrine' in contrast to ἱρόν 'temple'.
Did Mycenaean Greek make a similar distinction?

probable, either of two very different situations could have been contemplated by the writer of the tablet, namely: (i) the bronze was already in temples and was required to make the weapons specified in the following words (attributive use of *na-wi-jo*); or (ii) the bronze was intended for use in temples (predicative use of *na-wi-jo*). Although (ii) has rarely been considered the correct explanation, it does in fact yield better sense if the small quantities of bronze are taken into account: these quantities are more consistent with the need for 'dedicated' weapons than with that for equipment actually to be used in warfare. Again, if the scribe is merely recording amounts of bronze to be raised from various places, it is hard to see why the present use or location of the bronze is of much interest to him: his concern is with the *destination*, not with the *origin*, of the metal.

§ 214 Next in sense comes the last word of line 3, in the accusative plural and in apposition to 'bronze': *ai-ka-sa-ma* = αἰξμάνς (Attic αἰχμάς) 'points'. Finally we may take the dative plural words *pa-ta-jo-qe e-ke-si-qe*, which yield a good sense in Greek: παλταίοι-ϲ τε ἔγχεσί τε 'both for darts and for spears' (a word παλτόν is attested in later Greek).

§ 215 Thus the 'heading' of the tablet states the purpose for which the contributions of bronze are required and the classes of persons who are to make the contributions. The list which follows specifies how much bronze the *ko-re-te* and the *po-ro-ko-re-te* in each place will contribute. The names of two places in the Pylian domain have already been elicited from the A tablets (§ 199): *pu-ro* and *ro-u-so*. Although *pu-ro* does not figure in the present list, *ro-u-so* occurs in line 10. The first nine members of the list are arranged in an order which recurs on other tablets: a recurrence which facilitates the restoration of the damaged sections of our text. The remaining seven place-names do not form a list on any other extant tablet, although most of them are found individually on the Ma tablets, which record assessments of produce from named places (§§ 315-319). The correspondences may be expressed by means of a table:

Jn 829	Vn 20	Cn 608	Ma	
pi-*82	pi-*82-de	pi-*82	225	pi-*82
me-ta-pa	me-ta-pa-de	me-ta-pa	90	me-ta-pa
pe-to-no	pe-to-no-de	pe-to-no	120	pe-to-no
pa-ki-ja-pi	pa-ki-ja-na-de	pa-ki-ja-si	221	pa-ki-ja-pi
a-pu₂-we	a-pu₂-de	a-pu₂-we	124	a-pu₂-we
a-ke-re-wa	a-ke-re-wa-de	a-ke-re-wa	222	a-ke-re-wa
ro-u-so	e-ra-to-de	e-ra-te-i	365	ro-u-so
ka-]ra-do-ro	ka-ra-do-ro-de	ka-ra-do-ro	346	ka-ra-do-ro
ri-]jo	ri-jo-de	ri-jo	193	ri-jo
ti-mi-to-a-ke-e			123	ti-mi-to-a-ke-e
ra-]wa-ra-ta₂			216	ra-wa-ra-ta₂
sa-]ma-ra			378	sa-ma-ra
a-si-ja-ti-ja				
e-ra-te-re-wa-pi			333	e-ra-te-re-we
za-ma-e-wi-ja			393	za-ma-e-wi-ja
e-re-i				

§ 216 The names in Vn 20 contain the allative suffix -de, denoting the places to which wine has been distributed (§ 133). Three observations on the names themselves may be useful:
(i) The place-name standing fourth in the list appears sometimes as pa-ki-ja-ne (a plural in -ες), sometimes as pa-ki-ja-na (feminine singular or neuter plural?). In the above lists, pa-ki-ja-pi represents an ablative-instrumental in -φι, pa-ki-ja-si a locative plural in -σι.
(ii) The variation between ro-u-so and e-ra-to may be explained by assuming either that the same place had two different names or that one name refers to a town and the other to the district in which the town is situated: C.W. Shelmerdine AJA 77 (1973) 275.
(iii) Shelmerdine AJA 85 (1981) 319-325 identifies ti-mi-to-a-ke-e with Nichoria.

***

The distribution of bronze

§ 217 We have seen that Jn 829 records the assessment of bronze from sixteen named places. Nearly all the other tablets in the Jn set are concerned with the opposite transaction, namely the distribution of quantities of bronze to smiths for working. In theory, the 'full' form of these distribution-tablets consists of five paragraphs, which as a rule are carefully marked off from one another by means of blank lines:

Para. 1: (i) 'heading': place-name followed by the formula *ka-ke-we*
 ta-ra-si-ja e-ko-te (or *e-ko-si*), χαλκῆϝες ταλανσίαν
ἔχοντες (ἔχονσι); on one tablet, Jn 832.1, *ka-ke-we* is
put in apposition to *a-ke-te-re*, an agent-noun in
-τηρες, of unknown meaning;
(ii) a list of named smiths, each of whom is followed by a
weight of BRONZE;
(iii) the word *qa-si-re-u* = βασιλεύς, followed by a list of
named smiths.

Para. 2:   the total of the BRONZE allocated to the smiths, usually
introduced by the formula *to-so-de ka-ko* (τοσόσδε χαλκός) or *to-so-pa ka-ko* (τόσος πὰνς χαλκός).

Para. 3:   the formula (*to-so-de*) *a-ta-ra-si-jo* (*ka-ke-we*) =
(τοσοίδε) ἀταλάνσιοι (χαλκῆϝες), followed by a list of
named smiths, but without specification of weights of
BRONZE.

Para. 4:   a list of unnamed slaves attached to the foregoing
smiths; the list is sometimes preceded by the formula
to-so-de do-e-ro = τοσοίδε δοέλοι.

Para. 5:   the formula *po-ti-ni-ja-we-jo ka-ke-we ta-ra-si-ja*
e-ko-te = Ποτνιαϝείοι? χαλκῆϝες ταλανσίαν ἔχοντες, followed by a list of named smiths, each followed in turn
by a weight of BRONZE.

§ 218 Thus, apart from the perplexing *ka-ke-we a-ke-te-re* on Jn
832, three classes of bronze-smiths are distinguished: one group who
have *ta-ra-si-ja* (Para. 1); a second group who are *a-ta-ra-si-jo*
(i.e. who lack *ta-ra-si-ja*) and against whose names weights of
BRONZE are not recorded (Para. 3); and a third group who have some
connexion with Potnia, 'the Lady' (Para. 5).

§ 219 The meaning of the word *ta-ra-si-ja* cannot be fixed with
precision; but the fact that only those smiths with *ta-ra-si-ja* are
allotted amounts of bronze suggests that it contains a stem which
appears in later Greek τάλαντον and consequently means 'an amount
weighed out'.   It is a mark of the meticulous nature of the book-
keeping involved that the scribes record not only those smiths who
have quantities of bronze but also those who have none: *a-ta-ra-si-*
jo = 'men without *ta-ra-si-ja*'.   The association of the third
group with Potnia does not necessarily imply that such smiths are in
the service of a goddess.   The word *po-ti-ni-ja* 'lady' does not refer unequivocally to the divine sphere; and, since the Jn tablets
convey no hint that the smiths have cult-connexions, there is little
justification for insisting on their sacral function here.

§ 220   On Jn 431, 601, and 845 the word *qa-si-re-u* is found in
association with some smiths 'having *ta-ra-si-ja*'.   In 431.6 it is
written at the beginning of the line, followed by the names of two
smiths; in 601.8 it is followed by the name of one smith; in 845.7
it is used after the smith's name *e-ri-ko-wo*.   If we take these
facts into account and note the formal equivalence of *qa-si-re-u* to
βασιλεύς 'king' in alphabetic Greek, we can suggest that *qa-si-re-u*
signifies a local official of some kind.   The later extension of
the term to refer to a much more elevated status would by no means
invalidate such a suggestion.   Nor is the evidence of PY Jo 438 at
variance with it: among the persons, including *ko-re-te*, *po-ro-ko-re-te*,
and *mo-ro-qa* said by that text to contribute amounts of
GOLD, line 20 specifies the contribution by *a-ke-ro qa-si-re-u*.

§ 221   The following table gives in outline the structure of the
well-preserved distribution-tablets, by marking with × those of the
possible constituents which are actually present in each text:

	(i)	(ii)	(iii)	2	3	4	5
Jn 310	×	×			×	×	×
320	×	×		×	×		
389	×	×		×	×		
413	[×]	×		×	×	×	
415	×	×		×	×		
431	×	×	×	×	×	×	×
478	×	×		×	×		
601	×	×	×	×	×		
605	×	×			×	×	
658	×	×		×	×		
692	×	×			×		
693	×	×			×		
706	×	×		×	×	×	
725	×	×		×			
750	×	×			×	×	
832	×	×			×		
845	[×]	×	×	×	×		
881	×	×					
927	[	]			×		
937	×	×	[				

§ 222   There follow three examples of the Jn distribution-texts:

PY Jn 605

§ 223   This text falls into three distinct parts:

Part one shows amounts of bronze allotted to named smiths 'having
ta-ra-si-ja'.   The first word, a-pi-no-e-wi-jo, which occurs six
times elsewhere on the Pylos tablets, is probably an ethnic, indicating the place where the smiths in question carry on their work.

a-pi-no-e-wi[-jo] ka-ke-we ta-ra-si-ja e-ko-te

to-ri-jo BRONZE M1 N2 e-do-mo-ne-u BRONZE M1 N2

mi-ka-ri-jo BRONZE M1 N2 pu-ra-ta BRONZE M1 N2

u-wa-ta BRONZE M1 N2 ka-ta-wa BRONZE M1 N2

a-ta-ra-si-jo ka-ke-we

wi-ti-mi-jo 1 ma-no-u-ro 1 a-we-ke-se-u 1

to-so-de do-e-ro

pe-re-qo-no-jo 2 ai-ki-e-wo 2 mi-ka-ri-jo-jo 1

pu-ra-ta-o 1

Part two names three smiths 'without *ta-ra-si-ja*'.

Part three mentions six slaves attached to the smiths whose names
are present in the genitive case, *mi-ka-ri-jo-jo* in line 10 being
the genitive of the smith's name *mi-ka-ri-jo* (line 3) and *pu-ra-ta-o*
in line 11 being the genitive of *pu-ra-ta* (line 3).

§ 224 PY Jn 845

Four items are contained in this inscription: the first (lines 1-6)
specifying amounts of BRONZE allotted to named smiths 'having *ta-ra-si-ja*' (the place-name has been lost, because the top left-hand corner of the tablet is broken away); the second (line 8) adding *e-ri-ko-wo* the *qa-si-re-u;* the third (line 9) giving the total amount of BRONZE allotted (M 12); the fourth (lines 11-14) naming seven smiths who are without *ta-ra-si-ja.*

] ka-ke-we ta-ra-si-ja e-ko-te

po-ru-qo-ta BRONZE M1 N2 sa-ri-qo-ro BRONZE M1 N2

pu-ke-se-ro BRONZE M1 M 2 re-qo-we BRONZE M1 N2

qe-ta-ra-je-u BRONZE M1 N2 du-re-u BRONZE M1 N2

a-pa-je-u BRONZE M1 N2 pa-pa-ra-ko BRONZE M1 N2

e-ri-ko-wo qa-si-re-u 1

to-so-de ka-ko BRONZE M 12

to-so-de a-ta-ra-si-jo

po-so-ro 1 na-pu-ti-jo 1 ma-ta-ko 1

ku-ke-re-u 1 a-ti-ja-wo 1 wa-ra-ko-no 1

qe-re-me-ne-u 1

§ 225

PY Jn 310 = *Documents* no. 253 = *Interpretation* no. 174

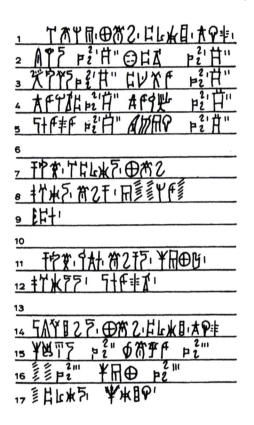

§ 226 The four parts of this text are marked off by means of blank lines:

Part one (lines 1-5) gives the amounts of BRONZE allotted to named smiths 'having *ta-ra-si-ja*' at *a-ke-re-wa,* one of the 'nine towns' already mentioned (§ 215).

a-ke-re-wà ka-ke-we ta-ra-si-ja e-ko-te

ti-qa-jo BRONZE M1 N2 qe-ta-wo BRONZE M1 N2

ai-so-ni-jo BRONZE M1 N2 ta-mi-je-u BRONZE M1 N2

e-u-ru-wo-ta BRONZE M1 N2 e-u-do-no BRONZE M1 N2

po-ro-u-te-u BRONZE M1 N2 wi-du-wa-ko BRONZE M1 N2

to-so-de a-ta-ra-si-jo ka-ke-we

pa-qo-si-jo 1 ke-we-to 1 wa [   ] re - u [

pe-ta-ro 1

to-so-de do-e-ro ke-we-to-jo 1 i-wa-ka-o 1

pa-qo-si-jo-jo 1 po-ro-u-te-wo 1

po-ti-ni-ja-we-jo ka-ke-we ta-ra-si-ja e-ko-te

i-ma-di-jo BRONZE M 2 tu-ke-ne-u BRONZE M 3

] BRONZE M 3 i-wa-ka BRONZE M 3

a-] ta-ra-si-jo pu$_2$-si-ja-ko 1

Part two (lines 7-9) names four smiths 'without *ta-ra-si-ja*'.

Part three (lines 11-12) records slaves belonging to the smiths *ke-we-to*, *i-wa-ka*, *pa-qo-si-jo*, and *po-ro-u-te-u* respectively.

Part four (lines 14-17) names four smiths 'of the Lady' who have *ta-ra-si-ja* and one smith who has not.

6   THE O-KA SET: PYLOS An TABLETS

General studies: H. Mühlestein *Die o-ka Tafeln von Pylos* (Basel 1956); L.R. Palmer *Eranos* 54 (1956) 1-13, *Minos* 4 (1956); E. Risch *Athenaeum* 46 (1958) 334-359; L. Deroy *Les leveurs d'impôts dans la royaume mycénien de Pylos* (Rome 1968); R. Schmitt-Brandt *SMEA* 7 (1968) 69-96.   *a₂-ru-wo-te:* A. Heubeck *BN* 11 (1960) 7.   *de-wi-jo:* A. Heubeck *SMEA* 11 (1970) 63-70.   *e-qe-ta:* G. Pugliese Carratelli *Minoica* 319-326; N. van Brock *RP* 34 (1960) 222-225; A.M. Ticchioni Jasink *SMEA* 17 (1976) 85-92; S. Deger-Jalkotzy *E-QE-TA: Zur Rolle des Gefolgschaftswesens in der Sozialstruktur mykenischer Reiche* (Vienna 1978).   *o-pi-a₂-ra:* O. Panagl *SMEA* 13 (1971) 156-165.   *o-u-ru-to:* P. Wathelet *SM* 105-111; F. Bader *BSL* 66 (1971) 148-149, 202-204.   *o-wi-to-no:* M.D. Petruševski *Klio* 58 (1976) 292-294.

***

§ 227   An important group of five texts, An 657, 519, 654, 656, and 661, are known as the *o-ka* tablets because of the presence in each of them of the word *o-ka*.   They were all written by the same scribe.   As they are closely similar to one another in structure, they may be represented by a single example:

PY An 657 = *Documents* no. 56 = *Interpretation* no. 43

§ 228 Since the publications of Mühlestein and Palmer in 1956, the *o-ka* tablets have generally been regarded as records of military dispositions: that is to say, the details of detachments of men who have been assigned to keep watch on the coast.   This interpretation still seems the most plausible one; although it should be pointed out that it rests on rather frail foundations, since many of the terms used (including the crucial word *o-ka* itself) resist exact identification, while it is impossible to mention a single term whose connotation is necessarily and unambiguously 'military'.   An entirely different line of interpretation is followed by Deroy in *Les leveurs d'impôts:* he sees the 'detachments of soldiers' as local dignitaries who are named for the purposes of taxation.   Although Deroy's interpretation is not accepted here, the very fact that his assumptions lead to an internally consistent analysis of the set should impose caution.   It is, therefore, only tentatively that the *o-ka* is here regarded as a military detachment.

o-u-ru-to o-pi-a₂-ra e-pi-ko-wo

ma-re-wo o-ka o-wi-to-no

a-pe-ri-ta-wo o-re-ta e-te-wa-ko-ki-jo

su-we-ro-wi-jo o-wi-ti-ni-jo o-ka-ra₃ MAN 50

ne-da-wa-ta-o o-ka e-ke-me-de

a-pi-je-ta ma-ra-te-u ta-ni-ko

a₂-ru-wo-te ke-ki-de ku-pa-ri-si-jo MAN 20

ai-ta-re-u-si ku-pa-ri-si-jo ke-ki-de MAN 10

me-ta-qe pe-i e-qe-ta ke-ki-jo

a-e-ri-qo-ta e-ra-po ri-me-ne

o-ka-ra ᵒ⁻ʷⁱ⁻ₜₒ.ₙₒ MAN 30 ke-ki-de-qe a-pu₂-ka-ne

MAN 20 me-ta-qe pe-i ai-ko-ta e-qe-ta

§ 229 Like the *jo-* at the beginning of PY Jn 829 (§ 207), the
o- at the beginning of An 657 indicates that this is the first tablet of a group. The scribe has carefully divided his text into
three 'paragraphs', each (apparently) dealing with one detachment.

§ 230 Para. 1 (lines 1-4). As on Jn 829, the 'heading' in line
1 indicates the occasion on which the record was drawn up. The word
-u-ru-to may represent a 3 plural present ρύνται, a deponent verb
found in Homer with the meaning 'guard, protect'. The subject of
this verb is *e-pi-ko-wo,* nominative plural masculine, which we may
equate with ἐπίκοροι 'watchers' (the stem κορ- being connected with
that of κορέω 'perceive, hear' and with Latin *caveo*). The object
of the verb is an accusative plural neuter *o-pi-a₂-ra,* which looks
like a spelling of ὀπί + ἅλα, 'those parts near the sea' — i.e.
'the coastal regions'. According to the usual interpretation, the
succeeding lines identify these 'watchers on guard over the coastal

regions'. Line 2 conveys a simple statement, with no verb expressed: o-ka is nominative, ma-re-wo the genitive of a man's name dependent upon it, and o-wi-to-no the dative-locative of a place-name.
The whole expression may mean something like 'detachment of ma-re-u
at o-wi-to-no'. Line 3 contains four names in the nominative (a-
pe-ri-ta-wo, o-re-ta, e-te-wa, and ko-ki-jo): these are presumed to
be officers subordinate to the 'commander' ma-re-u. The sense of
line 4 is difficult to grasp. The first word su-we-ro-wi-jo could
be nominative singular and so the name of another 'officer' (contin-
uing the list begun in line 3) or nominative plural describing the
fifty MEN specified by the ideogram. It is also conceivable that
it is locative singular, referring to the second place in parallel
with o-wi-to-no. Whatever the correct answer, it is probable that
o-wi-to-ni-jo is nominative plural of an ethnic, 'men of o-wi-to-no.'
o-ka-ra₃ too is opaque; with o-ka (line 2) and o-ka-ra (line 13) in
mind, we might regard it as being descriptive of the MEN.

§ 231 Para. 2 (lines 6-8). The 'detachment' of ne-da-wa-ta
(Νεδϝᾱτᾱς?) is said to contain the 'officers' e-ke-me-de, a-pi-je-ta,
ma-ra-te-u, and ta-ni-ko. The words comprising line 8 presumably
refer to the twenty MEN at the end. Of these, a₂-ru-wo-te is perhaps dative-locative of a place-name, ke-ki-de nominative plural of
a word in -ιδες (which appears elsewhere in the o-ka set and also on
PY Na 514), and ku-pa-ri-si-jo nominative plural of an ethnic, 'men
of Kyparissos'.

§ 232 Para. 3 (lines 10-14). Line 10 mentions ten more ku-pa-
ri-si-jo and ke-ki-de men, stationed this time at ai-ta-re-u-si,
the locative plural of a place-name in -εύς. Line 11 contains a formula which recurs in line 14 and frequently elsewhere in the o-ka
set: me-ta-qe pe-i e-qe-ta ke-ki-jo = μετά τέ σφεις ἐπέτᾱς Κέρκιος,
'and with them the Follower Kerkios'. The dative plural of the 3
personal pronoun pe-i = σφεις was mentioned in § 121. The word
e-qe-ta seems to be used as an honorific; as if a person of high
rank were attached to certain of the groups. Lines 12 and 13 mention another 'detachment': first the four 'officers' are named (a-e-
ri-qo-ta, e-ra-po, ri-me-ne, and o-ka-ra); then their location ('at
o-wi-to-no'); lastly the number of 'rank-and-file' soldiers, namely
thirty. Lines 13-14 describe yet another 'detachment', this time
consisting of twenty soldiers, specified as ke-ki-de and a-pu₂-ka-
ne; the latter word is probably the nominative plural of an ethnic,
because a singular a-pu₂-ka is used to describe the e-qe-ta named
ka-e-sa-me-no at An 656.19-20. At the end of line 14, an e-qe-ta
named ai-ko-ta is connected with this group.

7   INVENTORIES: PYLOS Ta TABLETS

General studies: M. Doria *Interpretazioni di testi micenei* I (Trieste 1956), *Varia Mycenaea* (Trieste 1973); L.R. Palmer *Minos* 5
(1957) 58-92, *BICS* 7 (1960) 57-63; D.H.F. Gray ib. 64-65; C. Gallavotti *RF* 90 (1962) 137-149, *SMEA* 15 (1972) 24-32; S. Hiller *Eirene*
9 (1971) 69-86.   Ta 641: C.W. Blegen *AE* (1953-1954/1) 59-62; V. Pisani *Minoica* 294-303.   Ta 716: J. Taillardat *REG* 73 (1960) 13-14.
a-ja-me-no in Ta 707 etc.: D.J.N. Lee *Glotta* 39 (1961) 195 n.1; P.
Chantraine *RP* 36 (1962) 11-15.   *ai-ke-u* in Ta 641: M.D. Petruševski
ZA 9 (1959) 154.   *da-mo-ko-ro* in Ta 711: J.-P. Olivier *Minos* 8
(1967) 118-122; L.R. Palmer ib. 123-124; A. Heubeck *AR* II 611-614.
di-pa in Ta 641: N.E. Collinge *BICS* 4 (1957) 55-59.   *e-ne-wo-pe-za*
in Ta 713: K. Giannoulidou *Platon* 15 (1963) 177-180.   *ke-re-si-jo*
we-ke in Ta 641: F. Bader *Les composés grecs du type de demiourgos*
(Paris 1965) 165-167.   *o-wo-we* in Ta 641: C. Gallavotti *PP* 11
(1956) 23-24; D.J.N. Lee *PP* 15 (1960) 407; M. Doria *PP* 16 (1961) 56-
62; O.J.L. Szemerényi *SMEA* 3 (1967) 56-58.   *qe-ra-na* in Ta 711:
M.D. Petruševski *ZA* 15 (1965) 60.   *qi-si-pe-e* in Ta 716: A. Heubeck
Minos 6 (1958) 55-60.   *se-re-mo-ka-ra-a-pi* in Ta 707 and 714: H.
Mühlestein *Glotta* 36 (1958) 152-156; E. Risch *SMEA* 1 (1966) 53-66.

                                   ***

    § 233 The Ta set consists of thirteen tablets, all written by
the same hand.   Only two of them will be discussed here.

PY Ta 711 = *Documents* no. 235 = *Interpretation* no. 248

o-wi-de pu₂-ke-qi-ri o-te wa-na-ka te-ke au-ke-wa da-mo-ko-ro

qe-ra-na wa-na-se-wi-ja qo-u-ka-ra ko-ki-re-ja JUG 1 qe-ra-na a-mo-te-wi-ja ko-ro-no-we-sa

qe-ra-na wa-na-se-wi-ja ku-na-ja qo-u-ka-ra to-qi-de-we-sa JUG 1

§ 234 Ta 711 is shown to be the first of its set by the presence of a 'heading', introduced by the prefix o-, in line 1. The
structure of line 1 is:
o-wi-de pu₂-ke-qi-ri o-te wa-na-ka te-ke au-ke-wa da-mo-ko-ro
-ϝίδε Φυ......... ὅτε ϝάναξ ϑῆκε Αὐγέϝᾶν? δᾱμοκλον?
The meaning of the line may be rendered thus: 'Phy....... (personal
name in the nominative) saw when the Lord appointed Augewas? as damoklos?' (An alternative interpretation, 'Phy....... saw when the
Lord buried the damoklos' is possible but seems less likely). The
da-mo-ko-ro is an official of some kind, unknown in later Greek but
evidently connected with the word da-mo = δᾶμος. On other tablets,
both at Pylos and at Knossos, the da-mo-ko-ro is present in the same
contexts as the du-ma-te.

§ 235 After the 'heading' there follows, on this and on the other
other twelve tablets of the Ta set, a list of objects which are described in considerable detail: many of these must have been of
great value, while others were ordinary utensils, sometimes in a damaged state. The heterogeneous collection includes jugs, tripods,
swords, tables, and foot-stools.

§ 236 The question has often been asked, what connexion there
was between the inspection, the appointment of Augewas, and the com-
pilation of such a list. It may be suggested that the connexion is
a purely temporal one — that the scribe fixed the date of this detailed inspection, or stock-taking, by reference to the induction of
a high official: so S. Hiller Eirene 9 (1971) 72.

§ 237 The list which occupies lines 2 and 3 of Ta 711 presents
many problems. The word qe-ra-na figures in each of the items of
the list, twice accompanied by the ideogram *204 and once not. The
shape of the ideogram shows plainly that qe-ra-na means a kind of
jug; but no corresponding Greek word is known. The list comprises:
qe-ra-na wa-na-se-wi-ja qo-u-ka-ra ko-ki-re-ja
qe-ra-na a-mo-te-wi-ja ko-ro-no-we-sa
qe-ra-na wa-na-se-wi-ja ku-na-ja qo-u-ka-ra to-qi-de-we-sa
In each item, qe-ra-na is accompanied by feminine adjectives. The
first of these, wa-na-se-wi-ja = ϝανασσηϝίᾱ, is formed from ϝάναξ or
ϝάνασσα and so must mean 'of the Lord' or 'of the Lady'; but it is
impossible to specify the nature of the connexion with the Lord or
the Lady. The qe-ra-na might have been a present to the Lord (or
Lady), a present from the Lord (or Lady), a possession of the Lord
(or Lady), etc. The interpretation 'decorated with a goddess' is
not plausible, since Mycenaean objects of the kind depicted here do
not (so far as is known) bear scenes of cult. There can be little
doubt that the next adjective, qo-u-ka-ra, describes the decoration
of the jug. It is composed of two elements which are well attested
in later Greek: qo-u- being the stem of βοῦς and -ka-ra the stem of

κάρᾱ 'head'. The kind of decoration this word suggests is that of
the 'bucrania' found on Late Minoan Ia pottery: A. Furumark *The Mycenaean pottery: analysis and classification* (Stockholm 1972[2]) 247.
No similar Mycenaean motif, however, is attested at the appropriate
period.   The third adjective in the first item, *ko-ki-re-ja*, is
perhaps connected with κόχλος, which means a kind of shell-fish
with spiral shell: if so, it would yield the meaning 'decorated
with a shell-pattern'.   The two adjectives describing the second
item, *a-mo-te-wi-ja* and *ko-ro-no-we-sa*, are completely opaque: spec-
ulation seems pointless here.   Of the four adjectives which go with
the third item, *wa-na-se-wi-ja* and *qo-u-ka-ra* have been discussed
already.   *ku-na-ja* fits exactly the syllables of γυναῖᾱ, an adjective formed from γυνή.   If that is indeed the word expressed, its
theoretical range of meanings is too wide for us to know what the
scribe intended: the sense 'belonging to a woman' is impossibly
vague, whereas if it means 'decorated with a woman' then the description refers to a motif hardly found in Mycenaean Greece; the
meaning 'for a woman's use' seems the least objectionable.   The stem
of *to-qi-de-we-sa* may be cognate with that of Latin *torqueo* 'twist':
hence τορκʷίδϝεσσα would mean 'decorated with a spiral pattern' and
would be synonymous with *to-qi-de-ja* (τορκʷιδεῖᾱ) at Ta 709.1.

§ 238   PY Ta 641 = *Documents* no. 236 = *Interpretation* no. 250

ti-ri-po-de ai-ke-u ke-re-si-jo we-ke TRIPOD 2 ti-ri-po e-me po-de o-wo-we TRIPOD 1 ti-ri-po ke-re-si-jo we-ke a-puke ke-re-a TRIPOD ke-u-ke-no

qe-to PITHOS 3 di-pa-me-zo-e qe-to-ro-we JAR 1 di-pa-e me-zo-e ti-ri-o-we-e JAR 2 di-pa-me-wi-jo qe-to-ro-we JAR 1

di-pa me-wi-jo ti-ri-jo-we JAR 1 di-pa me-wi-jo a-no-we JAR 1

Ta 641 lists the following items:
Line 1: (i) *ti-ri-po-de ai-ke-u ke-re-si-jo we-ke* TRIPOD 2
      (ii) *ti-ri-po e-me po-de o-wo-we* TRIPOD 1
      (iii) *ti-ri-po ke-re-si-jo we-ke a-pu ke-ka-u-me-no*
                              ke-re-a₂ TRIPOD [1
Line 2: (iv) *qe-to* PITHOS 3
      (v) *di-pa me-zo-e qe-to-ro-we* JAR 1
      (vi) *di-pa-e me-zo-e ti-ri-o-we-e* JAR 2
      (vii) *di-pa me-wi-jo qe-to-ro-we* JAR 1
Line 3: (viii) *di-pa me-wi-jo ti-ri-jo-we* JAR 1
      (ix) *di-pa me-wi-jo a-no-we* JAR 1

§ 239   (i) The writer has recorded the presence of two tripods:
hence the dual *ti-ri-po-de* = τρίποδε.   *ke-re-si-jo we-ke* possibly
represents a compound which would have been spelt as one word in alphabetic Greek, namely Κρησιοϝεργής 'of Cretan workmanship'. If this
analysis is correct, it carries with it the implication (which is
quite plausible on archaeological grounds) that special value was
placed on artefacts made by Minoan craftsmen or in the Minoan style
(since either of those meanings could be conveyed by the compound
word).   The scribe has failed to put his adjective in the dual, so
as to make it agree with *ti-ri-po-de*.   That is only one of several
incongruities displayed by the text.   For example, the word *ai-ke-u*
is in the nominative singular, and so cannot be directly in apposition to *ti-ri-po-de* (§ 160).   Two different explanations of the
function of *ai-ke-u* present themselves.   Either *ai-ke-u* is a proper
name (Αἰγεύς?) of a man who has some connexion with the tripods: perhaps their maker, their owner, or their consignee.   Or it has an adjectival function, describing the decoration of the tripod: *ai-ke-u*
has been thought to contain the stem αἰγ- 'goat' and so to mean
'decorated with goat-heads'.   The latter explanation presumes an
adjectival use of words in -εύς which is not found in historical
Greek; and there seems no good reason for assuming its existence in
Mycenaean.   A close parallel to *ai-ke-u* is provided by the entry on
another tablet of this set, Ta 709.3:
*ti-ri-po ke-re-si-jo we-ke *34-ke-u* TRIPOD 1
ti-ri-po ke-re-si-jo we-ke o-pi-ke-wi-re-je-u TRIPOD 1
If the writer of these tablets were in the habit of associating one
tripod 'of Cretan workmanship' with a word ending in -εύς, he would
be liable to write that word in the singular even when he was dealing with two tripods.   In this way the singular number of the word
ai-ke-u on Ta 641 is susceptible of a simple explanation.   The appearance of *34-ke-u*, like that of *ai-ke-u*, suggests that it is a
personal name.   By analogy, *o-pi-ke-wi-re-je-u* too is likely to be
a proper name: one in which the presence of the prefix *o-pi-* suggests an occupation-word which has been made into a man's name by
the addition of *-e-u*.   We may compare the occupation-term *o-pi-
te-ke-e-u* at PY Un 2.2.

§ 240 (ii) Here the tripod is described as *o-wo-we* and is accompanied by two words in the instrumental singular: *e-me po-de*. *o-wo-we* is one of four adjectival compounds in this text which have *-o-we* (i.e. -ώƑης, neuter -ῶƑες) as their second element. This element reflects the original Greek word for 'ear' *ὄƑός, from which Attic οὖς also is derived: P. Kiparsky *Language* 43 (1967) 627 and O.J.L. Szemerényi *SMEA* 3 (1967) 56. In the present text, the first element of the compound denotes the number of 'ears' or handles possessed by each vessel respectively (Theocritus' ἀμφῶες 1.28 'having a handle on either side' is a compound of exactly the same type). So in items (v) and (vii) *qe-to-ro-we* corresponds to τετρῶƑες 'four-handled'; in item (vi) *ti-ri-o-we-e* (dual) to τριώƑεε 'three-handled'; in item (viii) *ti-ri-jo-we* (singular) to τριῶƑες; and in item (ix) *a-no-we* (with alpha privative) to ἀνῶƑες 'handleless'. As would be expected, *qe-to-ro-we* is accompanied by an ideogram showing four handles, *ti-ri-o-we-e* by one showing three handles, and *a-no-we* by one showing no handles. The difficulty with *o-wo-we* is that the accompanying ideogram clearly displays a vessel with two handles. This makes one hesitate to accept the interpretation of *o-wo-we* as οἰƑώƑης 'with one handle' (whereby the first element is identified with the stem of οἶος 'sole, only'), compatible though that would be with the spelling. A simple (perhaps too simple) way out of the difficulty is to postulate a scribal error and assume that the writer intended the first sign to be *du*: *du-wo-we* (δυώƑης 'with two handles') would provide a satisfactory parallel to the other entries ending in *-o-we*. There is no doubt about the meaning of the phrase *e-me po-de*: it comprises the instrumental of the numeral 'one' (§ 123) and the instrumental of the word for 'foot' (πούς, ποδ-), therefore 'on one foot'. But why should the scribe append the phrase 'on one foot' to what is, by definition and by illustration, a three-legged vessel? The only plausible reason is that this tripod, like that mentioned in item (iii), has been damaged and has lost two of its feet.

§ 241 (iii) The description of this vessel may be expressed in alphabetic Greek as follows: τρίπως ΚρησιοƑεργὴς ἀπὸ κεκαυμένος σκέλεhα 'tripod of Cretan workmanship burnt off at the legs'. ἀπύ has its original meaning of a adverb of separation 'off, away'; κεκαυμένος is reduplicated perfect participle passive of καίω 'burn'; neuter plural σκέλεhα (contracted in Attic to σκέλη) is accusative of respect (§ 160).

§ 242 (iv) *qe-to* is nominative plural of an *o*-stem noun. *qe-to* was previously considered equivalent to πίθος, exemplifying the *i/e* alternation found in *di-pa*. The possibility remains, but strong objections to the identification are brought in *Documents* 493-494. In any case, it is highly probable that *qe-to* is a non-Greek word.

§ 243 (v) This and the rest of the items comprise a list of different types of vessel known as a *di-pa* (Homeric δέπας 'goblet').
The adjective *me-zo-e* is a comparative of the type described above
(§ 118).   The final *-e* is superfluous; it was written, we may pre-
sume, by a scribe who thought, for a moment, that he was recording
the presence of two vessels, as in item (vi)(§ 160).

§ 244 · (vi) Here the correctness of the dual forms *di-pa-e, me-
zo-e,* and *ti-ri-o-we-e* is certified by the numeral '2'.

§ 245 (vii) This *di-pa* is described as *me-wi-jo* = μείον 'smaller' (§ 118).

8   LAND TABLETS: E TABLETS FROM PYLOS AND TIRYNS

General studies: F.R. Adrados *Emerita* 24 (1956) 353-416, 29 (1961)
53-116; E.L. Bennett *AJA* 60 (1956) 103-133; W.E. Brown *Historia* 5
(1956) 385-400; E. Will *REA* 59 (1957) 5-50; S. Calderone *SG* 13
(1960) 81-102; L. Deroy and M. Gérard *Le cadastre mycénien de Pylos*
(Rome 1965); I. Tegyey *AC(D)* 1 (1965) 1-10; D.M. Jones *PCCMS* 245-249;
J. Masai *RBPH* 45 (1967) 97-115; C.J. Ruijgh *SMEA* 15 (1972) 91-104; Y.
Duhoux *Kadmos* 13 (1974) 27-38. PY Ea: M. Lejeune *Minos* 15 (1974) 81-
115. PY En: M. Lejeune *RP* 48 (1974) 247-266.   PY Ep: *Mémoires* III
107-111. PY Er: M. Lejeune *Minos* 14 (1973) 60-76; J.T. Hooker *Kadmos*
18 (1979) 101-105. PY Es: A. Heubeck *Sprache* 4 (1958) 80-95. TI Ef:
L. Godart and J.-P. Olivier *Tiryns* VIII (Mainz 1975) 43-50; M. Lejeune *RP* 50 (1976) 194-197. *da-ma-te:* A. Morpurgo *PP* 13 (1958) 322-
324; G. Maddoli *Minos* 13 (1972) 161-172; A. Moreschini Quattordio
Studi in onore di T. Bolelli (Pisa 1974) 217-224. *da-mo:* G. Maddoli
SMEA 12 (1970) 7-57; *Mémoires* III 137-154. *e-me* and *du-wo-u-pi:* A.
Heubeck *ZA* 19 (1969) 3-12. *e-ri-ta:* W.F. Witton *AJP* 81 (1960) 415-
421. *e-to-ni-jo:* J.-L. Perpillou *BSL* 76 (1981) 225-230.   *ka-ma* and
ka-ma-e-u: A. Heubeck *ZA* 15 (1965) 267-268; M.R. Cataudella *Ka-ma:
studi sulla società agraria micenea* (Rome 1973); *AVEM* 27-40; A.M.
Jasink Ticchioni *SMEA* 21 (1980) 231-245. *ke-ke-me-na* and *ki-ti-me-
na:* S. Luria *Minos* 6 (1958) 163-164; A. Heubeck *ZA* 17 (1967) 17-21;
O. Panagl *AC(D)* 9 (1973) 3-14; L.R. Palmer *Antiquitates Indogerma-
nicae: Gedenkschrift für H. Güntert* (Innsbruck 1974) 13-14; *AVEM* 9-
27. *ko-to-no-o-ko:* G.F. Polyakova *VDI* 139 (1977) 61-70. *o-na-to* and
e-to-ni-jo: E. Cantarella *RIL* 107 (1973) 844-862; *AVEM* 41-62. *o-ro-
jo:* J. Puhvel *Minos* 6 (1958) 61-63. *te-o-jo do-e-ro/-ra:* A. Tovar
Minos 7 (1961) 101-122. *te-re-ta:* A.I. Tyumenev *VDI* 70 (1959) 24-32;
F.R. Adrados *Minos* 10 (1969) 138-150. *wo-ro-ki-jo-ne-jo:* A. Heubeck
ZA 15 (1965) 268-270.

                                   ***

    § 246   A large number of E tablets from Pylos and two fragments
from Tiryns record various amounts of WHEAT.   In fact, these texts
are concerned only indirectly with wheat; amounts of grain are expressed in order to indicate the size of parcels of land which persons hold according to various tenures.   It appears, therefore,
that the scribes had no other means of describing the area of land:
we might suppose, in any case, that the productivity or yield of a
plot was more interesting to them than its area.   *pe-ma* or *pe-mo,*

which often precedes the WHEAT ideogram, properly means 'seed'
(σπέρμα/σπέρμο), whence the sense 'seed-corn' in the E texts; thus
each entry of WHEAT is more likely to refer to the amount of seed-
corn needed to sow a plot than to the yield.   The numerical relationship between amounts of WHEAT and areas of land is, of course,
unknown: it cannot have been a constant ratio from year to year or
from area to area.

§ 247 For convenience' sake, the large body of extant material
will be dealt with under two headings: simple land-holdings (Pylos
tablets) and more complex land-holdings (Pylos and Tiryns tablets).

***

Simple land-holdings

§ 248 The simplest type of land-holding tablet merely specifies
that certain parcels of land are reserved to certain persons:

PY Er 312 = *Documents* no. 152 = *Interpretation* no. 101

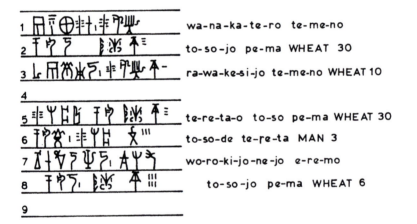

1   wa-na-ka-te-ro te-me-no

2   to-so-jo pe-ma WHEAT 30

3   ra-wa-ke-si-jo te-me-no WHEAT 10

4

5   te-re-ta-o to-so pe-ma WHEAT 30

6   to-so-de te-re-ta MAN 3

7   wo-ro-ki-jo-ne-jo e-re-mo

8   to-so-jo pe-ma WHEAT 6

9

This text may be divided into five 'paragraphs', as follows:

§ 249 Para. 1 (lines 1-2): *wa-na-ka-te-ro te-me-no to-so-jo*
pe-ma WHEAT 30.   This represents: ϝανάκτερον τέμενος· τοσοῖο σπέρμα
— viz. 'Lord's precinct, grain of such (an amount), 30 measures of
wheat'.   As in the Knossos tablets already discussed (§ 190), ϝανάκτερον is an adjective derived from ϝάναξ 'lord'.   Although, in
theory, the ϝάναξ in question could be a divine or a human lord, the
latter alternative is made more likely by the presence in the same
list of human persons.   Instead of the usual formula *to-so-de pe-ma*,
the scribe has expressed the first word in the genitive case, presumably with the meaning indicated in the above translation.

§ 250 Para. 2 (line 3): *ra-wa-ke-si-jo te-me-no* WHEAT 10 = λᾱϝᾱ-
γέσιον τέμενος, viz. 'Precinct of the Lawagetas, 10 measures of
wheat'.   *ra-wa-ke-si-jo* is an adjective formed from *ra-wa-ke-ta* =
λᾱϝᾱγέτᾱς: it is parallel in function to *wa-na-ka-te-ro* and similar
in formation to *e-qe-si-jo* (from *e-qe-ta*)(§ 188).   The word λᾱϝᾱγέτᾱς is easy to analyse in terms of Greek: it is a compound of the
stem of λᾱϝός 'people' (which in Attic proceeds to λεώς by regular
sound-changes) and the stem of ἄγω 'lead'; Pindar uses the contracted form λᾱγέτᾱς at *Olympian* 1.89 and elsewhere.   The word 'leader
of the people' is probably used here as an honorific, designating
the only person to have a τέμενος, apart from the ϝάναξ himself.   No
good reason exists for translating *ra-wa-ke-ta* as 'military commander' or 'leader of the war-host', a meaning proposed by Palmer at *TPS*
(1954) 35-37 and since repeated.   On the contrary, so far as can be
judged from the extant tablets, his affinities are with cult: thus
at PY Un 219.10 (in a list containing both human and divine members)
he appears as the recipient of offerings, while at Un 718.9 he is
the giver of offerings (§ 290).   *ra-wa-ke-ta* is mentioned again at
PY An 724.7, a tablet dealing with the absence of rowers; but that
text is too lacunose to allow any sound inference to be drawn about
the status of the *ra-wa-ke-ta*.

§ 251 Para. 3 (line 5): *te-re-ta-o to-so pe-ma* WHEAT 30. A further area of land (which does not, however, rank as a τέμενος) is
expressed in terms of 'seed-corn': it is occupied by, and is perhaps
in the possession of, a class of persons known as *te-re-ta*. In this
text they are in the genitive plural; elsewhere in the Pylos E texts
they appear (in the nominative singular or plural) as substantial
land-holders (cf. § 266); and in a single Knossos tablet, Am 826, at
least forty-five *te-re-ta* are recorded.   Although *te-re-ta* would be
the expected spelling of τελεστάς and might, indeed, represent that
very word, the identification must not be pressed.   The ambiguity
of the Linear B syllabary is such that other possibilities must be
left open.   Even if the equation *te-re-ta* = τελεστάς is sound, we
can only guess at the function of the *te-re-ta* in Mycenaean texts.
And in fact two quite different interpretations of the word have

been proposed: (i) that the *te-re-ta* is a religious functionary (because he is bound by τέλη 'religious obligations'); (ii) that he occupies a place in a 'feudal' structure of society (because he owes τέλος 'service, payment'). Neither meaning is imposed, or even suggested, by the Linear B contexts in which the word is found.

§ 252   Para. 4 (line 6): *to-so-de te-re-ta* MAN 3: 'so many te.... tai, three men'.

§ 253   Para. 5 (lines 7-8): *wo-ro-ki-jo-ne-jo e-re-mo to-so-jo pe-ma* WHEAT 6.   No remotely plausible suggestion for the meaning of the first word has yet been made.   Its very form is unknown, since in theory it could equally well be nominative plural masculine (referring to the persons who hold this parcel of land) or nominative singular neuter (referring to the land itself).   However that may be, the word *e-re-mo* = ἐρῆμον 'desert, uninhabited' indicates that this part of the text is concerned with winning land from the waste.

§ 254   If there is a thread linking the five paragraphs of Er 312, it is probably that of locality.   The scribe seems to have grouped together several holdings of land which are heterogeneous in character but which have in common the fact that they were all situated in the same area.

***

More complex tenures

§ 255   Most of the E tablets are concerned with transactions involving parcels of land.   In the Ea set the situations described are quite straightforward; they are less so in Eb, Eo, Ep, and En. The work of writing the majority of these tablets was divided among three scribes, who may be represented arbitrarily thus: scribe A wrote the Ea set; scribe B wrote the Eb and Eo sets; scribe C wrote the Ep and En sets.

§ 256   Some typical texts from the Ea set (which contains in all sixty-seven tablets) are taken first, since their terminology provides a good introduction to that of the longer and more detailed documents:

PY Ea 811

du-ni-jo e-ke o-na-to WHEAT T 6

PY Ea 754

ti-ri-da-ro e-ke o-na-to ko-do-jo ko-to-na WHEAT T 6

PY Ea 806

ke-re-te-u e-ke o-na-to ke-ke-me-na ko-to-na WHEAT1 T 2

PY Ea 821

ta-ra-ma-ta-o   ko-to-na ki-ti-me-na WHEAT 5   T 7 V 3

PY Ea 28

ti-ri-da-ro ra-pte e-ke ka-ma WHEAT[

PY Ea 778

ta-ra-ma-ta   e - ke   o na to pa ro da mo WHEAT T 9

PY Ea 800 = *Documents* no. 110

ke-re-te-u   e - ke   o-na-to pa-ro mo-ro-qo-ro po-me-ne WHEAT 2

§ 257 First in our selection comes a text of a simple kind: Ea
811 records the fact that a man named *du-ni-jo* 'holds' (*e-ke* =
ἔχει) an *o-na-to*.   The word *o-na-to* occurs repeatedly in the E
series.   It is conventionally interpreted as a neuter noun ὄνᾱτον,
which did not survive in classical Greek but which would refer to a
beneficial use of land (perhaps corresponding roughly to the English
term 'lease'), if its stem is correctly identified with that of the
verb ὀνίνᾱμι 'confer a benefit upon'.

§ 258 The second tablet, Ea 754, may be analysed thus:
ti-ri-da-ro ra-pte e-ke o-na-to ko-do-jo ko-to-na
Τι.......ος ῥαπτὴρ ἔχει ὄνᾱτον· Κο...οιο κτοίνᾱ
'Ti.......os the stitcher holds a 'lease': the plot of Ko...os'
Alphabetic Greek offers an agent-noun ῥάπτης from ῥάπτω 'stitch,
sew'; ῥαπτήρ is not attested, but it is hard to think of any other
possible equivalent of *ra-pte*.

§ 259 The word *ko-to-na* is readily identifiable with κτοίνᾱ 'a
plot (of land)'.   In Ea 754, *ko-to-na* has no descriptive term attached to it; but in many other E texts two types of *ko-to-na* are
distinguished from each other.   We may have either *ke-ke-me-na*
ko-to-na (as in Ea 806) or *ko-to-na ki-ti-me-na* (as in Ea 821).
These two types are mutually exclusive, and they may be described
as follows:

§ 260 *ke-ke-me-na ko-to-na* refers to a kind of common land, most often 'leased' from the *da-mo*.   The latter word is formally equivalent to δᾶμος (Attic δῆμος), which in the Mycenaean context may perhaps be rendered 'local community'. The form of the word *ke-ke-me-na* has been the subject of much debate; it is plainly a perfect passive participle, but of what verb it is impossible to say.   The way in which it is used in Linear B texts makes a connexion with κοινός 'common' or with κεάζω 'cut' seem likely.   The word *ka-ma*, which appears as the object of *e-ke* on Ea 28, is apparently a special kind of *ko-to-na ke-ke-me-na;* while *ka-ma-e-u* means 'holder of a *ka-ma'*.

§ 261 *ko-to-na ki-ti-me-na,* on the other hand, refers to private land, which is often said by the tablets to be 'leased' from named individuals.   *ki-ti-me-na* is the present passive participle of an unknown verb; it may be formed from an athematic verb κτίημι or κτεῖμι, which was later replaced by the thematic form κτίζω ('found, establish, inhabit').

§ 262 The last tablet to be discussed here, Ea 800, adds a piece of information to that given by Ea 811 and similar texts.   It states not simply that *ke-re-te-u* holds a 'lease', but that he holds it παρὸ M.......ωι ποιμένει, viz. 'from M.......os the shepherd' (for the construction *pa-ro* with dative, see § 163).

***

§ 263 Although the E series is sometimes loosely described as a 'land-register', the tablets do not in fact record the location of plots of land; and it would not be possible to learn from them who was in possession of a given plot of land.   The only clue to the location of any land is given in En 609, where the first word shows that this tablet (and hence the other En tablets as well, 74, 659, and 467, which together form a connected group) refer to Pakijana, already identified as one of the 'nine' towns (§ 216).   There is no way of telling which, if any, of the other E tablets similarly refer to Pakijana.   A number of personal names recur from one tablet to another; but, except where a man's status or occupation is mentioned as well as his name, the same name does not necessarily denote the same person.

§ 264 As soon as the E tablets were collated and studied in detail, it became evident that a special relationship obtained between the Eo and the En sets on the one hand and between the Eb and the Ep sets on the other.   Broadly speaking, we can see that Eo contains shorter tablets and En longer tablets and also that the En tablets

recapitulate, and put into definitive form, the information already
given in the Eo tablets.   In the same way, the long Ep tablets represent a 'later edition' of the short Eb tablets.   The principal
difference between the 'earlier' (Eb and Eo) tablets and the
'later' (Ep and En) is that the earlier more often use *e-ke-qe* to
express the meaning 'has, holds', the later more often simple *e-ke*
(compare, for instance, Eb 846 with its later version Ep 301.2 and
Eo 211.3 with its later version En 609.6); but there are several exceptions to this rule — thus Ep 301, though a 'later' tablet, shows
e-ke-qe in lines 8-14.   Since *e-ke* and *e-ke-qe* are sometimes present on one and the same tablet and since the occurrence of *-qe* always affects the word-order of the entry in which it appears, there
must be some difference in meaning between *e-ke* and *e-ke-qe,* but it
is not obvious in what the difference consists.

§ 265 The comparison of an 'earlier' with a 'later' set may begin with two earlier tablets, Eo 211 and Eo 224, of which the damaged tablet En 609 is a later recension:

PY Eo 211 = *Documents* no. 118 = *Interpretation* no. 79

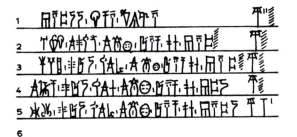

wa-na-ta-jo-jo ko-to-na ki-t i-me-na   WHEAT 2[

a – t u-ko e-te-do-mo e-ke-qe o-na-to pa-ro wa-na-ta[-jo]   WHEAT[

i-ni-ja te-o-jo do-e-ra e-ke-qe o-na-to pa-ro wa-na-ta[-jo]   WHEAT[

e-65-to te-o-jo do-e-ro e-ke-qe o-na-to pa-ro wa-⟨na⟩ta-jo   WHEAT[

si-ma te-o-jo do-e-ra e-ke-qe o-na-to pa-ro wa-na-ta-jo   WHEAT T1

PY Eo 224 = *Documents* no. 119 = *Interpretation* no. 80

a-ma-ru-ta-o ko-to-na ki-ti-me-na WHEAT 2 T [

so-u-ro-te-o-jo do-e-ro e-ke-qe o-na-to pa-ro pa-ra-ko WHEAT V 3

e-do-mo-ne-u te-o-jo do-e-ro e-ke-qe o[-na-to]pa-ro pa-ra-ko WHEAT T 1

e-sa-ro te-o-jo do-e-ro e-ke-qe o-na[-to]pa-ro a-ma-ru-ta WHEAT V 3

wa-na-ta-jo te-re-ta e-ke-qe o-na-to pa-ro a-ma-ru-ta WHEAT T 1

e-ra-ta-ra i-je-re-ja do-e-ra pa-ki-ja-na e-ke-qe pa-ro a-ma-ru-ta WHEAT T 1

po-so-re-ja te-o-jo do-e-ra e-ke-qe o-na-to pa-ro ta-ta-ro WHEAT T1 V 3

i-je-re-ja pa-ki-ja-na e-ke-qe o-na-to pa-ro a-ma-ru-ta WHEAT T 3

PY En 609 = *Documents* no. 114 = *Interpretation* no. 78

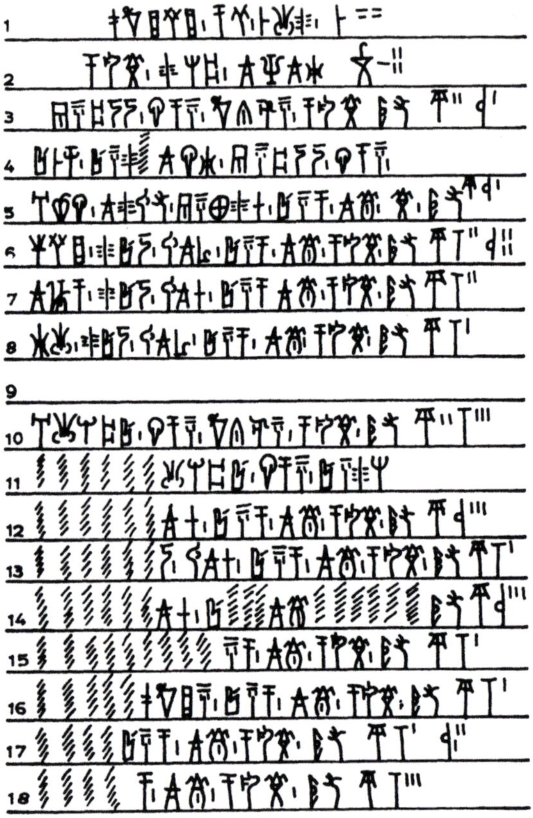

pa-ki-ja-ni-ja to-sa da-ma-te DA 40

to-so-de te-re-ta e-ne-e-si MAN 14

wa-na-ta-jo-jo ko-to-na ki-ti-me-na to-so-de pe-mo WHEAT 2 V 1

o-da-a₂ o-na-te[-re] e-ko-si wa-na-ta-jo-jo ko-to-na

a-tu-ko e-te-do-mo wa-na-ka-te-ro o-na-to e-ke ⟨to-so⟩de pe-mo WHEAT V 1

i-ni-ja te-o-jo do-e-ra o-na-to e-ke to-so-de pe-mo WHEAT T 2 V 4

e-ⁿ5-to te-o-jo do-e-rc o-na-to e-ke to-so-de pe-mo WHEAT T 2

si-ma te-o-jo do-e-ra o-na-to e-ke to-so-de pe-mo WHEAT T 1

a-ma-ru-ta-o ko-to-na ki-ti-me-na to-so-de pe-mo WHEAT2 V3

]-ma-ru-ta-o ko-to-na o-na-te-re

]-e-ro o-na-to e-ke to-so-de pe-mo WHEAT V 3

]-jo-do-e-ro o-na-to e-ke to-so-de pe-mo WHEAT T 1

]-e-ro o[   ]e-ke[   ]pe-mo WHEAT V3

]-na-to e-ke to-so-de pe-mo WHEAT T 1

]pa-ki-ja-na o-na-to e-ke to-so-de pe-mo WHEAT T 1

]o-na-to e-ke to-so-de pe-mo WHEAT T1 V 3

]-to e-ke to-so-de pe-mo WHEAT T 3

§ 266   En 609 is the first in its set.   It begins with an over-
all 'heading' referring to forty *da-ma-te;* line 2 records the presence of fourteen *te-re-ta* (τε....ται).   There follow, spread over
this and the three other En tablets, thirteen 'paragraphs', marked
off from one another by blank lines, which describe lands owned by
the *te-re-ta* and the 'leases' which other persons hold from them.
It is unknown why the tenure of only thirteen *te-re-ta* is described,
whereas fourteen are mentioned in En 609.2.   Either the scribe
wrote the wrong number by mistake, or a tablet is missing from the
set.

§ 267   In the 'heading' of En 609 (lines 1-2), line 1 contains
three words in the nominative plural feminine.   *da-ma-te* is evidently the plural of a consonant-stem noun ending in -ες; it may be
affiliated to δᾶμος or to δόμος: no translation should be attempted,
but the meaning may approach that of 'family-groups' or 'households'
(*familiae*).   Whatever the meaning of the word, its first syllable
seems to have been taken up and used as a quasi-ideogram before the
numeral 40.   *pa-ki-ja-ni-ja* is the feminine plural of an ethnic adjective formed (in the usual way) from the place-name *pa-ki-ja-na*.
Line 1 thus conveys the general meaning: 'so many family-groups at
Pakijana, namely 40'.   Line 2 (*to-so-de te-re-ta e-ne-e-si* MAN 14)
may be transliterated: τοσοίδε τε....ται ἐνέενσι, 'so many te....tai
are in (them), namely 14'.

§ 268   Para. 1 (lines 3-8).   The lay-out of this paragraph is
followed closely by that of the following paragraphs.   Line 3 specifies the size of the *ko-to-no ki-ti-me-na* ('private plot') owned
by a *te-re-ta:* his name is put into the genitive (*wa-na-ta-jo-jo*).
Line 4 introduces the list of persons who hold an *o-na-to* from
wa-na-ta-jo.   For the 'itemizing' word *o-da-a$_2$* see § 131.   The subject is expressed by the nominative plural word *o-na-te-re* (an
agent-noun formed from *o-na-to*, so 'lease-holders' or the like).
e-ko-si = ἔχονσι '(they) hold'.   *ko-to-na* κτοίνᾱν is the object of
the verb.   Thus the sentence means roughly: 'item, lease-holders
hold the plot of W.'.   Lines 5-8 name the four persons who hold
'leases' from W.   A man named *a-tu-ko* receives the description
e-te-do-mo wa-na-ka-te-ro: the first word surely denotes the man's
occupation, but the compound resists convincing analysis in terms of
Greek; *wa-na-ka-te-ro* means 'in the service of the lord' (whether
human or divine we cannot say).   The description appended to the
persons in lines 6-8 means that a divine lord cannot be discounted
here.   The appellations *te-o-jo do-e-ra* (θεοῖο δοέλᾱ 'female slave
of the god') and *te-o-jo do-e-ro* ('male slave') occur on many of the
E tablets.   But the persons so described must have been of a higher
status than the women recorded on the Pylos A tablets.   There, the
women are never named, and only their numbers, their occupation, and
(sometimes) their place of work are of concern to the scribes.   On

the other hand, the 'slaves of the god' in the E series are always given individual mention, are always named, and are always classed as land-holders. That being so, the description 'slave of the god' appears to be an honorific title, perhaps that of a priestly caste (cf. lines 16 and 18, § 269). The presence of such a caste at Pakijana could be expected, since other Pylos tablets (notably Tn 316 and Un 2) make it plain that this place was an important centre of cult.

§ 269 Para. 2 (lines 10-18). The structure is exactly the same as that of Para. 1, with the exception of the changed word-order in line 11. Seven persons are said to hold a 'lease' from a man named *a-ma-ru-ta*. Four of these (*so-u-ro, e-do-me-ne-u,*[1] *e-sa-ro,* and *po-so-re-ja*) are described as 'slaves of the god'. The entry in line 15 is interesting, because the *te-re-ta* named *wa-na-ta-jo,* who in Para. 1 (§ 268) appeared as owner of a plot, here holds a 'lease' from another *te-re-ta*. In line 16 the word *i-je-re-ja* is genitive (ἱερείᾱς), depending on the nominative *do-e-ra,* while *pa-ki-ja-na* is probably nominative of the place-name, put vaguely in apposition to the rest of the entry: '*e-ra-ta-ra* the slave of the priestess (at) Pakijana holds a lease, so much seed-corn...' The fact that the priestess's slave is included in the same list with the priestess herself (line 18) corroborates the suggestion made in § 268 that the expression 'slave' in the E tablets does not refer to servile status in the strict sense, but may even denote a privileged class.

***

§ 270 Whereas the En/Eo sets describe the holdings of *ko-to-na ki-ti-me-na* ('private land'), the Ep/Eb sets deal with *ke-ke-me-na ko-to-na* ('common land'). The following examples show how the entries on a single Ep tablet (301) are built up from the information contained in twelve tablets of the earlier Eb set:

[1] The alternation between *e-do-me-ne-u* ('Εδομενεύς) and Homeric 'Ιδομενεύς is similar to that between *di-pa* and δέπας (§ 167).

PY Eb 818 = *Documents* no. 132

ke-ke-me-na ko-to-na a-no-no to-so-de pe-mo WHEAT 1 T1

PY Eb 846 = *Documents* no. 133 = *Interpretation* no. 182

ai-ti-jo-qo e-ke-qe o-na-to ke-ke-me-na ko-to-na

pa-ro da-mo ko-to-no-o-ko   to-so-de pe-mo WHEAT1 T 4   V 3

PY Eb 369

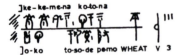

]jo e-ke-qe o-na-to ke-me-na ko-to-na

]mo ko-to-no-o-ko   to-so-de pe-mo WHEAT   T 5

PY Eb 747

a-da-ma-o e-ke-qe o-na-to ke-me-na ko-to-na

pa-ro da-mo ko-to-no-o-ko   to-so-de pe-mo WHEAT T 4

PY Eb 874 + 902

]ke-ke-me-na ko-to-na

]o-ko   to-so-de pe-mo WHEAT V 3

PY Eb 496

pi-ke-re-u e-ke-qe ke[

ko-to-no-o-ko   [

PY Eb 566

ra-ku-ro e-ke-qe ke-ke-me-na ko-to-na[

ko-to-no- o -ko   to-so[

PY Eb 893 + 897

ku -so   e[   ]ke-me-na ko-to-na

ko-to-no[to-so-de pe-mo WHEAT V 3

PY Eb 501

ke-ra-u-jo e-ke-qe ke-ke[

ko-to-n o-o -ko—   [

PY Eb 377

pa-ra-ko   e - ke-qe   ke - ke-me[

ko-to- no-   o - ko   [

PY Eb 892 = *Interpretation* no. 86

ko-tu-ro₂ pa-da-je-u   e-ke[

ke - ke-me-na   ko-to-na [

PY Eb 895 + 906 = *Documents* no. 134 = *Interpretation* no. 83

a - i-qe-u e-ke-qe ke-ke-me-na ko-to-na

ko-to- no- o - ko   to-so-de pe-mo WHEAT T 6

PY Ep 301 = *Documents* no. 131 = *Interpretation* no. 81

§ 271 Ep 301 falls into three 'paragraphs':

§ 272 Para. 1 (line 1).   So much land, being *ke-ke-me-na ko-to-na,* is described as *a-no-no;* since this is a compound adjective, its feminine has the same form as the masculine.   As all the entries in Para. 2 refer to persons who 'hold *o-na-to*', the probability is that *a-no-no* means a plot 'which is not leased out' or, perhaps, one 'which is not subject to lease'; so *a-no-no* is thought to consist of alpha privative and the stem ὀν- found in ὄνᾱτον, but no analogous Greek compound is actually attested.

§ 273 Para. 2 (lines 2-6).   Five persons are described as holding *o-na-to pa-ro da-mo,* 'a lease from the local community', and the land they hold is called *ke-ke-me-na ko-to-na.*   *a-tu-ko* the *e-te-do-mo* was encountered on En 609 (§ 268).   Both in this tablet and in Eb 846, on which the entry is based, the first member of the list is called a *ko-to-no-o-ko.*   It is hard to assess the significance of this term ('plot-holder') in its context since everyone named

ke-ke-me-na ko-to-na a-no-no to-so-de pe-mo [

      ko-to-no-   -o-ko
ai-ti-jo-qo o-na-to e-ke pa-ro da-mo ke-ke-me-na ko-to-na to-so[ ]WHEAT 1 T 4 V 3

wa-na-ta-jo o-na-to e-ke pa-ro da-mo ke-ke-me-na ko-to-na to-so-de pe-mo WHEAT T 5

a-da-ma-o o-na-to e-ke pa-ro da-mo ke-ke-me-na ko-to-na to-so pe-mo WHEAT T 4

a-tu-ko e-te-do-mo o-na-to e-ke pa-ro da-mo ke-ke-me-na ko[

ta-ta-ro o-na-to e-ke pa-ro da-mo ke-ke-me-na ko-to-na to-so pe [

pi-ke-re-u e-ke-qe ke-ke-me-na ko-to-na ko-to-no-o-ko to-so pe-mo[

ra-ku-ro e-ke-qe ke-ke-me-na ko-to-na ko-to-no-o-ko to-so pe-mo WHEAT [

ku-so e-ke-qe ke-ke-me-na ko-to-na ko-to-no-o-ko to-so pe-mo WHEAT V 1[

ke-ra-u-jo e-ke-qe ke-ke-me-na ko-to-na ko-to-no-o-ko to⟨so⟩ pe-mo WHEAT T 4

pa-ra-ko e-ke-qe ke-ke-me-na ko-to-na ko-to-no-o-ko to-so pe-mo WHEAT T 7

ko-tu[-ro]e-ke-qe ke-ke-me-na ko-to-na ko-to-no-o-ko to-so pe-mo WHEAT T 1

a-i-qe-u e-ke-qe ke-ke-me-na ko-to-na ko-to-no-o-ko to-so pe-mo WHEAT T 6

here is, by definition, a plot-holder. The obvious inference is
that in the Linear B texts the word *ko-to-no-o-ko* conveys some special, technical sense which now escapes us. (For the analysis of
this compound, cf. § 150).

§ 274 Para. 3 (lines 8-14). Seven men are described as holders
of *ke-ke-me-na ko-to-na*. The chief difference between this and the
preceding paragraph is that here the *e-ke-qe* of the Eb versions is
preserved in every item; the fact that this form is consistently
kept in this paragraph and consistently changed to *e-ke* in Para. 2
constitutes the strongest single argument in favour of the premise
that *e-ke* differs in meaning from *e-ke-qe*. Each of the seven is
called a *ko-to-no-o-ko;* unlike the persons mentioned in Para. 2,
these are not said to hold their plots *pa-ro da-mo*.

***

§ 275 Two of the inscribed fragments from Tiryns certainly belong to land-tablets:

TI Ef 2   TI Ef 3

]qo-u-ko-ro DA 1 to-sa-pe-mo WHEAT 6

di- ko-na-re-ja   ke-ke-me[

The combination of DA with the WHEAT ideogram on Ef 2 and the appearance of a word on Ef 3 which can be nothing else than some form
of *ke-ke-me-na* suffice to show that the Tirynthian scribes kept a
set of land-tablets of very similar type to that of the large archive dedicated to this subject at Pylos.

9   RELIGIOUS TEXTS FROM KNOSSOS PYLOS AND THEBES

General studies: G. Pugliese Carratelli *PP* 12 (1957) 81-96; L.A.
Stella *Numen* 5 (1958) 18-57; W.K.C. Guthrie *BICS* 6 (1959) 35-46;
M. Gérard-Rousseau *Les mentions religieuses dans les tablettes mycé-
niennes* (Rome 1968), *SMEA* 13 (1971) 139-146; F.R. Adrados *AM* I 170-
203. *pe-re-*82:* P. Scarpi *BIFG* 2 (1975) 230-251. *ti-ri-se-ro-e:* B.
Hemberg *Eranos* 52 (1954) 172-190. KN Fp: A. Sacconi *SMSR* 35 (1964)
137-159; J. Chadwick *PCCMS* 27-30; L. Baumbach *CM* 197-205.   PY Fr:
E.L. Bennett *The olive oil tablets of Pylos* (Salamanca 1958); L.R.
Palmer *TPS* (1958) 1-35; C. Gallavotti *PP* 14 (1959) 87-105; N. van
Brock *RP* 34 (1960) 229-231; M. Doria *PP* 15 (1960) 188-202; F.R. Adrados *Minos* 7 (1961) 49-61; M. Gérard *AC* 35 (1966) 207-209; M.D. Petru-
ševski *SMEA* 12 (1970) 127-130, *AM* II 122-137; M. Wylock *SMEA* 11 (1970)
116-133; J.T. Hooker *Kadmos* 18 (1979) 107-111. TH Of: T.G. Spyropoulos and J. Chadwick *The Thebes tablets* II (Salamanca 1975) 86-107;
J.T. Hooker *Minos* 16 (1977) 174-178; A.M. Jasink Ticchioni *SMEA* 21
(1980) 205-220. PY Tn 316: A. Furumark *Eranos* 52 (1954) 51-53; P.
Meriggi *Glotta* 34 (1955) 19-22; L.R. Palmer *Eranos* 53 (1955) 1-13;
C. Gallavotti *RF* 84 (1956) 225-236, *PP* 12 (1957) 241-249, 14 (1959)
96-98; G. Pugliese Carratelli *PP* 12 (1957) 352-354, *SCO* 7 (1958) 27-
31; W. Merlingen *Athenaeum* 46 (1958) 383-388; I. Chirassi *AR* II 945-
991; M. Gérard ib. 596-597; E.L. Bennett, H. Mühlestein *CM* 221-237.
PY Un 718: H. Mühlestein *SM* 114-115; M. Lejeune *Minos* 14 (1973) 60-
76; J. Chadwick *Le monde grec: hommages à C. Préaux* (Brussels 1975)
450-453; P. de Fidio *I dosmoi pilii a Poseidon: une terra sacra di
età micenea* (Rome 1977) 77-129.

***

The Knossos Fp tablets

    § 276 The Fp tablets at Knossos record disbursments of oil for
the benefit of persons (some of whom are certainly divine) and for
dispatch to named places.   The name of a month is usually given
in the 'heading' of each text.   The set may be represented by the
longest extant Fp tablet:

KN Fp 1 + 31 = *Documents* no. 200 = *Interpretation* no. 116

1	de-u-ki-jo-jo ^{me-}no
2	di-ka-ta-jo diwe OIL S 1
3	da-da-re-jo-de OIL S 2
4	pa-de OIL S 1
5	pa-si-te-o-i OIL 1
6	qe-ra-si-ja OIL S 1 [
7	a-mi-ni-so pa-si-te-o-i S 1 [
8	e-ri-nu OIL V 3
9	*47-da-de OIL V 1
10	a-ne-mo i-je-re-ja V 4
11	
12	to-so OIL 3 S 2 V 2

§ 277 This text falls into three parts: a heading, stating the
month in which the disbursments were (or are to be) made; a list of
recipients, together with the quantity of oil disbursed to each; the
total of the amount of oil disbursed.

§ 278 The heading (line 1).   *me-no* (μηνός) 'in the month'; *de-
u-ki-jo-jo* 'of Deukios?'

§ 279 The list (lines 2-10).   Three forms of words occur: the
nominative or the dative (used of personal recipients) and the accusative with allative suffix *-de* (used of places to which the oil was
delivered).   Nominative (apparently) is *e-ri-nu*.   Dative are *di-we,
pa-si-te-o-i, qe-ra-si-ja,* and *i-je-re-ja*.   Allative are *da-da-re-
jo-de* and **47-da-de*.   It is impossible to be certain whether *pa-de*
is dative or accusative + *-de*.   The two words in line 2, *di-ka-ta-
jo di-we,* represent Δικταίωι Διϝεί 'to Dictaean Zeus': an entry
which shows that by the time this text was written some degree of
assimilation had already taken place between Helladic and Minoan
cult.   'Dictaean Zeus' may indicate the Zeus who had a cult at

Mount Dicte or the Zeus who was thought to rule over Dicte as one of his special domains. *da-da-re-jo-de* in line 3 probably stands for the allative of a place, Δαιδαλειόνδε: if it does, the association of Knossos with Daedalus (or at least with *a* Daedalus) is shown to go back to the Bronze Age. Line 5 contains an entry which recurs on this tablet and on other tablets of the Fp set: *pa-si-te-o-i* = πᾶνσι θεοῖς 'to all the gods'. The *qe-ra-si-ja* of line 6 may very well stand for a word which would be written θηρασίαι 'to the Huntress' in later Greek, with regular development of the labio-velar, § 96; there is no means of knowing whether this word ought to be regarded as a title of Artemis, appropriate though it would be to her. Since in this set of texts the dative case seems to be reserved for personal recipients, the word *a-mi-ni-so* in line 7 is more likely to be nominative than dative; it is not clear whether the entry 'Amnisos' refers merely to *pa-si-te-o-i* or acts as a 'sub-heading', introducing the recipients named in lines 7-10. As for *e-ri-nu* in line 8, the Greek word 'Ερινύς fits the syllables perfectly; if the equation is correct, our knowledge of Aegean cult is not thereby enlarged, for the functions of 'Ερινύς and 'Ερινύες are not clearly defined even in later Greek: cf. A.H. Krappe *RhM* 81 (1932) 305-320. Line 9 contains the allative of an unknown place-name. Line 10 records the dispatch of oil *a-ne-mo i-je-re-ja* ἀνέμων ἱερείαι 'to the priestess of the winds': a phrase which seems to imply the existence of a cult centred on the forces of wild nature.

§ 280 The total (line 12). *to-so* (τόσον) 'so much (oil) — 3 full measures, 2 medium measures, 2 small measures'. The large amounts mentioned in the aggregate on the F tablets from Knossos and Pylos testify to the widespread use of oil in cult, but the precise nature of its employment is unknown; perhaps (as has been suggested) it was intended for ritual anointing.

§ 281 Other divinities mentioned on the Knossos tablets as recipients of offerings are: *e-re-u-ti-ja* ("Ελευθία) at Amnisos (Gg 705.1); *a-ta-na-po-ti-ni-ja* ('Αθάνα πότνια or 'Αθάνας πότνια), *e-nu-wa-ri-jo* ('Ενυϝάλιος), *pa-ja-wo-ne* (Παιᾱϝόνει), *po-se-da-o-ne* (Ποσειδάονει)(V 52 + 8285). On the lower edge of the latter tablet the word *e-ri-nu-we* (in erasure) can be read: this is either nominative plural or dative singular of *e-ri-nu*.

***

The Pylos Fr tablets

§ 282 The Fr set contains short texts accounting for the dispatch of oil to persons, many of whom are divinities. For example:

PY Fr 1219 = *Interpretation* no. 140

wa-no-so-i po-se-da-o-ne OIL⁺A V 2

PY Fr 1220 = *Documents* no. 307 = *Interpretation* no. 141

ro-u-si-jo a-ko-ro pa-ko-we OIL⁺PA V 4

di-pi-si-jo-i wa-na-ka-te OIL⁺PA S 1

§ 283 In Fr 1219, the scribe has written *wa-no-so-i* in error
for *wa-na-so-i* (which is correctly spelt elsewhere in the Fr set).
What is the meaning of this text? It has sometimes been suggested
that both *wa-no-so-i* and *po-se-da-o-ne* are in the dative case, as
recipients of the oil, and that *wa-no-so-i* is the dual of *wanassa*
'queen': thus, it is said, the oil is intended for a divine triad,
comprising two goddesses and a god (similarly with the phrase
wa-na-ka-te wa-na-so-i on Fr 1227). The absence of a copula linking the two words (to say nothing of the difficulty of explaining
the phrase in terms of cult) makes this theory implausible. It is
better to regard *wa-no-so-i* as a locative, which might mean 'at the
(place of the) *wanax*'; but it is conceivable that the resemblance
between *wa-no-so-i* and *wa-na-ka* is fortuitous and that *wa-no-so-i*
is the locative of a place-name. The OIL ideogram is here ligatured with the syllabic sign *a*, which may be the abbreviation of
a-ro-pa (ἀλοιφά) 'unguent'.

§ 284 Fr 1220 contains two entries, which may or may not be connected. *ro-u-si-jo a-ko-ro* represents either the nominative or the
dative of Λούσιος ἀγρός 'the region of Lousos'. *pa-ko-we* is probably the spelling of a neuter singular adjective σφακόϝεν 'scented
with sage (σφάκος)'; this is neuter, in agreement with *e-ra₃-wo* =
ἔλαιϝον, which is understood. It is possible that the *pa* ligature
is an abbreviation of *pa-ko-we*. Line 2 has a structure similar to
that of Fr 1219: *wa-na-ka-te* being a dative recipient 'to the *wanax*'
(here, in all likelihood, the divine 'Lord') and *di-pi-so-i* being
the locative of a place-name, perhaps that of a cult-centre.

The Thebes Of tablets

§ 285   The Of tablets from Thebes are concerned with amounts of
wool.   They differ from the Knossos L tablets, discussed in §§ 185-
194, in that they record not the assessment of wool but its dispatch
to persons (often divine persons), who are put in the dative case,
and to places which appear in the accusative with allative -*de*: they
are thus closely analogous to the Fp tablets from Knossos (§§ 276-
281).   Two disbursments of WOOL are recorded by:

TH Of 36

no-ri-wo-ki-de   ku WOOL 1 a-ke-ti-ra₂wa-na-ka[

1

2

po-ti-ni-ja wo-ko-de a-ke-ti-ra₂ ku WOOL 1

Line 1 mentions the dispatch of one unit of WOOL to *no-ri-wo-ki-de*:
a word of unknown meaning which could represent either the nominative plural of 'rubric' (ending in -ιδες) or the allative of a
place-name (ending in -ινδε) or the dative singular of a personal
recipient (ending in -ιδει).   The adjunct *ku*, put before the WOOL
ideogram, recalls the appearance of the same sign inside the CLOTH
ideogram on the L series from Knossos.   The other two words in line
1 presumably refer to the women responsible for working the wool:
a-ke-ti-ra₂ wa-na-ka[-te-ra.   A double ambiguity resides in these
words: first, it is uncertain whether they are nominative singular,
nominative plural, or dative singular; second, there is no way of
telling whether the *wanax* with whom the women are connected is the
king or a god.   The same ambiguity attends *a-ke-ti-ra₂* in line 2;
but at least the two words which precede it are clear enough. *po-ti-
ni-ja wo-ko-de* must stand for Ποτνίας ϝοικόνδε 'to the house of the
Lady': it is possible that early Greek ϝοῖκος, like Latin *aedes*,
could mean either 'house' or 'shrine'.

***

Records of cult-practices at Pylos

§ 286 PY Un 718 = *Documents* no. 171 = *Interpretation* no. 102

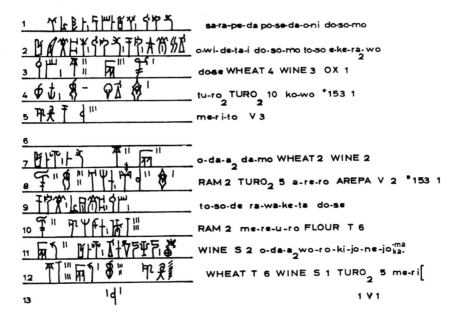

1	sa-ra-pe-da po-se-da-o-ni do-so-mo
2	o-wi-de-ta-i do-so-mo to-so e-ke-ra₂-wo
3	do-se WHEAT 4 WINE 3 OX 1
4	tu-ro₂ TURO₂ 10 ko-wo ⁺153 1
5	me-ri-to V 3
6	
7	o-da-a₂ da-mo WHEAT 2 WINE 2
8	RAM 2 TURO₂ 5 a-re-ro AREPA V 2 ⁸153 1
9	to-so-de ra-wa-ke-ta do-se
10	RAM 2 me-re-u-ro FLOUR T 6
11	WINE S 2 o-da-a₂wo-ro-ki-jo-ne-jo ka⁻ma
12	WHEAT T 6 WINE S 1 TURO₂ 5 me-ri[
13	1 V 1

This text may be broken down into a 'heading' and four 'paragraphs':

§ 287 Heading (line 1). The heading specifies the offerings to be mentioned in the body of the text as *po-se-da-o-ni do-so-mo* = Ποσειδάονι δοσμός 'a contribution to Poseidon'. The word *sa-ra-pe-da,* which is presumably a place-name, may be in the nominative case in apposition to the rest of the inscription (like *pu-ro* and *ro-u-so* in the Pylos A series, § 195) or in the genitive, depending on *do-so-mo* — 'the gift of S.....'.

§ 288 Para. 2 (lines 2-5). The meaning of *o-wi-de-ta-i* is completely obscure. In form, the word can hardly be anything other than a dative plural, but it is incomprehensible why a dative plural should be written as well as the dative *po-se-da-o-ni*: are the *o-wi-de-ta-i* perhaps priests or priestesses, or even satellite deities,

associated with the cult of Poseidon?   *e-ke-ra₂-wo* (nominative) is
the name of a man of high standing.   The words may be represented
thus in alphabetic Greek: δοσμὸν τόσον Ἐχελᾱϝων? δώσει, 'E. will
give so great a contribution'.   The separate constituents of the
offering are then enumerated: 4 measures of grain, 3 measures of
wine, 1 bull, 10 measures of cheese, and a *ko-wo*.   The last item
is perhaps a by-form of the Homeric word κῶας 'fleece', and the following ideogram (*153) does appear to depict a skin or hide.   The
final member of this list of offerings comprises 3 weights 'of
honey': *me-ri-to* = μέλιτος.

§ 289   Para. 2 (lines 7-8).   This paragraph is introduced by
the 'itemizing' word *o-da-a₂*.   The subject is *da-mo,* and with this
word there must be understood *do-se* from para. 1: 'the local community is to give...'.   The offerings are to consist of grain, wine,
rams, and cheese: items which give rise to no difficulty.   But an
enigmatic entry follows.   The phonetic rendering of the word
a-re-ro is accompanied by a 'monogram' formed from the three signs
a + re + pa.   It therefore seems that the scribe meant to write ⳨
as the last sign of the word, but wrote † in error: *a-re-pa* is probably equivalent to ἄλειφαρ 'unguent', which would be highly appropriate in this context (cf. § 75).

§ 290   Para. 3 (lines 9-11).   A new entry begins in line 9, although this time it is not marked off by a blank line or introduced
by *o-da-a₂*.   The subject is *ra-wa-ke-ta:* the λᾱϝᾱγέτᾱς (§ 250) 'is
to give so much': 2 rams, 6 measures of *me-re-u-ro,* and 2 measures
of wine.   The meaning of *me-re-u-ro* is not known for certain: it
may be a variant of μάλευρον, which is itself an alternative form
of ἄλευρον 'flour'.

§ 291   Para. 4 (lines 11-13).   The last paragraph is introduced
by *o-da-a₂*.   Here the subject is *wo-ro-ki-jo-ne-jo ka-ma,* the obscure entity already encountered on PY Er 312.7 (§ 253).   The offering comprises grain, wine, cheese, and honey.

                                   ***

§ 292   We come now to the most important single Mycenaean document to give evidence of cult-practices.   It is inscribed on both
sides, the front (recto) and the back (verso):

PY Tn 316 = *Documents* no. 172 = *Interpretation* no. 162

Recto

Verso

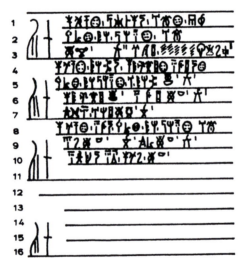

po-ro-wi-to-jo

      i-je-to-qe pa-ki-ja-si do-ra-qe pe-re po-re-na-qe.

pu-ro

      a-ke po-ti-ni-ja GOLD 2-HANDLED GOBLET 1 WOMAN 1

ma-na-sa GOLD DISH 1 WOMAN 1 po-si-da-e-ja GOLD DISH 1 WOMAN 1

ti-r i-se-ro-e GOLD CUP 1 do-po-ta GOLD 2-HANDLED GOBLET 1

pu-ro

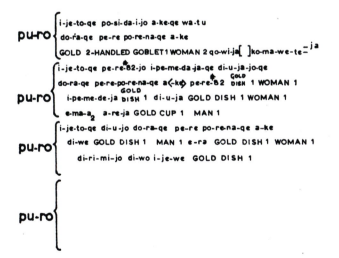

puro

i-je-to-qe po-si-da-i-jo a-ke-qe wa-t u
do-ra-qe pe-re po-re-na-qe a-ke
GOLD 2-HANDLED GOBLET 1 WOMAN 2 qo-wi-ja[ ]ko-ma-we-te−^{ja}

pu-ro

i-je-to-qe pe-re-82-jo i-pe-me-da-ja-qe di-u-ja-jo-qe
do-ra-qe pe-re-po-re-na-qe a(-k◊) pe-re-82 ᴅɪꜱʜ 1 WOMAN 1
    GOLD
i-pe-me-de-ja ᴅɪꜱʜ 1 di-u-ja GOLD DISH 1 WOMAN 1
e-ma-a$_2$ a-re-ja GOLD CUP 1 MAN 1

pu-ro

i-je-to-qe di-u-jo do-ra-qe pe-re po-re-na-qe a-ke
di-we GOLD DISH 1 MAN 1 e-ra GOLD DISH 1 WOMAN 1
di-ri-mi-jo di-wo i-je-we GOLD DISH 1

pu-ro

§ 293 *Recto:*   Heading (line 1).   This consists of the single
word *po-ro-wi-to-jo,* genitive singular of the masculine noun *po-ro-
wi-to,* which occurs in the nominative on some Pylos Fr tablets.   The
word is usually diagnosed as the name of a month, like *de-u-ki-jo-jo*
at KN Fp 1.1 (§ 278).   Thus we would have a genitive of time, 'in
(the month of) Porowitos'; but there is no certainty about this interpretation, and *po-ro-wi-to* is likely to be a personal name in PY
Fr 1221 and Fr 1232.

§ 294 Para. 1 (lines 2-5).   The exact significance of the large
characters at the left is not clear.   If the meaning is that the
ceremonies described in the text were held at Pylos, then Pylos and
Pakijana must have lain very close to each other, for the locative
of the latter name, *pa-ki-ja-si,* is found in line 2, and must refer
to the cult-place.   The paragraph contains three clauses, each with
a finite verb, and the clauses are linked by copulative *-qe:* clause
1, *i-je-to-qe;* clause 2, *do-ra-qe pe-re;* clause 3, *po-re-na-qe a-ke.*
The meaning of the three verbs *i-je-to, pe-re,* and *a-ke* is very difficult to ascertain.   When attempts were first made to explain this
text, *i-je-to* was usually regarded as a 3 singular middle ἵετοι or a
3 plural middle ἵεντοι (from ἵημι 'send'); then *pe-re* would spell
φέρει and *a-ke* ἄγει: '(someone) sends to Pakijana and leads offerings (*po-re-na* perhaps being a neuter plural noun, connected with
φέρω)'.   Alternatively, the spelling *i-je-to* might conceal a verb
connected with ἱερός, so that it would mean '(someone) performs an
act of consecration'.   With either meaning, *i-je-to* yields a tol-
erable sense, but it and the two other verbs lack an explicit subject; possibly a subject is to be understood out of *po-ro-wi-to-jo*
or *pu-ro.*   Palmer has advanced a different suggestion (*Interpretation* 264-267): he regards *i-je-to* as a medio-passive verb containing
the stem of ἱερός and understands it to mean 'a consecration takes
place'.   In the second clause, Palmer takes *do-ra* = δῶρα as the
subject; the neuter plural is, as usual, construed with a singular
verb, and Palmer suggests that *pe-re* represents an aorist passive
*φρή (from φέρω), so that the clause will mean 'gifts were brought'.
Palmer thinks *a-ke* is another 3 singular aorist passive: *ἄγη, containing the stem found in ἁγνός 'ritually pure, sanctified'.   The
meaning of this clause would then be 'the offerings were purified'.
The principal objections to Palmer's theory are that it necessita-
tes the construction of hypothetical forms and that it puts the
present *i-je-to* in parallel with aorists; but the latter objection
might perhaps be met by reference to the stereotyped character of
ritual language.   Lines 3-5 contain five words in the dative, each
of which is accompanied by an ideogram depicting a gold vessel and
three of them also by the WOMAN ideogram.   The words in the dative
appear to be the names of divine persons, while the ideograms represent offerings made to each god respectively.   *po-ti-ni-ja* =

Ποτνίαι 'to the Lady' — a goddess in her own right, or the title of
a goddess?   The presence of the WOMAN ideogram may indicate that,
as part of the ceremony, a woman was sacrificed or dedicated to her
service.   The remaining words are likewise the names of divinities:
their meaning is unknown, except that *po-si-da-e-ja* is a feminine
name formed from *po-si-da-o*: this goddess is not attested in later
Greek cult.

§ 295 *Verso:*   Para. 1 (lines 1-3).   This paragraph consists
of four clauses, followed by ideograms.   As on the front of the
tablet, the clauses are linked by copulative *-qe: i-je-to-qe po-si-*
da-i-jo; a-ke-qe wa-tu; do-ra-qe pe-re; po-re-na-qe a-ke. po-si-da-
i-jo = Ποσειδαῖον 'the shrine of Poseidon'.   Palmer's theory is
especially attractive in respect of the second clause: *ἄγη τε
ϝάστυ 'and the town was purified'.   Unlike the corresponding entries on the front, these clauses do not contain the dative case of
the deity to whom the gold vessel and the woman of line 3 are dedicated.   The function and meaning of the words *qo-wi-ja...ko-ma-we-*
te-ja are uncertain; they may be adjectives describing the vessel
(*ko-ma-we-te-ja* recurs at TH Of 35.1).

§ 296 Para. 2 (lines 4-7).   Three clauses, together with a list
of deities and offerings to them, make up this entry.   The clauses
have the following structure:
(i) *i-je-to-qe pe-re-*82-jo i-pe-me-de-ja < -jo >-qe di-u-ja-jo-qe;*
(ii) *do-ra-qe pe-re;*
(iii) *po-re-na-qe a< -ke >.*
The scribe has omitted one syllable in clause (i) and another in
clause (iii).   In clause (i) the words *pe-re-*82-jo, i-pe-me-de-ja*
< -jo >, and *di-u-ja-jo* are probably nominative: 'the shrine of *Pere*82*
is consecrated (?) and the shrine of Iphemedeia and the shrine of
Diwia'.   Clauses (ii) and (iii) add the customary items of information about the gifts and the *porena*.   The three divinities whose
shrines have been mentioned are now named in the same order; they
are put into the dative case, being the recipients of the offerings
depicted by the ideograms: 'to *Pere*82* one gold vessel and one woman;
to Iphemedeia one gold vessel; to Diwia one gold vessel and one
woman'.   *Pere*82* is the name of an unknown goddess.   Iphemedeia
does not appear in later cult, but she is mentioned in the *Odyssey,*
in the form Ἰφιμέδεια, as a concubine of Poseidon (λ 305); thus her
connexion with Poseidon seems to go back to the Mycenaean age.   The
name of the goddess Diwia is formed from the stem of Zeus, Διϝ-: this
formation is parallel to that of *po-si-da-e-ja* from *po-si-da-o* (line
4 of the recto).[1]   The dative of a god's name is now added to the

---

[1] Διϝία recurs in the Pamphylian dialect of later Greek: C.
Brixhe *Le dialecte grec de Pamphylie* (Paris 1976) 139.

list, *e-ma-a₂ a-re-ja;* one gold vessel and one man are offered to
him.   There is little doubt that the first word represents Ἑρμάαι,
the dative of the divine name Hermes (Homeric Ἑρμείας, Doric
Ἑρμᾶς): *a-re-ja* would then act as epithet to the god's name, but
its meaning is uncertain (could it be a form of 'Ares'?)

§ 297 Para. 3 (lines 8-10).   Again three clauses are followed
by the names of deities and offerings to them: (i) *i-je-to di-u-jo* =
'the shrine of Zeus is consecrated (?)'; (ii) and (iii) then repeat
the pattern set in Para. 2.   The juxtaposition in line 9 of *di-we* =
Διϝεί 'to Zeus' and *e-ra* = Ἥραι 'to Hera' strongly suggests that
Hera was already regarded as the consort of Zeus.   The word *di-ri-
mi-jo* in line 10 represents the name of an otherwise unknown god;
he is described as a 'son of Zeus': *di-wo i-je-we* = Διϝὸς (υ)ἱεϝεί,
the latter word being a dative of *i-jo* = (ὐ)ἱός 'son'.

10   WHEEL AND CHARIOT TABLETS: THE KNOSSOS S SERIES

General: P. Chantraine *Minos* 4 (1956) 50-65; D.J.N. Lee *BICS* 5 (1958) 61-64, *PP* 15 (1960) 401-414; M. Lejeune *Mémoires* I 25-44, III 285-330; R. Wild *Kadmos* 1 (1962) 126-129; M. Doria *ZA* 25 (1975) 369-380; C.J. Ruijgh *Chars et roues dans les tablettes mycéniennes: la méthode de la mycénologie* (Amsterdam 1976), *CM* 207-220. *a-ra-ru-ja a-ni-ja-pi:* D.M. Jones *Glotta* 37 (1958) 117-118.   *o-pa:* C. Consani *SSL* 17 (1977) 31-66.

***

Wheel tablets

§ 298 The WHEEL and CHARIOT tablets come from the so-called Arsenal, to the north-west of the palace of Knossos.   Twenty-four short tablets make up the So set; they comprise an inventory of pairs of wheels, and also single wheels, which were present (or which ought to have been present) when the inventory was drawn up. The WHEEL ideogram is carefully drawn, and it evidently represents wheels of different types, as the following examples will show:

KN So 4439 = *Documents* no. 280 = *Interpretation* no. 219

a-mo-ta e-ri-ka te-mi-dwe-ta WHEEL ZE MO WHEEL

KN So 4430 = *Documents* no. 282 = *Interpretation* no. 223

ko-ki-da o-pa   ne-wa

e-ri-ka   o-da-twe-ta a-ro₂-a   WHEEL ZE 22 MO WHEEL 1

KN So 4440 = *Documents* no. 281 = *Interpretation* no. 220

de-do-me-na

a-mo-ta pte-re-wa o-da-twe-ta WHEEL ZE 6

KN So 4442 = *Documents* no. 283 = *Interpretation* no. 222

o-pe-ro

]-ja a-mo-te pe-ru-si-nwa ta-ra-si-ja WHEEL ZE 1

§ 299 The first tablet, So 4439, may be analysed as follows:
a-mo-ta e-ri-ka te-mi-dwe-ta WHEEL ze   3   1
ἄρμοτα ἑλἱϰᾱς τε....ὄϝεντα· WHEEL ζε(ὐγεα) 3 μό(νϝον) 1
wheels of wil- ?   ?: 3 pairs of   1 single
        low   wheels;   wheel
a-mo-ta is the nominative plural of a neuter noun a-mo = ἄρμο,which
is found in the singular at KN Sg 1811. It is equivalent to later
Greek ἄρμα: for the ἄρμο/ἄρμα alternation, cf. σπέρμο/σπέρμα (§ 167).
In Homer the noun ἄρματα means 'an assemblage of wheels, a chariot';
as will be seen in § 304, Mycenaean uses a different word for 'chariot', but one which can be paralleled in later Greek.   The word
which follows a-mo-ta is a descriptive genitive formed from a noun
cited by Theophrastus as meaning a species of willow.   te-mi-dwe-ta
is a neuter plural adjective ending in -ὄϝεντα, describing ἄρμοτα:
no plausible meaning has yet been proposed for it.   ze is likely to
be an abbreviation of ze-u-ko = ζεῦγος 'yoke, pair' (the dative plural ze-u-ke-si = ζεύγεσι is found at PY Ub 1318.4). Since the syllabic sign mo is always associated with the numeral 'one', it is
probably an abbreviation of μόνϝον 'single'.

§ 300 So 4430 contains two introductory words, ko-ki-da o-pa, in
apposition to the rest of the text.   ko-ki-da might be a personal
name in the nominative or genitive; the meaning of o-pa is quite unknown.   a-mo-ta has to be understood with the following words, thus:
ne-wa (a-mo-ta) e-ri-ka o-da-twe-ta a-ro₂-a
νέϝα (ἄρμοτα) ἑλἱϰᾱς ο....τϝεντα ἀρίοha
new (wheels) of wil- ?   ? better
              low
ne-wa = νέϝα is neuter plural of νέϝος (> Attic νέος) 'new'; o-da-
twe-ta is an adjective similar in formation to te-mi-dwe-ta in So
4439, and its meaning is equally unknown; a-ro₂-a is neuter plural
of a comparative adjective, 'better, of superior quality' (§ 118).

§ 301 So 4440 begins with the comment de-do-me-na, neuter plural
of a perfect passive participle δεδομένα 'given, handed over'; thus
the task assigned has been carried out.   These a-mo-ta are pte-re-
wa = πτελέϝᾱς 'of elm'.

§ 302 So 4442 records the absence of wheels which the inventory-
taker expected to find: the text begins with o-pe-ro = ὄφελος 'deficit'.   If line 2 is correctly restored, it starts with a place-name
se-to-i-ja. Dual a-mo-te = ἄρμοτε is in harmony with the 'one pair'
of wheels denoted by the ideogram + ze. pe-ru-si-nwa ta-ra-si-ja is
descriptive of the wheels: for ta-ra-si-ja,see § 219; pe-ru-si-nwa =
περυσινϝᾱ́ 'belonging to last year'.   It seems that, in the year preceding the one in which the text was written, materials were allocated for so many pairs of wheels, but one pair was not manufactured.

Chariot tablets

§ 303 The eighteen Sd tablets, all by the same hand, describe chariots of various types: as with the WHEEL tablets, the scribe has not drawn a stereotyped ideogram, but has rendered the details of construction. The Sf texts, which are distinguished by the presence of *242 (the CHARIOT-FRAME ideogram), show some resemblance to the Sd tablets. The recurrent formulae may be illustrated by the following examples:

KN Sd 4409 + fragments = *Documents* no. 267

wi-ri-ne-o o-po-qo ka-ke-ja-pi o-pi-i-ja-pi WHEEL-LESS CHARIOT 1

a

b

i-qi-ja po-ni-ki-ja a-ra-ro-mo-te-me-na a-ja-me-na

KN Sd 4404 + fragment = *Documents* no. 269

]jo i-qo-e-qe wi-ri-ni-jo o-po-qo ke-ra-ja-pi o-pi-i-ja-pi

a

WHEEL-LESS [CHARIOT

b

i-qi-ja ku-do-ni-ja mi-to-we-sa-e a-ra-ro-mo-te-me-na

KN Sd 4422 = *Documents* no. 271

o-pa o-u-qe pe-qa-to u-po WHEEL-LESS [CHARIOT

a

b

i-qi-ja a-ro-mo-te-me-na o-u-qe a-ni-ja po-si e-e-si

KN Sf 4420 = *Documents* no. 273 = *Interpretation* no. 218

i - qi - ja   a - na - ta   a-na-mo-to CHARIOT 80

§ 304 In Sd 4409, as in the other members of the Sd set, the
lower line must be read before the upper. The subject is defined
by the first word of the second line, *i-qi-ja:* this is formally
equivalent to ἱππία, a feminine noun formed from the adjective ἵπ-
πιος 'to do with horses'. This noun is used in the collective
sense of 'chariot' (by a somewhat similar linguistic development,
Homer uses dual ἵππω or plural ἵπποι with the meaning 'chariot').
po-ni-ki-ja is a feminine adjective describing *i-qi-ja;* it represents φοινικία 'crimson, purple', but we cannot know whether the use
of this word implies that the whole chariot was painted such a colour, or only parts of it. *a-ra-ro-mo-te-me-na* and *a-ja-me-na* are
passive participles in the feminine (-μένα), further describing the
chariot: the first almost certainly contains the stem of ἀραρίσκω
'fit out, equip', but the details of the formation (especially that
of the *-mo-te-* element) are obscure; likewise, the general meaning
of *a-ja-me-na* ('decorated') is indicated by its use in this set and
also in the Pylos Ta tablets, but no corresponding Greek word is attested.   In the upper line, the words *wi-ri-ne-o o-po-qo* are presumably in the nominative; they could be plural or dual. Both words
are susceptible of analysis in terms of later Greek: *o-po-qo* = ὄπωποι
(or dual ὀπώπω) 'things on the eyes' (ὀπ- + ὠπ-), i.e. 'blinkers';
wi-ri-ne-o = Ϝρίνειοι (or dual Ϝρινείω) 'made of leather'. The last
two words also are transparently Greek formations, each with the instrumental suffix *-pi* = -φι: *o-pi-i-ja-pi* = ὀπι- + ἷαφι 'with things
on the bridle' (if the stem of ἷαφι is identical with that of ἱμάς
'thong'): probably 'bits'.   *ka-ke-ja-pi* is an adjective describing
o-pi-i-ja-pi: χαλκείαφι 'made of bronze'.   A tentative translation
of the whole text would be: 'chariot, crimson, equipped, decorated;
leather blinkers with bronze attachments'.

§ 305 Sd 4404 has a very similar structure.   It is interesting
that the scribe has applied the adjective *ku-do-ni-ja* to this chariot, but the word is too vague for any sound historical inference to
be drawn: it probably means 'from Kydonia'.   *mi-to-we-sa-e* contains

a scribal error, in that -e is otiose; perhaps it was added by a
writer who thought for a moment that he was dealing with a dual of
the third declension.   *mi-to-we-sa*, like *po-ni-ki-ja*, is an adjective of colour, and it is impossible to tell how the two colours
differ from each other, for in Homer they are used interchangeably:
mi-to-we-sa = μιλτόϝεσσα 'red'.   In the upper line, *do-we-jo i-qo-
e-qe* are probably nominative dual.   *do-we-jo* = δορϝείω 'wooden' is
restored from Sd 4413.   *i-qo-e-qe* is a compound which (to judge
from its first element) must denote some part of the equipage; the
meaning 'saddles' suggested in both *Documents* and *Interpretation* is
no better than a guess.

§ 306   On Sd 4422 the *i-qi-ja* is probably specified as an *o-pa*,
but this is not certain since the left-hand side of the tablet is
damaged.   After the usual entry *a-ro-mo-te-me-na*, a new clause is
written:
o-u-qe a-ni-ja po-si e-e-si o-u-qe pe-qa-to u-po
οὔτε   ἄνίαι   ποσὶ   ἔενσι   οὔτε   ?   ? ὑπό
neither reins are present upon (it) nor ?? beneath
Both ποσί and ὑπό have their original adverbial force.   No completely satisfactory explanation of *pe-qa-to* has yet been offered; but
Wild's suggestion that *pe-* conceals a stem πεδ- would harmonize well
with the lower part of the chariot demanded by ὑπό.

§ 307   Sf 4420 describes eighty chariot-frames as the *o-pa* of a
man's name in the genitive, *a-re-ki-si-to-jo*.   The fact that in the
Sf set a chariot is described either as *a-ja-me-na* or as *a-na-(i-)ta*
but never as both has suggested that *a-na-(i-)ta* means 'undecorated';
but the total number of Sf tablets is hardly sufficient to allow the
truth of this suggestion to be confirmed.   It is troublesome, in
particular, that the scribe has regarded this negative adjective (if
that is what it is) as a word of three terminations (hence the ending -a), whereas the one immediately following has only two terminations, for *a-na-mo-to* may be regarded, with some confidence, as a
spelling of ἀν-άρμοστοι (with the stem of ἀρμόζω), 'not equipped'.

11   SPICE TABLETS: THE MYCENAE Ge SET

Editions and commentaries: E.L. Bennett and others *The Mycenae tab-lets* II (Philadelphia 1958) 64, 65, 79, 80, 108; J. Chadwick and others *The Mycenae tablets* III (Philadelphia 1963) 71; J.-P. Olivier *Kadmos* 8 (1969) 51-52; A. Sacconi *Corpus delle iscrizioni in lineare B di Micene* (Rome 1974) 48-49.   *sa-pi-de:* L. Deroy *AC* 29 (1960) 315-318.

***

§ 308 The Ge tablets were found in the 'House of Sphinxes', due south of Grave Circle B at Mycenae: they appear to record transact-ions between individuals.   The text chosen to represent the Ge set is formed from two broken fragments which do not meet in the middle:

MY Ge 602 = *Documents* no. 105 = *Interpretation* no. 166

jo-o-po-ro a-ro[   ]mi-jo pe-se-ro

pu-ke ma-ra-tu-wo Z 1 [

pe-ke-u ku-mi-no   Z [   ] tu-wo V1 sa-sa-ma Z2 sa-pi-de 6

　　　　e-ru-ta-ra[   ] sà-ma V 1
ka-e-se-we ka-na-ko L   ] ra-tu-wo V1 sa-pi-de 6

　　　　e-ru-ta-ra
ke-po ka-na-ko M[   ]V1 mi-ta PE 2 ko-no-a-po-te[

                        ]V1 DE 1 RECEPTACLE[

Line 1.   As usual, the 'introductory' particle *jo-* has brought the
main verb with it to the beginning of the inscription.   *-o-po-ro*
probably stands for ὦφλον, 3 plural aorist of ὀφείλω 'owe'.   The
word beginning *a-ro-* is likely to be the object of this verb, and
the word ending *-mi-jo* (nominative plural in -μιοι?) its subject.
pe-se-ro seems to be the dative of a man's name.   Hence: 'the .....
-mioi owed a.... to Psellos(?)'.   The names of two of the .....
-mioi are then given in large characters at the left of lines 2 and
3.
Line 2.   A man named *pu₂-ke* (owed) an amount of *ma-ra-tu-wo:* compare later Greek μάραθ(ρ)ον 'fennel'.
Line 3.   A man named *pe-ke-u* (owed) amounts of *ku-mi-no* (κύμῑνον
'cummin'), *[ma-ra]-tu-wo*, *sa-sa-ma* (σᾱσάμᾱ 'sesame'), and six *sa-
pi-de* (perhaps σαρπίδες 'boxes').
Line 4.   The structure of this line differs from that of lines 2
and 3.   It begins with a dative, as if the name of a new 'creditor'
(which would appear in the nominative as *ka-e-se-u*) had been introduced.   This man is 'owed' amounts of *e-ru-ta-ra ka-na-ko* (ἐρυθρᾱ̀
κνᾱκος 'red safflower'), of *[sa]-sa-ma*, and of *ma-ra-tu-wo*, and six
sa-pi-de.
Line 5.   It is impossible to say whether the name *ke-po* is nominative (as in lines 2 and 3) or dative (as in line 4).   The items involved in this transaction are red safflower, two *pe* ('bundles'??)
of *mi-ta* (μίνθα 'mint'), and others which are obscure.   The vessel
depicted by the ideogram *155* is presumably a container for the
spices.

12   ASSESSMENTS OF VARIOUS COMMODITIES: M AND N TABLETS FROM PYLOS
     AND KNOSSOS

PY Ma: M. Lejeune *Mémoires* I 65-91,   147-150; W.F. Wyatt *AJA* 66
(1962) 21-41; C.W. Shelmerdine *AJA* 77 (1973) 261-275; P. de Fidio
SMEA 23 (1982) 84-106.   KN Mc: L. Baumbach *AC(CT)* 14 (1971) 1-16;
J.L. Melena *Minos* 13 (1972) 29-54; C.G. Thomas *AC(CT)* 22 (1979) 145-
148; P. de Fidio *SMEA* 23 (1982) 116-121.   PY Ma and KN Mc: J.-P.
Olivier *BCH* 98 (1974) 23-35.   PY N: *Mémoires* I 127-155; W.A. McDon-
ald *Minos* 6 (1960) 149-155; J.T. Killen *BICS* 26 (1979) 134.

                              ***

Pylos Ma tablets

    § 309 The Ma tablets number eighteen.   Each records the assess-
ment of six commodities in one town of the Pylian state.   The commodities are always mentioned in the same order: *146, RI, KE, *152,
O, ME.   The first five of these signs are accompanied by comparatively small numbers, the last often by large ones; but none of the
signs can be identified with certainty.   As was seen in § 215,
fourteen of the Ma texts refer to places named in the list on PY Jn
829.   The principal types are represented by the following examples:

    § 310   PY Ma 333 + 526

e-ra-te-re-we *146 46 RI M 46 KE M[   ] M 10 ME 1000[

This text contains a place-name in the dative case and amounts of
the standard commodities.   In view of the structure of the other Ma
tablets, these commodities probably represent the 'assessment' of
what is due from the place in question.

§ 311 PY Ma 222 = *Documents* no. 173

a-ke-re-wa *146 23 RI M 23 KE M 7 *152 10 0 M 5 ME 500

a-pu-do-si *146 10 o 13 RI M 22 o M 1 KE M 7 *152 8 o 2 0 M 5 ME 500

A more complex type is seen on this tablet.   The 'assessment' for
the place *a-ke-re-wa* is stated in line 1.   Line 2 is introduced by
the word *a-pu-do-si* = ἀπύδοσις 'delivery': this shows that the first
amount associated with each commodity has actually been delivered,
while the second amount is marked *o*, that is, it is still owing or
'in deficit'.   In the case of each commodity, the amount delivered
plus the amount in deficit equals the 'assessment' recorded in line
1:

commodity	units delivered	units in deficit	units assessed
*146	10	13	23
RI	22	1	23
KE	7	0	7
*152	8	2	10
O	5	0	5
ME	500	0	500

§ 312   PY Ma 123 = *Documents* no. 176

ti-mi-to-a-ke-e ⸜146 24 RI M 24 KEM 7 ⸜152 10 0 M 5 ME 500

a-pu-do-si ⸜146 21 o 2 RI M   KE M ⸜152 0 M   ME

o-da-a₂ ka-ke-we o-u-di-do-si ⸜146 1 RI M 1 ME 10

On Ma 123, and on eight other tablets of the set, a third line has
been added.   This is introduced by the 'itemizing' particle *o-da-a₂*
and states that a certain class of artificers (usually, as here, the
ka-ke-we = χαλκῆϝες 'bronze-smiths') 'do not give': *o-u-di-do-si* =
οὐ δίδονσι.   In the case of the commodities denoted by *146, RI,*
and *ME,* the units which the smiths 'do not give' have to be added to
the units 'in deficit' in order to arrive at the total assessment.
In line 2, the scribe has not stated what amounts of *O* and *ME* were
actually delivered, and so it is to be presumed that there was no
deficit:

commodity	units not given	units delivered	units in deficit	units assessed
*146	1	21	2	24
RI	1	23	0	24
KE	0	7	0	7
*152	0	10	0	10
O	0	5	0	5
ME	10	490	0	500

§ 313 PY Ma 393 = *Documents* no. 175 = *Interpretation* no. 195

za-ma-e-wi-ja *146 28 RI M 28 KE M 8 *152 12 0 M 5 ME 600

a-pu-do-si *146 20 a-ne-ta-de *146 1 RI M 21 KEM 5 o M 1 *152 8 0M 6 ME   450

o-da-a₂ ma-ra-ne-ni-jo o-u-di-do-si *146 7 RI M 7 KE M 2 *152 3 0 M 2ME 150

In this text, the word *a-ne-ta-de* is placed in opposition to *a-pu-do-si*. *a-ne-ta-de* is usually thought to contain ἄνετα suffixed with the adversative particle δέ, ἄνετος being a verbal adjective formed from ἀνίημι 'let go, set free'. In the present context, *a-ne-ta* means presumably that the items placed after it are 'remitted': that is, they will not after all have to be contributed, in spite of the assessment. The meaning of *ma-ra-ne-ni-jo* in line 3 is unknown: it is the nominative plural of a word which may be an ethnic or an occupation-term. Following is the analysis of Ma 313:

commodity	units not given	units delivered	units remitted	units in deficit	units assessed
*146	7	20	1	0	28
RI	7	0	21	0	28
KE	2	0	5	1	8
*152	3	0	0	8	12
O	2	0	0	6	5
ME	150	0	0	450	600

It will be noticed that the books do not balance in respect of items *152 and O: the units of *152 fall one short of the number assessed, while the units of O exceed the assessment by three.

✳✳✳

Knossos Mc tablets

§ 314 Most of the twenty-three extant Mc tablets from Knossos
are very fragmentary. They resemble the Pylos Ma texts in that
they record amounts of standard commodities: here the items are represented by the four ideograms *150, SHE GOAT, HORN, and *142. The
signification of the first and fourth ideograms is unknown. The recurrent type of inscription is exemplified by:

KN Mc 4455 + fragments

It is known from other Knossos texts that the word ku-ta-to, written
in large characters at the left of this tablet, is a place-name (§
181).   Analogy with the Pylos Ma set suggests that we have here the
assessment of so many commodities at the place ku-ta-to: but, unlike
the Pylos tablets, this text brings in a personal name a-pa-sa-ki-jo
as well.   This might be the name of the man responsible for contri-
buting the items in the locality of ku-ta-to or, conceivably, the
name of the supervisor or census-taker.

                                    ***

Pylos N tablets

§ 315 The N tablets are concerned with the assessment of a commodity which is represented by the sign SA: this has been identified
as 'flax' on the evidence of Nn 228.1 (below).[1]   The Na set comprises a large number of short texts, each showing the assessment of
amounts of SA at a named place; sometimes details are added about
payment or non-payment by certain classes of persons.   Nn 228 is a
totalling tablet, bringing together information contained in a number of Na texts.   The two Ng tablets present grand totals of the
amounts of SA contributed, or not contributed, by two great divi-
sions of the Pylian kingdom.   Representative texts are considered
in the following order:

[1] Cf. A.L.H. Roskin AJA 83 (1979) 469-474.

PY Na 245 = *Documents* no. 195 = *Interpretation* no. 200

o-u-di-do-si   SA 10

e-wi-te-wi-jo SA 20 to-sa-de ma-ra-te-we ra-wa-ke-si-jo

PY Nn 228 = *Documents* no. 184 = *Interpretation* no. 211

1 o-o-pe-ro-si ri-no o-pe-ro

2 u-ka-jo SA 20 ro-o-wa SA 35

3 pu_2-ra-a-ke-re-u SA 10 ke-i-ja-ka-ra-na

4 SA 5 di-wi-ja-ta SA 60

5 a-pi-no-e-wi-jo SA 28

6 po-ra-pi SA 10 e-na-po-ro SA 33

7 te-tu-ru-we SA 38

PY Ng 319 = *Documents* no. 198 = *Interpretation* no. 209

de-we-ro-ai-ko-ra-i-ja SA 1239

1

2

to-sa-de o-u-di-do-to SA 457

PY Ng 332 = *Documents* no. 199 = *Interpretation* no. 210

pe-ra_3-ko-ra-i-ja SA 200[

1

2

to-sa-de o-u-di-do-to SA[

§ 316 Na 245 gives an assessment for the place *e-wi-te-wi-jo* of
twenty units of *SA*.   Then comes the entry:
to-sa-de ma-ra-te-we ra-wa-ke-si-jo o-u-di-do-si   SA 10
τοσάδε   Μαλαθῆϝες? λᾱϝᾱγέσιοι   οὐ δίδονσι   *SA* 10
This records the non-contribution of ten units of *SA* by the *Mala-
thēwes(?)* belonging to the *lāwāgetas*.   *ma-ra-te-we* is the nominative plural of an occupation-word, whose meaning is not known.   Elsewhere on the Pylos tablets, *ma-ra-te-u* is a man's name (§ 231);
presumably the occupation-word can function as a personal name, as
with English *Smith*, etc.   The craftsmen are described as belonging
to the *lāwāgetas*: like some of the bronze-smiths mentioned by the Mc
tablets, they 'do not contribute' so many units of the assessment,
but the text does not say whether their payment has been waived or
is still outstanding.

§ 317 Nn 228 begins with a 'heading' introduced by *o-*, recalling the *jo-* at the opening of MY Ge 602 (§ 308):
o-o-pe-ro-si ri-no o-pe-ro
ὀ-ὀφείλονσι λίνον ὄφελος
they owe   flax? as a deficit
The words which follow are place-names, each with its deficit expressed in units of *SA*.

§ 318 Ng 319 and Ng 332 show the assessment of *SA* at *de-we-ro-
ai-ko-ra-i-ja* and *pe-ra₃-ko-ra-i-ja* respectively.   Whatever the
meaning of the second element of these compounds, there is little
doubt that the first elements are complementary to each other: *de-
we-ro-* representing later Greek δεῦρο 'hither, here'[1] and *pe-ra₃-
πέρᾱ-* 'farther'.   They accordingly denote parts of the kingdom,
de-we-ro- lying closer to the palace of Pylos and *pe-ra₃-* farther
away.   In just the same way, the Romans spoke of Cisalpine and
Transalpine Gaul respectively; and probably *-ai-ko-ra-i-ja* too is
the name of a geographical feature.   The first line of both tablets records the total assessment; then line 2 indicates that:
to-sa-de o-u-di-do-to
τοσάδε   οὐ δίδοτοι
so many are not given

---

[1] Cf. C.J. Ruijgh *AM* II 441-450.

13   INSCRIBED JARS SEALINGS AND LABELS

Inscribed jars from Thebes: G. Björck *Eranos* 52 (1954) 120-124; H.W.
Catling and A. Millett *Archaeometry* 8 (1965) 3-85; J. Raison *Les
vases à inscriptions peintes de l'âge mycénien* (Rome 1968) 61-117;
A. Heubeck *Athenaeum* 57 (1969) 144-153; L.R. Palmer *Kadmos* 11
(1972) 27-46; C. Sourvinou-Inwood *Minos* 13 (1972) 130-136; J. and J.
McArthur *Minos* 15 (1974) 68-80; A. Sacconi *Corpus delle iscrizioni
vascolari in lineare B* (Rome 1974) 121-173; A.L. Wilson *Archaeometry* 18 (1976) 51-58.   Inscribed sealings: J. Chadwick *BICS* 5
(1958) 1-5, *Eranos* 57 (1959) 1-5; J.-P. Olivier *Minos* 9 (1968) 173-
183.

***

Inscribed jars

   § 319 More inscribed jars have been found at Thebes than at any
other Mycenaean site.   The best-preserved inscriptions can be put
into a series:

TH Z 839 = *Interpretation* no. 171   TH Z 852

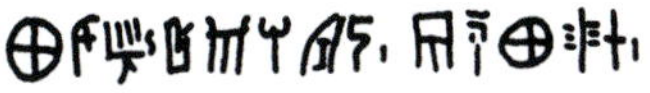

⊕ⴼⴘⵀ�ⵝⵟⵉ⸵, ⵀⵜ⊕ⵝⵜⵏⵉ   ⵝⵉⴹⵉⵀⵜ⸵ ⵉⴼⵟⵝⵘ
ka-u-no o-du-ru-wi-jo wa-na-ka-te-ro   a-re-me-ne wa-to re-u-ko-jo

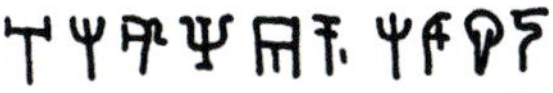

TH Z 853   TH Z 854

ⴽⴼⵉⵟⵉ, ⵀⵜ, ⵣⵏⵜⵀⵟ   ⵣ ⵜ, ⵀⵜ, ⵌⵝⵉ
e-u-da-mo wa-to ri-ˢ82-ta-o   pi-pi wa-to su-ro-no

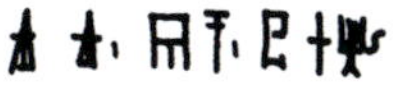

All of the foregoing texts contain the same three elements arranged
in the same order, namely:
(i) a man's name in the nominative case;
(ii) a place-name, also in the nominative;
(iii) either a man's name in the genitive or the word *wa-na-ka-te-ro*.
It does not seem possible to form any conclusion about the function
of the personal names; but it might reasonably be conjectured that
(i) is the name of the consignor responsible for the dispatch (and
perhaps also the manufacture) of the oil which the jars originally
contained.   The presence of *wa-na-ka-te-ro* as third element in Z
839 strongly suggests that, just as the man named *ka-u-no* 'worked
for' the *wanax*, so *a-re-me-ne* 'worked for' *re-u-ko*, *e-u-da-mo* for
*ri-*82-ta*, and *pi-pi* for *su-ro*.   But it is (ii) which arouses the
greatest interest.   It takes the form either of *wa-to* or of *o-du-
ru-wi-jo*.   Both words are used as place-names on the Knossos tablets: in KN C 902, the *ko-re-te* at *o-du-ru-wi-jo* and the *ko-re-te*
at *wa-to* are mentioned in successive lines in connexion with cat-
tle.   It thus becomes very likely that the jars and their contents
were exported to the mainland from Crete and that *wa-to* and *o-du-ru-
wi-jo* are the names of places at which the jars were manufactured
and filled with oil.

***

Inscribed sealings

§ 320 Lumps of clay bearing seal-impressions and incised with
Linear B characters were found at Knossos, Pylos, and Mycenae.   The
close similarity between these inscriptions and those on the Linear
B tablets shows that the sealings played a part in the scribal bur-
eaucracy of the palaces.   It is to be presumed that the one or two
words inscribed on a sealing served as a kind of index to a class
of tablets, while the seal-impression itself was made by the signet
of an important official or overseer, who had checked the contents
of the archive in question.

KN Ws 1704 = *Documents* no. 264

α   ⟶   JAVELIN
β   𝕳 ‡   o-pa
γ   ‡ 𝕳 𝕭   pa-ta-ja

This and other sealings come from the Arsenal at Knossos, which
yielded also the tablets recording numbers of weapons and chariots.
The meaning of the word *o-pa* (encountered already in §§ 303-307) is

unknown; but the inscription is nevertheless of interest in that a connexion is established between the word *pa-ta-ja* and the ideogram depicting a dart. It is evident that *pa-ta-ja* and *pa-ta-jo* are alternative forms of a word which appears later as παλτόν 'light missile' (cf. § 214). The sealing acts as a check on the run of tablets which record numbers of these weapons.

§ 321 MY Wt 504

⊙Λ 𝐁

qe-ti-ja

The single word on this sealing suffices to make the connexion with MY Ue 611, a tablet which contains a list of words and numerals. No ideograms are written, but the presence of two words (*a-po-re-we* = ἀμφορῆϝε and *ti-ri-po-di-ko* = τριποδίσκοι) indicates that the words in the list are vessel-names. Furthermore, the word *qe-to* is found in line 4 of the tablet. From its appearance in the Pylos Ta tablets, this too is known to be a vessel-name (§ 242); *qe-ti-ja,* in line 3 of the tablet, is obviously a different form of the same word, indicating a vessel similar to a *qe-to*. *qe-ti-ja* has been extracted from its context and written on our sealing as an indication that the archive deals with vessels; other vessel-names are similarly used on other sealings.

※※※

Inscribed labels

§ 322 PY Wa 114

me-ni-jo WOMAN

pe-ra₃-ko-ra-i-ja ko-[

The word in line 2, *pe-ra₃-ko-ra-i-ja,* was met on PY Ng 332, where it denotes the 'farther' part of the kingdom (§ 318). This label is thus likely to refer to a class of tablets concerned with contributions from, or outgoings to, the remoter areas. The ideogram shows that the contributions or outgoings are connected with women. *me-ni-jo* cannot describe the women directly, and it may indicate the item(s) levied or distributed. The association with μήν 'month' rests on a mere guess, and is unsafe.

PART THREE

INDEX 1: LINEAR B WORDS

In this and the following indexes, the numbers refer to paragraphs.

a-da-ra-ti-jo   145
a-e-ri-qo-ta   232
a-e-ti-to   149
a-ja-me-na   304, 307
a-ka-ma-no   153
a-ka-si-jo-ne   159
a-ka-ta-jo   153
a-ka-wi-ja-de   159
a-ke   294-296
a-ke-ra-wo   153
a-ke-re-wa   159, 226, 311
a-ke-ro   220
a-ke-te-re   217
a-ke-ti-ri-ja   198
a-ke-ti-ra$_2$ 138, 285
a-ke-ti-ra$_2$-o   199
a-ke-u   152
a-ki-ti-to   149
a-ko-ro   284
a-ko-to   ˙152
a-ku-ro   84
a-ma-ru-ta   269
a-mi-ni-si-jo   146
a-mi-ni-so   49, 50, 84, 159
a-mo   117, 299
a-mo-si   117
a-mo-ta   84, 117, 141, 299-302
a-mo-te   117, 302
a-mo-te-wi-ja   237
a-na-i-ta   149, 307
a-na-i-to   149
a-na-mo-to   149, 307
a-na-pu-ke   149
a-na-ta   149, 307
a-ne-mo   103, 279
a-ne-ta-de   313
a-ne-u-te   159, 173
a-ni-ja   87, 103, 306
a-ni-ja-pi   103

a-ni-ja-to   179
a-no-no   272
a-no-we   149, 240
a-no-wo-to   149
a-nu-ko   179
a-nu-to   152
a-pa-re-u-pi   159
a-pa-sa-ki-jo   314
a-pa-ta-wa   159
a-pe-do-ke   128
a-pe-ri-ta-wo   230
a-pi   84, 129
a-pi-e-ke   129
a-pi-a$_2$-ro   153
a-pi-do-ro   153
a-pi-je-ta   231
a-pi-me-de   153
a-pi-no-e-wi-jo   223
a-pi-po-re-we   109
a-po-ne-we   159
a-po-re-we   109, 321
a-po-te-ro-te   133
a-pu-   129, 164
a-pu-do-ke   128
a-pu-do-si   311, 313
a-pu$_2$-ka(-ne)   232
a-qe-mo   179
a-ra-ro-mo-te-me-na   304
a-ra-ru-ja   57
a-ra-ru-wo-a   57, 128, 171
a-re-ja   296
a-re-ke-se-u   178
a-re-ki-si-to-jo   307
a-re-ku-tu-ru-wo   145, 152
a-re-me-ne   319
a-re-pa   289
a-ro-mo-te-me-na   306
a-ro-pa   283
a-ro$_2$-a   118, 188, 300

a-ro$_2$-e   118
a-ro$_2$-jo   118
a-ta-na-po-ti-ni-ja   281
a-ta-no   153
a-ta-ra-si-jo   217-219
a-te-mo   179
a-tu-ko   268, 273
a$_2$-ka-a$_2$-ki-ri-jo   156
a$_2$-ru-wo-te   231
ai-ka-sa-ma   103, 214
ai-ke-u   239
ai-ki-pa-ta   139
ai-ki-po   153
ai-ko-ta   232
ai-mi-re-we   176
ai-ta-re-u-si   232
ai-ta-ro-we   153
ai-ti-jo-qo   153
ai-to   152
au-de-we-sa   141
au-ke-wa   234
au-ta$_2$ 179

da-da-re-jo-de   159, 279
da-i-qo-ta   153, 179
da-ja-ro   179
da-ma-te   210, 266, 267
da-mi-ni-jo   181
da-mo   103, 260, 273, 274, 289
da-mo-ko-ro   234
da-ta-ja-ro   179
da-we-u-pi   159
da-wo   179, 180
da-*22-to   179
-de   133, 216, 313
de-do-me-na   301
de-so-mo   103, 171
de-u-ka-ri-jo   152
de-u-ki-jo-jo   278, 279, 293
de-we-ro-ai-ko-ra-i-ja   318
di-do-si   101
di-do-to   127, 318
di-ka-ta-de   159
di-ka-ta-jo   146, 279
di-ko-na-ro   145
di-pa   113, 166, 243, 245, 269
di-pa-e   244
di-pi-so-i   284

di-ri-mi-jo   297
di-ro   179
di-u-ja   148
di-u-ja-jo   148, 296
di-u-jo   120
di-we   110, 279, 297
di-wi-je-u   152
di-wi-jo   120
di-wo (Διϝός)   90, 110, 297
di-wo (Δίϝων?)   152
do-e-ra   202, 268
do-e-ro   268
do-e-ro-i   103
do-ra-qe   294
do-ro-me-u   152
do-se   288, 289
do-so-mo   103, 287
do-so-si   208
do-we-jo   305
du-ma-te   115, 210
du-ni-jo   104, 257
du-ru-to-mo   84
du-ta-so   179
du-wo-u-pi   123
du-wo-we   240

e-do-me-ne-u   269
e-e-si   101, 306
e-ka-ra   86, 141
e-ka-ra-e-we   176
e-ke   134, 257, 258, 264, 274
e-ke-da-mo   153
e-ke-e   126
e-ke-me-de   153, 231
e-ke-qe   264, 274
e-ke-ra$_2$-wo   153, 288
e-ke-si-qe   214
e-ki-no   152
e-ko   84
e-ko-me-na-ta-o   152
e-ko-me-no   159
e-ko-si   101, 134, 217, 268
e-ko-so   179
e-ko-so-no   159
e-ko-te   217
e-ko-to   152
e-ma-a$_2$ 296
e-me   123, 240

e-ne-e-si   129, 267
e-ne-ka   93, 129
e-ne-wo-   123
e-ni-pa-te-we   159
e-nu-wa-ri-jo   281
e-o   126
e-pi   129
e-pi-ja-ta   152, 153
e-pi-ki-to-ni-ja   192
e-pi-ko-wo   230
e-qe-si-ja   188
e-qe-si-jo   250
e-qe-ta   96, 108, 139, 188,
     232, 250
e-qe-ta-e   108
e-qe-ta-i   108
e-ra-po   232
e-ra-ta-ra   203, 269
e-ra-te-i   159
e-ra-to   216
e-re-e   159
e-re-e-u   159
e-re-i   159
e-re-mo   253
e-re-pa   115
e-re-pa-te   115
e-re-pa-to   115
e-re-ta   139
e-re-ta-o   108
e-re-u-ti-ja   281
e-ri-ke-re-we   153
e-ri-ko-wo   220, 224
e-ri-nu   279, 281
e-ri-nu-we   281
e-ro-ma-to   159
e-ru-ta-ra   308
e-ru-to-ro   152
e-ra$_3$-wo   103, 141, 284
e-sa-ro   269
e-ta-wo-ne-u   152
e-te-do-mo   268, 273
e-te-wa   230
e-te-wo-ke-re-we-i-jo   145
e-ti-we   141
e-u-da-mo   153, 319
e-u-de-we-ro   156
e-u-ke-to   97, 127

e-u-ko-me-no   152
e-u-me-de   151, 153
e-u-me-ne   153
e-u-me-ta   152, 153
e-u-po-ro-wo   153
e-u-ru-da-mo   153
e-wi-te-u   159
e-wi-te-wi-jo   159, 316

i-do-me-ne-ja   152
i-ja-te   138
i-ja-wo-ne   152
i-je-re-ja   136, 202-204, 269, 279
i-(j)e-re-u   87, 109, 136
i-je-re-wi-jo   147
i-je-re-wo   109
i-je-ro-jo   202
i-je-to-qe   294-296
i-je-we   111, 297
i-jo   297
i-jo-te   87
i-pe-me-de-ja-jo   296
i-qi-ja   141, 304
i-qi-jo   304
i-qo   99, 103
i-qo-e-qe   305
i-to-we-sa   141
i-wa-ka   226
i-wa-so   152

jo-   87, 130, 308

ka-e-sa-me-no   232
ka-e-se-u   308
ka-ke-ja-pi   304
ka-ke-u   152
ka-ke-u-si   109
ka-ke-we   109, 217, 218, 312
ka-ko   84, 103, 213
ka-ma   260, 291
ka-ma-e-u   260
ka-na-ko   308
ka-pa-ti-ja   211
ka-ra-do-ro   159
ka-ra-do-wa-ta   153
ka-ra-pa-so   152
ka-ra-u-ko   152

ka-ra-wi-po-ro   211
ka-to   152
ka-u-no   319
ka-zo-e   100, 108
ke-e   159
ke-i-ja-ka-ra-na   156
ke-i-jo   159
ke-ke-me-na   259, 260, 270,
     272-275
ke-ki-de   231, 232
ke-po   308
ke-ra-a   113
ke-ra-e   113
ke-ra-me-ja   136, 152
ke-ra-me-u   136
ke-ra-so   152
ke-ra-ti-jo-jo   157
ke-re-si-jo we-ke   239
ke-re-te-u   262
ke-re-ti-wo   159
ke-u-sa   182
ke-we-to   226
ki-ni-di-ja   200
ki-ri-ta   103
ki-ti-me-na   259, 261, 268,
     270
ki-to   191, 192
ko-do-jo   258
ko-ka-ro   152
ko-ki-da   300
ko-ki-jo   230
ko-ki-re-ja   237
ko-ma-we   153
ko-ma-we-te-ja   295
ko-no-si-jo   146
ko-no-so   51, 84, 159
ko-re-te   138, 220, 319
ko-re-te-re   209
ko-re-te-ri-jo   147
ko-ri-to   159
ko-ro   179
ko-ro-jo-wo-wi-ja   158
ko-ro-no-we-sa   141, 237
ko-so-u-to   152
ko-to-na   103, 258, 259, 268,
     270, 272-274
ko-to-na-o   103

ko-to-no-o-ko   150, 273, 274
ko-tu-ro$_2$ 152
ko-tu-we   159
ko-wa   103, 197
ko-wo ('boy, son')   90, 103, 197,
     199
ko-wo ('skin, hide')   288
ku-do-ni-ja   159, 305
ku-ka-ro   171
ku-ke-re-u   152
ku-mi-no   308
ku-na-ja   237
ku-na-ke-ta-i   139
ku-pa-ri-si-jo   231, 232
[ku-]pa-ri-so   159
ku-pa-ro-we   141
ku-pe-se-ro   152
ku-ra-no   152
ku-ru-me-no   152
ku-ru-so   84
ku-su   84, 129
ku-ta-(i-)to   159, 166, 179,
     182, 314
ku-te-re-u-pi   109, 159
ku-tu-qa-no   179
ku-wa-no   87

ma-di   179
ma-ka-wo   152
ma-na-si-we-ko   153
ma-ni-ko   140
ma-ra-ne-ni-jo   313
ma-ra-te-u   231, 316
ma-ra-te-we   316
ma-ra-tu-wo   308
ma-re-wo   230
ma-ri-ta   152
ma-ro-pi   173
ma-te   114
ma-to-(ro-)pu-ro   156
me-ka-o   157
me-ni-jo   322
me-no   278, 279
me-re-u-ro   290
me-ri-du-ma-te   210
me-ri-to   288
me-ta   129

me-ta-pa 159
me-to-qe-u 153
me-u-jo 92, 118, 120
me-u-jo-e 118
me-u-jo-a$_2$ 118
me-wi-jo 92, 118, 120, 245
me-zo 118
me-zo-e 118, 243, 244
me-zo-a$_2$ 118
-mi 121
mi-ka-ri-jo(-jo) 223
mi-ra-ti-ja 200
mi-ta 308
mi-ti 182
mi-to-we-sa 141, 305
mi-to-we-sa-e 305
mo-qo-so 96, 152
mo-ro-qa 220

na-u-si-ke-re[153
na-wi-jo 213
na-wi-ro 152
ne-de-wa-ta 153, 231
ne-de-wa-ta-o 231
ne-de-we 159
ne-do-wo-te 159
ne-wa 300
ne-wo 90
no-ri-wo-ki-de 285

o- 87, 130, 229, 234, 317
o-a$_2$ 131
o-da-a$_2$ 131, 268, 289, 291,
        312
o-da-ke-we-ta 141
o-da-ku-we-ta 141
o-da-tu-we-ta 141
o-da-twe-ta 300
o-de-qa-a$_2$ 131
o-du-ru-wi-jo 319
o-ka 227, 228, 230, 232
o-ka-ra 230, 232
o-ka-ra$_3$ 230
o-ki-ro 179
o-na-te-re 268
o-na-to 257, 258, 268, 272,
        273
o-no (ὄνοι) 85

o-no ('payment'?) 143
o-pa 300, 306, 307, 320
o-pe-ro 199, 302, 317
o-pe-ro-si 317
o-pe-ta 152
o-pi 129
o-pi-a$_2$-ra 230
o-pi-i-ja-pi 304
o-pi-ka-pe-e-we 212
o-pi-ke-wi-re-je-u 239
o-pi-ri-mi-ni-jo 153
o-pi-su-ko 212
o-pi-te-ke-e-u 239
o-po-qo 304
o-po-ro 308
o-re-mo-a-ke-re-u 156
o-re-ta 152, 230
o-ru-ma-to 159
o-te 98, 160
o-u- 132
o-u-di-do-si 312, 316
o-u-di-do-to 318
o-u-ki- 132
o-u-qe 132, 306
o-wi-de-ta-i 288
o-wi-to-ni-jo 230
o-wi-to-no 159, 230, 232
o-wo-we 240

pa-de 279
pa-di-jo 153
pa-i-ti-jo 146
pa-i-to 159, 178-180
pa-ja-wo-ne 281
pa-ka-na 86, 103
pa-ki-ja-na 159, 216, 267, 269
pa-ki-ja-ne 216
pa-ki-ja-ni-ja 146, 267
pa-ki-ja-pi 216
pa-ki-ja-si 216, 294
pa-ko-we 141, 284
pa-qo-si-qo 226
pa-ro 129, 163, 174, 273, 274
pa-si 101
pa-si-te-o-i 279
pa-ta-ja 320
pa-ta-jo-qe 214
pa-te 84

pa-we-a   188, 190
pa-we-pi   113
pe-da   129
pe-de-we-sa   141
pe-i   121, 232
pe-ke-u   308
pe-ko-to   190
pe-ma   117, 166, 249, 253
pe-mo   86, 117, 166
pe-ne-we-ta   188
pe-qa-to   306
pe-re   294-296
pe-re-qo-ta   97
pe-re-u-ro-na-de   159
pe-re-*82-jo   296
pe-ri-   129
pe-ri-me-de   153
pe-ri-ta   153
pe-ru-si-nu-wo   181
pe-ru-si-nwa   302
pe-ra$_3$-ko-ra-i-ja   318, 322
pe-se-ro   308
pe-ta-ro   152
pe-to-no   159
pi-pi   319
pi-ri-e-te-si   114
pi-ri-je-te(-re)   171
pi-ro-we-ko   153
pi-sa-wa-ta   153
pi-ti-ro$_2$-we-sa   141
po-de   115, 240
po-ki-ro-nu-ka   188
po-me   114
po-me-ne   114
po-me-no   114
po-ni-ke-(j)a   144
po-ni-ki-ja   144, 304
po-pi   115
po-re-na(-qe)   294-296
po-ri-wo   152
po-ro   103
po-ro-   84, 129, 209
po-ro-du-ma-te   210
po-ro-ko-re-te(-re)   209, 220
po-ro-te-u   152
po-ro-u-te-u   226
po-ro-wi-to(-jo)   293, 294

po-ru-ka-to   153
po-se-da-o   94, 102
po-se-da-o-ne   166, 167, 281, 283
po-se-da-o-ni   166, 167, 287, 288
po-si   102, 129, 306
po-si-da-e-ja   294, 296
po-si-da-i-jo   295
po-so-re-ja   269
po-ti-ni-ja   87, 148, 182, 285,
                294
po-ti-ni-ja-we-(i-)jo   148, 182,
                217, 219
po-ti-ni-ja-wi-jo   148
po-ti-ni-ja-wo   148
pu-ra-so   152
pu-ra-ta(-o)   223
pu-ro   159, 199, 202, 215, 294
pu$_2$-ke-qi-ri   234
pu$_2$-te   308
pte-re-wa   301

qa-da-so   152
qa-nu-wa-so   152
qa-ra   159
qa-ra-i-so   152
qa-si-re-u   85, 96, 217, 220, 224
-qe   96, 134
qe-ra-na   141, 237
qe-ra-si-ja   279
qe-re-qo-ta-o   97
qe-te-a   143
qe-te-a$_2$ 143
qe-te-(j)o   143, 192
qe-ti-ja   321
qe-to   242, 321
qe-to-ro-   123
qe-to-ro-we   240
qi-si-pe-e   84, 113, 170
qo-o   112
qo-u-ka-ra   237
qo-u-qo-ta   139, 153
qo-wi-ja   295

ra-ja   159
ra-pi-ti-ra$_2$ 138
ra-pte   258
ra-su-to   159

ra-to 159
ra-wa-ke-si-jo 147, 250, 316
ra-wa-ke-ta 108, 139, 250, 290
ra-wo- 90
ra-wo-do-ko 153
re-qa-se-wo 157
re-u-ka-so 152
re-u-ko 319
re-u-ko-nu-ka 188
ri-jo 159
ri-me-ne 232
ri-no 103, 317
ri-*82-ta 319
ro-o-wa 159
ro-u-si-jo 146, 284
ro-u-so 159, 199, 215, 216,
        284
ru-ke-wo-wo-wi-ja 158
ru-ki-to 159, 179
ru-na-so 152

sa-ma-ra 159
sa-ma-ri-wa 159
sa-pa 192
sa-pi-de 308
sa-ra-pe-da 287
sa-ri-nu-wo-te 159
sa-sa-ma 308
se-ri-no-(wo-)te 159
se-to-i-ja 159, 302
si-a$_2$-ro 103
si-ja-du-we 159, 182
si-ri-jo 104
si-to 201
so-u-ro 269
su-di-ni-ko 179
su-qo-ta(-o) 108, 139
su-ro 319
su-we-ro-wi-jo 230
su-za 201

ta-ni-ko 231
ta-ra-mi-ka 140
ta-ra-si-ja 217-220, 223, 224,
        226, 302
-te 133
te-ke 234

te-me-no 113, 249, 250
te-mi-dwe-ta 141, 299
te-mi-ti-ja 159, 166
te-o(-jo) 103, 104, 269
te-re-ne-we 159
te-re-ta(-o) 251, 252, 266-269
ti-mi-ti-ja 159, 166
ti-mi-to 159, 166
ti-mi-to-a-ke-e 216
ti-ri-da-ro 258
ti-ri-o-we-e 240, 244
ti-ri-po 115
ti-ri-po-de 115, 239
ti-ri-po-di-ko 140, 321
ti-ri-si 123
to-e 122
to-jo 122
to-ko-so-ta 139
to-me 122
to-pe-za 100, 141
to-pe-zo 103, 107
to-qi-de-ja 237
to-qi-de-we-sa 141, 237
to-sa-de 316, 318
to-so 251, 280
to-so-de 122, 217, 252, 267
to-so-jo 249, 253
to-so-ne 122
to-so-pa 217
to-to 122
tu-na-no 190
tu-qa-ni-ja-so 152
tu-ri-si-jo 146
tu-ri-so 159
tu-we-a 87, 113
tu-we-ta 152

u-ka-jo 159
u-pa-ra-ki-ri-ja 159
u-po 129, 306
u-po-di-no 157
u-po-ra-ki-ri-ja 159
-u-ru-to 230
u-ta-jo(-jo) 179
u-ta-no 159

wa-na-ka 86, 90, 116, 234

wa-na-ka-te   116, 283, 284
wa-na-ka-te-ra   188, 190, 285
wa-na-ka-te-ro   116, 142, 249,
          250, 268, 319
wa-na-ka-to   116
wa-na-se-wi-ja   148, 237
wa-na-so-i   283
wa-na-ta-jo(-jo)   268, 269
wa-no-jo   173
wa-no-so-i   283
wa-to   159, 319
wa-tu   90, 295
wa-tu-o-ko   153
we-pe-za   123
we-te-i   113
we-te-i-we-te-i   162
we-to   90, 113, 162
we-we-si-jo(-jo)   178-180
-wi-de   90, 234
wi-jo-ka-de   179
wi-pi-no-o   153

wi-ri-ne-(j)o   144, 304
wi-ri-ni-jo   144
wi-se-jo   179
wo-do-we   141
wo-i-ko-de   166
wo-ko-de   166, 285
wo-no-qe-we   159
wo-no-qo-so   153
wo-qo-we   159
wo-ra-we-sa   141
wo-ro-ki-jo-ne-jo   253, 290
wo-wo   157, 173
wo-*82-ni-jo   179

za-we-te   100, 181
ze-u-ke-si   299
ze-u-ko   299

*34-ke-u   239

*47-da-de   279

INDEX 2:   GREEK WORDS

marks a reconstructed or hypothetical form.
†*marks a word which contains a Greek stem but which is not actually attested in historical Greek.*

ἄγει   294
*ἄγη   294
ἀγνός   294
ἀγρεύς   156
ἄγριος   156
ἀγρός   284
ἄγω   250
'Αθᾶνᾱ?   281
αἰγ-   239
Αἰγεύς?   239
αἰγι-   139
†Αἰγίπως?   153
†Αἰθαλόϝενς?   153
Αἰθίοψ   153
Αἴθων   152
†αἰξμάνς   103, 214
αἰχμάς   214
'Ακταῖος   153
"Ακτωρ   152
ἄλειφαρ   289
'Αλεκτρύϝων   152
ἄλευρον   290
'Αλκεύς?   152
ἀλκή   152
'Αλκμάνωρ   153
ἀλοιφᾶ   283
†'Αμνίσιος   146
'Αμνισός   49, 50, 84, 159
ἀμφί   84, 129
'Αμφίαλος   153
'Αμφίδωρος   153
ἀμφιέχει   129
'Αμφιμήδης   153
†ἀμφιφορῆϝε   109
†ἀμφορῆϝε   109, 321
ἀμφοτέρωθεν   133
ἀμφῶες   240

ἀνάμπυκες   149
ἀνάρμοστοι   149, 307
ἀνδρόμεος   148
ἀνέμων   103, 279
ἄνετα   313
ἅνίαι   87, 103, 306
†ἁνίᾱφι   103
ἀνίημι   313
'Αντάνωρ   153
†"Ανυτος   152
†ἀνῶϝες   149, 240
†ἀνώϝοτος   149
ἀπέδωκε?   128
ἀπό   164
†"Απταρϝα?   159
ἀπύ   129, 164, 241
ἀπύδοσις   311
ἀπύδωκε   128
†ἀραρϝόα   57, 171
ἀραρυῖα   57
ἀραρίσκω   171, 304
ἄργυρος   84
ἀρείων   120, 188
†ἀρίοα   118
†ἀρίοες   118
†ἀρίοος   118
†ἀρίων   120
ἄρμα   117, 299
†ἄρμο   117, 299
ἁρμόζω   307
†ἄρμοσι   117
†ἄρμοτα   84, 117, 141
†ἄρμοτε   117
ἀσκέω   198
ἀσκητριῶν   199
†ἀταλάνσιοι   217
†'Αχαιϝιᾶνδε?   159

194

Ἀχέλᾱϝος? 153

βαίνω 95
βασιλεύς 56, 85, 96, 217, 220
βίος 95
Βουβόται 153
Βουβότᾱς 139
βοῦς/βῶς 112, 237

Γλαῦκος 152
γυναίᾱ 237
γυνή 237

Δαιδαλεῖόνδε 159, 279
Δᾱιφόντᾱς 153
†δᾱμοκλον? 234
δᾱμος 260, 267
δᾱμωι 103
δέ, -δε 133, 313
δεδομένᾱ 301
δέπας 113, 166, 167, 243, 269
δεσμοῖς 103, 171
Δευκαλίων 152
δεῦρο 318
δίδονσι 101, 312, 316
δίδοτοι 318
Διϝεί 110, 279, 297
Διϝείφιλος 114
†Διϝιεύς 152
Διϝός 90, 152, 297
Δίϝων? 152
Δικταῖος 146
Δικταίωι 279
Δίκτᾱνδε 159
†δοέλᾱ 268
†δοέλαι 202
†δοέλοι (dat. plur.) 103
†δοέλοι (nom. plur.) 217
†δοέλος 268
δόμος 267
†δορϝείω 305
δοσμόν 103
δοσμός 287
Δρομεύς 152
δρόμος 152
δρυτόμος 84
†δυώϝης 240
δῶρα 294

δώσει 288
δώσονσι 208
ἔγχεσι 214
ἔγχος 84
†Ἐδομενεύς 269
ἔενσι 101, 306
ἐκεῖ 114
Ἕκτωρ 152
ἔλαιϝον 103, 141, 284
†Ἐλάτει? 159
†Ἐλέει? 159
Ἐλευθίᾱ 281
†ἐλεφάντει 115
ἐλέφαντος 115
ἐλέφᾱς 115
†ἐμεί 123
†ἐνέενσι 129, 267
ἔνεκα 93, 129, 202, 203
ἐνί 123
ἐννεϝο- 123
Ἐνυϝάλιος 281
†ἐπέταε 108
ἐπέται 108
ἐπέτᾱς 96, 108, 188
ἐπί 129
Ἐπιάλτᾱς 152, 153
†Ἐπικλέϝης 153
†ἐπίκοϝοι 230
ἔπομαι 95
ἐρέτᾱς 139
ἐρετάων 108
ἐρῆμον 253
†Ἐρικλέϝης 153
Ἐρινύς 279
Ἐρμᾱᾱι 296
ἐρυθρά 308
Ἔρυθρος 152
†Ἐρχομενάτᾱο 152
†Ἐρχόμενος 159
ἐσχάρᾱ 86, 141
†Ἐταϝωνεύς 152
ἔτεισα 143
εὔδᾱμος 153
†Εὐδείϝελος? 156
Εὐμένης? 153
Εὐμήδης 151, 153
Εὐμήτᾱς 152, 153

†Εὔπλοϝος 153
Εὐρύδᾱμος 153
εὔχετοι 97
†Εὐχόμενος 152
'Εχέδᾱμος 153
ἔχεεν 126
ἔχει 134, 257, 258
ἔχειν 126
†'Εχελάϝων/-ᾱϝος? 153, 288
'Εχεμήδης 153
'Εχῖνος 152
ἔχουσι 101, 134, 217, 266
ἔχοντες 217
ἐών 126

†ϝανάκτει 116
†ϝανάκτερον 249
†ϝανάκτερος 268, 319
ϝάνακτος 116
ϝάναξ 86, 90, 116, 234, 237
ϝάνασσα 237
†ϝανασσηϝίᾱ 148, 237
†Ϝαρναταῖος? 268
ϝάστυ 90
Ϝαστύοχος 153
†ϝέκπεζα 123
ϝέτει 113
ϝέτος 90, 113, 162
ϝίδε 90, 234
Ϝῑϝίνοος 153
ϝοῑκόνδε 285
Ϝοῑνοψ 153
†ϝορϑόϝεν 141
*ϝόρϝια 158
*ϝόρϝος 157, 173
*ϝόρϝωι 173
ϝρῑν- 144
†ϝρῑνειοι/-ω 304
†ϝρύντοι 230

ζεύγεσι 299
ζεῦγος 299

ἡδίων 119
Ἥρᾱι 297

θέμις 167

-θεν 133
θεοῖο 103, 104, 268
θῆκε 234
†θηρασίᾱι 279
†θύϝεα 87, 113
†θυϝέστᾱι 152

'Ιάϝονες 152
ἰᾱτήρ 138
†ἴᾱφι 304
†'Ιδομένεια 152
'Ιδομενεύς 152, 269
†ἰεϝεί 297
ἰε(ν)τοι 294
ἰέρεια 136
ἰερείᾱι 279
ἰερείᾱς 202, 269
ἰερεύς 87, 136
†ἰερήϝιος 147
†ἰερῆϝος 109
ἰεροῖο 202
ἰερός 294
ἴημι 294
ἰόντες 87
ἰππίᾱ 141, 304
ἴππος 99, 103, 304
ἴπποι/-ω 304
ἰρόν 213
'Ιφιμέδεια 296

καίω 241
†κακίοες 118
κακίονες 100
καλυψαμένω 107
κάρᾱ 237
Κάστωρ 152
κεάζω 260
κεκαυμένος 241
κέραα/-ε 113
†Κεράμεια 136, 152
κεραμεύς 136, 152
*κλᾱϝιφόροι 211
κλᾱικοφόρωι 211
Κλύμενος 152
κνᾱκος 308
†Κνίδιαι 200
Κνώσ(σ)ιος 146

Κνωσ(σ)ός 84, 159
κοϝέω 230
κοινός 260
†Κομάϝενς? 153
κόρϝᾱ 103
κόρϝαι 197
κόρϝοι 197
κόρϝος 90, 103
κορίαννον 54
Κόρινθος 159
Κότυλος 152
κόχλος 237
κρανᾱ 156
†Κρηθεύς? 262
†Κρησιοϝεργής? 239, 241
κρῑθάν 103
*κτεῖμι 261
κτίζω 261
*κτίημι 261
κτοίνᾱ 259
κτοίνᾱν 268
κτοίνᾱς 103
κτοινάων 103
†κτοινόοχος 150
Κυδωνίᾱ 159
κύϝανος 87
†Κυθηρεῦφι? 109
Κυκλεύς 152
κύκλος 152
Κύλλᾱνος 152
κύμῑνον 308
κυναγέται 139
Κυπαρίσσιοι 231
Κυπαρισσός 159
†κυπαρόϝεν 141
†Κύταιστος? 159
Κύψελος 152
Κώκαλος 152

λᾱγέτᾱς 250
†λᾱϝᾱγέσιοι 316
†λᾱϝᾱγέσιον 250
†λᾱϝᾱγέσιος 147
†λᾱϝᾱγέται 108
†λᾱϝᾱγέτᾱς 139, 250, 290
λᾱϝο- 90
Λᾱϝόδοκος 153
λᾱϝός 250

Λᾱτώ 159
λείπω 95
†λευκόνυχα 188
λεώς 250
λίνον 103, 317
Λούσιος 146, 284
Λουσός/-οί? 159, 199
Λύκτος 159, 179

†Μαλαθῆϝες? 316
μάλευρον 290
Μαλίτᾱς 152
μάραθ(ρ)ον 308
μάτηρ 114
†Ματρόπυλος 156
Μαχάϝων 152
†μέζοα/-ε/-ες 118
μέζων 118, 119
μείζονες 100
μείζων 119
†μείοα/-ε/-ες 118
μεῖον 118, 245
μείων 92, 118
μέλιτος 288
μετά 129
Μέταπα 159
†Μετωπεύς? 153
μήν 322
μηνός 278
†Μῑλάτιαι 200
†μιλτόϝεσσα 141, 305
μιν 121
μίνθα 308
Μνᾱσίϝεργος 153
μόνϝον 299
Μόψος 96, 152

†Νᾱϝιλος? 152
*νᾱϝιον 213
νᾱϝός 213
ναῦς 213
Ναυσικλε-[153
†Νεδϝᾱτᾱς? 153, 231
†Νεδϝόντει? 159
νέϝα 300
νέϝος 90
νέος 300
νηός 213

†ξίϝεε 84, 113
ξίφος 170
Ξοῦθος 152
ξύν 84, 129

ὅ 130
ὁδούς 141
*ὁϝός 240
οἶϝος 240
†οἰϝώϝης 240
†ὄνᾱτα 103
†ὀνᾱτῆρες 268
†ὄνᾱτον 257, 272
ὀνίνᾱμι 257
ὄνοι 85
ὄνυξ 188
ὀπι- 129, 212, 304
†ὀπίhαλα 230
†'Οπιλίμνιος? 153
†ὄπωποι/-ω 304
'Ορέστᾱς 152
ὅρος 157, 173
†'Ορύμανθος 159
ὅτε 98, 160, 234
οὐ 132
οὐκι- 132
οὖς 240
οὔτε 132, 306
ὀφείλονσι 317
ὀφείλω 308
ὄφελος 199, 302, 317
'Οφέλτᾱς 152

Παιᾱϝόνει 281
†παλταίοιι 214
παλτόν 214, 320
Πανδίων? 153
πάνς 217
πᾶνσι θεοῖς 279
πάντες 84
παρά 129
†παρό 262
πεδά 129
†πέδϝεσσα 141
πέρᾱ 318
περι- 129
Περιμήδης 153

Περίτᾱς? 153
περυσινϝᾶ 302
Πέταλος 152
πίθος 242
†Πισϝᾱτᾱς? 153
Πλευρῶνάδε 159
†ποδεί 115
ποῖ 95
†ποικιλόνυχα 188
†ποιμένει 114, 262
ποιμένες 114
ποιμένος 114
ποιμήν 114
Πόλιϝος 152
†Πολύκαστος 153
†πόπϕι 115
†Ποσειδᾱονι 287
†Ποσειδᾱϝων 94
†Ποσειδᾱόνει 281
Ποσειδᾱων 102
Ποσειδῶν 94
†ποσί (preposition) 102, 306
Ποτεδᾱϝονι/-ονος 94
Ποτειδᾱν 102
πότνια 87, 148, 182, 281
ποτνίαι 294
ποτνίᾱς 285
πρίω 171
πρό 84, 129, 209
πρόμαντις 209
πρόξενος 209
πρός 129
Πρωτεύς 152
πρῶτος 152
†πτελέϝᾱς 301
Πύλος 159, 199, 294
πώλω 103

†ῥαπτήρ 258
ῥάπτης 258
ῥάπτω 258
'Ρίον 159

σαρπίδες 308
σᾱσάμᾱ 308
†Σελινοϝόντει? 159
σῆτες 100

σίαλονς 103
σῖτος 201
†σϰέλεhα 241
σϰέλη 241
σπέρμα 117, 249, 251,
253, 299
†σπέρμο 86, 299
συβώταο 108
συβώτᾱς 139
σῦϰον 212
*σῦϰγαι 201
†σφαϰόϝεν 141, 284
σφάϰος 284
σφεις 121, 232
†ταλανσίᾱν 217
τάλαντον 219
τε 95, 96
Τελαμώνιος 145
τελεστᾱ́ς 251
τέλη, τέλος 251
τέμενος 113, 249-251
†τερμίδϝεντα 141
†τετρῶϝες 240
τίς 95
τοξότᾱς 139
†τόρπεζα 100, 141
†τορπέζω 103
†τορπίδϝεσσα? 141, 237
τοῖο 122
τόσ(σ)α/-αι/-οι/-ον/-ος 53, 86,
122, 217, 251, 280
τοσ(σ)άδε 316, 318
τοσ(σ)οῖο 249, 253
†τοσ(σ)όνε 122
τοσ(σ)όσδε/-οίδε 122, 133,
217, 267
τράπεζα 100
τρίποδε 115, 239
τριποδίσϰοι 140, 321
τρίπως 115, 241
τρισί 123

†τριώϝεε/-ϝες 240
Τυλίσ(σ)ιος 146
Τυλισ(σ)ός 159

υἱός 111
ὑπό 129, 306

Φαίστιος 146
Φαιστός 159, 178, 179
†φάρϝεα 188
†φάρϝεσφι 113
φᾶρος 188
φάσγανον/-να 86, 103, 168, 170
φᾱσί 101
φατειός 143
φέρει 294
φέρω 294
Φιλόϝεργος 153
φοινῑϰ- 144
φοινῑϰίᾱ 304
*φρή 294

†χαλϰείᾱφι 304
χάλϰε(ι)ος 144
Χαλϰεύς 152
χαλϰεῦσι 109
†χαλϰῆϝες 109, 217, 312
χαλϰόν 213
χαλϰός 84, 152
χαλϰῶι 103
†Χαραδοϝᾱ́τᾱς? 153
Χάραδρος 159
χείρων 119
χιτών 191, 193
χλαῖνα 192
χλαμύς 192
χρυσοῖο 202
χρυσός 84

ὦν 126
ὤφλον 308

INDEX 3:   LINEAR B INSCRIPTIONS DISCUSSED

KN Da 1156 + 7236	178	
KN Db 1159	179	
KN Df 1121 + 7689	181	
KN Dl 463	182	
KN Dl 946	182	
KN Dn 1094 + 1311	180	
KN Do 927	181	
KN Fp 1 + 31	276	
KN L 693	191	
KN Lc 525, 526	190	
KN Ld 571, 572	187	
KN Mc 4455	314	
KN Ra 1540	168-170	
KN Ra 1548	171	
KN Sd 4404	303	
KN Sd 4409	303	
KN Sd 4420	303	
KN Sd 4422	303	
KN So 4430	298-302	
KN So 4439	298-302	
KN So 4440	298-302	
KN So 4442	298-302	
KN Ws 1704	320	
MY Ge 602	308	
MY Wt 504	321	
PY Aa 85	195	
PY Aa 189	195	
PY Aa 573	195	
PY Aa 666	195	
PY Aa 717	195	
PY Ae 303	202	
PY An 657	227	
PY Cn 40	172	
PY Ea 28	256	
PY Ea 754	256	
PY Ea 778	256	
PY Ea 800	256	
PY Ea 806	256	
PY Ea 811	256	

PY Ea 821	256	
PY Eb 369	270	
PY Eb 377	270	
PY Eb 496	270	
PY Eb 501	270	
PY Eb 566	270	
PY Eb 747	270	
PY Eb 818	270	
PY Eb 846	270	
PY Eb 874 + 902	270	
PY Eb 892, 893	270	
PY Eb 895 + 906	270	
PY En 609	265	
PY Eo 211	265	
PY Eo 224	265	
PY Ep 301	270-274	
PY Er 312	248	
PY Fr 1219, 1220	282	
PY Jn 310	225	
PY Jn 605	222	
PY Jn 829	206	
PY Jn 845	224	
PY Ma 123	318	
PY Ma 222	317	
PY Ma 333	316	
PY Ma 393	319	
PY Na 245	316	
PY Ng 319	315, 318	
PY Ng 332	315, 318	
PY Nn 228	315, 317	
PY Ta 641	238	
PY Ta 711	233	
PY Tn 316	292-297	
PY Un 718	286-291	
PY Wa 114	322	
TH Of 36	285	
TH Z 839	319	
TH Z 852-854	319	
TI Ef 2, 3	275	

1. KN As 1516:

large 'page'-tablet
4 x 7in.

2. KN V 831:

smaller 'page'-tablet
4 x 5½in.

3. KN Uf 839: 'palm-leaf' tablet   5 x 1 in.

4. PY Wa 114: clay label   2 x 1 in.

5. TH Z 839:

inscribed jar
height: 17½in.
diameter (max.): 12½in.

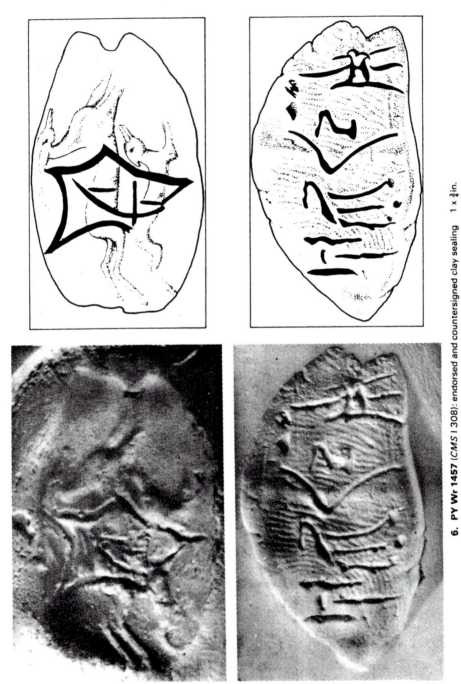

6. **PY Wr 1457** (*CMS* I 308): endorsed and countersigned clay sealing   1 x ¾in.